Social Work and Assessment with Adolescents

**Ruth Sinclair, Louise Garnett
and David Berridge**

The National Children's Bureau was established as a registered charity in 1963. Our purpose is to identify and promote the interests of all children and young people and to improve their status in a diverse society.

We work closely with professionals and policy makers to improve the lives of all children but especially young children, those affected by family instability, children with special needs or disabilities and those suffering the effects of poverty and deprivation.

We collect and disseminate information about children and promote good practice in children's services through research, policy and practice development, publications, seminars, training and an extensive library and information service.

The Bureau works in partnership with Children in Wales and Children in Scotland.

Contents

Acknowledgements

We would like to express our thanks to the Research Authority for agreeing to participate in the study and for the very generous way in which they facilitated our task throughout the three years that we worked with them. In particular we would like to thank the staff in the Children and Families Division and most especially those from the Adolescent Assessment Service, who were always most welcoming. Our thanks also to the young people, families and carers who generously allowed us to attend their meetings and who gave of their time to be interviewed.

The Department of Health was not only instrumental in the creation of the project by granting the necessary funding; through its continued encouragement and support it helped to sustain it and bring it to a satisfactory conclusion. In particular we wish to thank Dr Carolyn Davies, from the Research and Development Division, for her help in steering the project through, and to other Department colleagues who sat on the Steering Group. We mention in particular John Rowlands who offered enormously valuable comments on early drafts.

We also received advice from research colleagues, Pat Cawson, Marion Hundleby and Peter Marsh; our thanks to them for their interest and support.

It is impossible to undertake and publish a large research project like this without a great deal of help from other Bureau colleagues. Our thanks to Roger Grimshaw for help in the research design; to the secretarial staff in the Research Department, especially Janine Gregory and Sabina Collier; to the Publications Department and to the Library and Information Service.

Ruth Sinclair
January, 1995

List of Figures

List of Tables

Introduction

The welfare of the nation's children is a subject that rightly arouses a high degree of public concern. Within this diverse group can be identified specific categories of young people, whose well-being gives particular cause for disquiet. One such group forms the subject matter of this research report: namely young people who have been referred or seek help from social services or who are unable to live with their own parents and are looked after by the local authority.

The exact circumstances of this group – of whom around 50,000 are being looked after by local authorities in England and Wales on any one day – is very variable. Some are separated from their families for a matter of days before being reunited; others live apart for years or even, on some occasions, forever. They range from fragile babies to the troublesome adolescent. Their short lives have frequently been both unfulfilling and unenviable: they stem from the poorest sections of society with associated material disadvantage and family stress. Breakdown in relationships is common and neglect, exploitation and/or physical injury may have been inflicted upon them. These experiences will have influenced children's development, who in turn often display signs of insecurity and defiance.

The quality of child care practice

A subject of particular concern in recent years to legislators, policy makers and social researchers alike has been the quality of child care and wider social work support available to these young people and their families. The Children Act 1989 has been a positive and widely supported measure aimed at enhancing, where justified, state involvement in family life. This legislation was firmly based on the main conclusions of a significant body of child care research through the 1980s (see DHSS, 1985; Department of Health, 1991a).

These research studies reinforced a number of common findings. For example, child separations might sometimes have been averted if more effective preventive work had been undertaken in advance. Parental involvement was also undervalued and barriers to contact were frequent when children moved to foster families or residential settings. Once living away from home, too many placements were precarious and unrewarding. Other commentators pointed to particular deficiencies in services for children and their families from minority ethnic groups (House of Commons Social Services Committee, 1984).

Assessment in child care

However, a main theme running through many of these research studies was concern about the quality of **decision making** in cases where family breakdown occurred or was threatened. In view of this, a research programme based at the National Children's Bureau focusing on **assessment in child care** was significant: this report forms the third, and indeed main, publication to stem from this programme of enquiry (see Fuller, 1985; Grimshaw and Sumner, 1991). Later chapters in this report provide a more detailed account of the background, specific focus, main findings and implications of the current work. But it may be useful at the outset for readers to have a general overview.

Concerns about aspects of assessment practice in child care had been around for some time beforehand but were highlighted in the report of the DHSS Working Party on Observation and Assessment chaired by Norman Tutt (DHSS, 1981). Relevant questions include, for example, what is assessment and what relationship should it have to other aspects of social work practice with children? What is the appropriate balance between assessment and the provision of services? Why, exactly, is assessment undertaken? What form should the assessment take? Who should undertake it? What is its professional basis? Do formal periods of 'observation and assessment' lead to improved outcomes for children and families? Why has so much formal assessment activity been undertaken in large residential centres and what are the consequences of this approach: indeed do residential assessments tend to lead to recommendations for subsequent residential care? What does assessment cost and can these costs be justified? What do participants in assessment, particularly young people and their parents, make of the process?

One consequence of this heightened interest in assessment was a desire for better quality research information. Indeed, it was evident that hitherto the subject had attracted little research interest; furthermore most previous work had focused on *residential* observation and assessment (see, for example, Reinach, Lovelock and Roberts, 1976; Walker and Xanthos, 1982). The newer, more community-based forms of assessment, in contrast, were largely unexplored. Due to the complexity of the subject and relative absence of previous work, it was agreed with the Department of Health, which was providing funding, that before any evaluative research could be undertaken a number of theoretical and methodological issues should first be addressed.

The initial stage of research, therefore, was undertaken by Fuller (1985), who summarised existing thinking in this field and sought to clarify conceptually what is meant by assessment in child care. This work was continued by Grimshaw and Sumner (1991), who operationalised some of these theoretical developments and undertook pilot work in six agencies which demonstrated contrasting approaches to assessment. These researchers paved the way for the current evaluative stage of the research programme, which has sought to examine systematically different formal and informal, community- and residentially-based approaches to assessment, together with an investigation of their outcomes. In this task we have worked alongside colleagues from the University of Kent Personal Social Services Research Unit, who have concentrated specifically on the costs of different methods of assessment.

The research study

Our research was located in an inner London Borough, described in more detail in Chapters 4 and 5, which contained a range of assessment approaches. It accommodated a diverse population, including membership of a variety of different minority ethnic groups. We followed a sample of 75 adolescents through the assessment process: scrutinising case records and interviewing social workers, a wide range of professionals and a number of young people themselves. We also were able to observe assessment meetings in progress. Cases were followed-up a year later, at which time we examined the relationship between the assessment and the subsequent development of the case. We chose adolescents specifically, first, because of their predominance in the child care population – indeed 63 per cent of children and young people looked after by local authorities in 1993 were 10 years and over

(Department of Health, 1994). Secondly, as many readers will no doubt be aware, this is a group that poses particular problems to many agencies and for whom residential care is a significant service. Thirdly, we did not want to overlap to too great a degree with assessment in child protection. But also finally we felt it necessary to begin to disaggregate the larger population of children being looked after and focus more specifically on the situation and experiences of a more discrete group.

Aims of the study

To summarise, therefore, the broad aim of this study is to analyse the role and contribution which assessment currently plays in social work decision making with adolescent young people and their families. More specifically, by examining several different forms of assessment, both residential and community-based, the study aims to explore the following questions:

- what are the main components of the different forms of assessment for adolescents;
- which children or young people are allocated to which form of assessment and why;
- who participates in the assessment and what are the participants' perspectives on the assessment process;
- what is the outcome of these assessments in terms of their impact on young people's circumstances one year later;
- what are the relative costs of the various assessment packages – is there a relationship between costs and outcomes in terms of the child's subsequent care career?

The research report

To appreciate the implications of any research findings it is necessary to have an understanding of the context in which the study was conducted. In this report that context is presented in three dimensions. We start first with a very general overview of developments in child care policy and practice over the past two decades. This is followed by a discussion of assessment – how the concept has been interpreted and applied within social services, particularly since the Tutt Report in 1981. Lastly we describe, in some detail, the context of the local authority in which the research was conducted.

The characteristics of our sample of 75 young people are set out in Chapter 6. In describing the assessment process Chapters 7, 8 and 9 present a very realistic picture of current social work practice with adolescents. Chapters 10 and 11 report on the circumstances of the young people one year later and gauge the outcomes for them from the assessment process. The relative cost implications of undertaking assessments in different forms is explored in Chapter 12. In the final chapter, we highlight the major themes to emerge from the research and identify key issues for the future in the role of assessment within child care services.

1. Child care in the past two decades

Assessment has played an important but variable role in the provision of social services to children and young people over the past two decades. To appreciate the way in which both the concept and the practice of assessment have developed, it is necessary to be aware of current issues in child care and of the very significant changes in child care policy and practice over the past 20 or so years.

An overview of child care

This study of child care assessment, therefore, starts with an overview of the major developments in child care, culminating with the implementation of the Children Act 1989 late in 1991. This overview takes a broad perspective on child care, rather than concentrating solely on assessment – that will be the subject of the next chapter. Its purpose is to establish the context in which the subsequent discussion of assessment and the findings of the research study can best be understood. The brief sketch presented here has, of necessity, to be a broad brush one. However the need to summarise national trends should not disguise the large measure of variation that has existed between local authorities in the way in which they have responded to a changing environment. While social services departments still display significant variation in their structures, policies and the quality of their social work practice, the degree of prescription contained within the Children Act 1989 and its accompanying Regulations and Guidance, has had a more unifying influence.

Nor has the period under review been free from major philosophical differences. The present level of professional consensus around the principles of the Children Act, is in marked contrast to earlier conflict. First, between the 'state as parent' protagonists and the 'kinship defenders', an ideological discussion that has been broadened to include a laissez-faire and children's rights perspective (Fox, 1982; Fox-Harding, 1991; Frost and Stein, 1989). Second, between those who argued for broad preventive welfare strategies against those concerned with the coercive impact of social work intervention and the care system in particular (see Hardiker, Exton and Barker, 1991).

Child care statistics

One indicator of shifts over time in child care policies and practices is changes in the numbers of children in care. As with all uni-dimensional indicators this can raise as many questions as it answers. Nonetheless, the significant variations in the care population do require explanation (Sinclair, 1987; Parker, 1987). In statistical terms the two decades, the 1970s and the 1980s, show almost contrary trends, as illustrated in Figure 1.1A, which shows the numbers of children in care in England on 31 March each year. (The source of this and other statistical information related to children in care is *Annual Statistical Returns on Children in Care of Local Authorities,* DHSS/Department of Health.)

Although the number of children in care in England and Wales rose very gradually during the 1960s (from 61,729 in 1960 to 71,210 in 1970, or by 1.5 per cent per annum), during the 1970s the numbers rose dramatically, reaching a peak of 101,200 children in care in England and Wales on 31 March 1977. With the fall in the total number of young people under 18 in the population, the actual proportion of the child population in care on any one day continued to rise until 1980. In that year, the average rate of children in care per thousand in England and Wales was 7.8 – although this average disguises the wide variations across authorities, from 24.6 per 1,000 in Tower Hamlets to 3.1 in Barnet (see Figure 1.1B).

Child care in the 1970s

So despite the high hopes of the new preventive powers within the Children and Young Persons Act 1963, the creation of the unified social services departments in 1971, the attendant growth in social work staff, changes in dealing with juvenile offenders following the 1969 Act – in particular, the redesignation of approved schools as CHE's (Community Homes with Education) – all had the effect of increasing the number of children within the care system (Packman, 1981). This growing number in care on any one day not only reflected more admissions to care, but also a greater use of com-

Figure 1.1A   Number of children in care, England 1967–1991

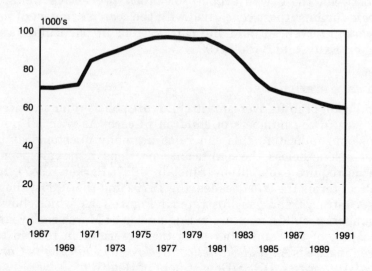

Figure 1.1B   Proportion of Children in Care, England 1967–1991

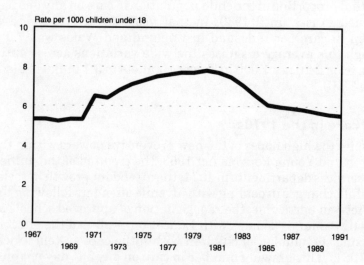

Note: Figures for 1966-70 apply to both England and Wales

pulsory orders with many children spending a longer time away from home (Aldgate, 1980).

It seems that in the 1970s the consequences of trying to provide a broader welfare service to families in difficulty, often rooted in poverty and poor housing, was to bring their children into the net of the care system (Holman, 1980). Similarly, welfare approaches to minor offending and the widespread practice of 'assessing' children brought many young people into care, most often into residential care (DHSS, the Tutt Report, 1981; Morris and Giller, 1987). And once in that net, the operation of the care system made it difficult for many young people to return home. Many families seeking the help and support of social services found instead the hand of the coercive social worker, however unintended that coercion may have been (Rowe and Lambert, 1973; Wilding, 1982; DHSS, 1985; Packman and others, 1986).

Child care in the 1980s

The new decade saw the development of child care policies influenced by a different range of internal and external factors:

- the changed philosophy towards the welfare state and local government as the values of the government led by Mrs Thatcher achieved domination;
- a different resource climate, typified by the 1981 reductions in local authority budgets;
- awareness of the seemingly inexorable rise of the number of children in care during the 1970s;
- the apparent success of a systematic approach to juvenile justice which greatly reduced the number of offenders being committed to care and custody;
- the growing strength of the voices of the consumer, transmitted through organisations such as the Children's Legal Centre; the Family Rights Group; the Who Cares? project at the National Children's Bureau and the National Foster Care Association;
- dissemination of a growing body of proven research that indicated limited effectiveness of much past social work practice; a lack of focused interventions; limited emphasis on planning and decision implementation; the great stigma and powerlessness felt by many clients; and insufficient understanding of the need for a range of policies to deal with the very heterogeneous care population.

Many of these new policies focused on older children, the 'beyond control' teenagers. Not only did this group cause considerable public concern, but looking at the age distribution of the care population it can be seen that they were a numerically important and visible group. Figure 1.2 shows the proportion of boys and girls from different age groups who were in care on 31 March 1985. Given this age profile, it was inevitable that responses to older children should dominate not only resources, but more significantly thinking in child care.

However, if most innovative thinking in social work was focused on work with teenagers, the issue of the physical abuse and death of younger children was never far from the public eye. To this was added the problems of the management of sexual abuse as demonstrated by events in Cleveland in 1987. Inquiries into the deaths of Tyra Henry, Kimberley Carlile but perhaps most notably that of Jasmine Beckford gave many social services departments cause to think. Indeed, the downward trend in admissions to care, particularly of under fives, was halted following the publication of *A Child in Trust* (Brent Borough Council, 1985).

Services for minority ethnic group children

Another area of growing concern throughout the late 1970s and 1980s related to services for children and their families who are black and from minority ethnic groups. This issue is of particular concern to the current study because the fieldwork was undertaken in a London Borough with a diverse ethnic population: indeed, the majority of our study population were from a variety of minority ethnic groups.

Several official and other reports in the 1970s and 1980s highlighted the deficiencies of social work services for children and families from minority ethnic groups (see, for example, Ahmed *in* Cheetham and Small, 1986). The Association of Directors of Social Services together with the Commission for Racial Equality (CRE) published a report in 1978 expressing strong concern about social services departments' relevance to minority ethnic clients (ADSS/CRE, 1978). The CRE followed this up in 1989 with a survey of social services/social work departments, which revealed that two-thirds of the departments did not have written equal opportunities policies (CRE, 1989 and 1990). These concerns had previously been highlighted in the Short Report by the House of Commons Social Services Committee (1984), which pinpointed the low take-up of services by certain minority ethnic groups. However other studies have pointed to the varying distribution of children from different ethnic groups among those in care, most noticeably

Figure 1.2 Number of children in care by age group on 31 March 1985

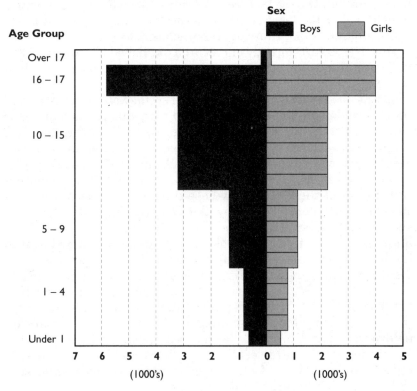

the over representation of children of mixed parentage (Bebbington and Miles, 1989; Rowe, Hundleby and Garnett, 1989). Throughout the past decade much of the discussion has focused on the respective merits and deficiencies of 'same race' or 'transracial' adoptive or foster placements for black children, although there were also wider concerns especially around assessment (Ahmed, 1980; Rhodes, 1992; Smith and Berridge, 1994).

Departmental responses

As the influence of all these factors became more discernible, new policies were introduced in many authorities, although the changes were by no means uniform. Three important threads in these new approaches were the continued transfer of resources away from costly residential provision towards community assessment and community-based 'alternatives to care'; an emphasis on permanency planning aligned with new gatekeeping procedures to reduce inappropriate stays in care; and social work responses that were more likely to be task-centred and contract-based and which aimed to offer the least obtrusive statutory intervention (Adcock, 1980; Hussell, 1983; Bunyan and Sinclair, 1987).

However, a further body of research published in the mid 1980s indicated some discrepancy between the new approaches to child care with what was happening in practice. These studies raised concerns about the general standard of social work practice and in particular demonstrated that 'drift' in care, due to inadequate or non-existing planning, was still a major issue. However, they also suggested that poor practice was caused more often by omission rather than commission (Vernon and Fruin, 1986; Sinclair, 1984; Fisher and others, 1986; Millham and others, 1986). The cumulative impact of these studies, whose common messages were distilled into a single volume by the Department of Health, was significant (DHSS, 1985). The very active dissemination of the findings through the 'Pink Book' prompted many authorities into further reappraisals of their child care policies and practices, some resulting in comprehensive statements or Child Care Strategies (Robbins, 1990). Many departments accompanied the introduction of these new policies with departmental restructuring. For some this was to bring together managerially the formerly separated fieldwork and care branches (as many of the divisions responsible for providing care within establishments were called); for others it represented a move away from genericism, towards greater specialisation of child care social work.

Despite an array of procedural arrangements and nomenclature introduced by different authorities, the thrust of many of these Child Care Strategies was broadly similar:

- a reaffirmation that where possible a child is best placed with their family;
- a preference for community-based solutions over institutional ones;
- a need to avoid drift by speedy decision making and regular, active reviewing of the cases of all children in care;
- a sharper distinction between voluntary and compulsory care.

The same principles often informed the creation of new procedures for assessing the needs of children and families. For instance one authority declared its philosophy on community assessment in the following terms:

The child's best placement is within his or her own family; that intervention should be the minimum necessary to secure the child's well being; and that the child's needs should be approached individually and decisions based on professional judgement. (Stockport SSD, 1983)

Coupled with these policies were new approaches to the management of social work practice: tighter procedures, greater accountability, regular statistical monitoring, and the removal of decision making discretion from individual social workers to more senior managers or to collectives in the form of panels or meetings (Bilson and Thorpe, 1987).

Yet despite these changes within departments there was a need for further action to address several important issues: the different concerns generated by 'beyond control' teenagers compared to younger children at risk of abuse; securing the appropriate balance in 'gatekeeping' care to reduce the risk of unnecessary separation or damaging care experiences, while adequately protecting children and supporting families; the danger that too limited a use of voluntary care could lead to more emergency and compulsory admissions to care with all the detrimental effects this has on child/family relationships; and the need to develop appropriate services and practice for children from minority ethnic groups.

Specialist Child Care Teams

One response was the creation of new specialist teams of workers. A key message taken from the research and from the continuing child abuse inquiries, was the difficulties faced by case workers in area teams (DHSS, 1985). If the minimum statutory requirements were to be met on all cases then there could be insufficient opportunity for the intensive work that was necessary to achieve change at crucial points in the child's history. A common response to this dilemma was the creation of specialist teams. So within an increasingly fragmented child care service there was the growth of further specialisms dealing either with particular age groups or particular presenting problems. These took many forms – child protection teams, intervention teams, children's services teams, family placement teams, juvenile justice teams, and assessment teams (Challis and Ferlie, 1987; Shaw and Hipgrave, 1983; Morris and Giller, 1987).

A common aspect of many of these teams was that their input was to be additional to that of the area worker. Work would still be channelled through area offices and area workers would hold case responsibility, but the additional, intensive input was to be provided by specialist workers with particular skills.

Some variation of this pattern of service development, while not universal, was found in a great many social services departments (see Cliffe with Berridge, 1991; Bunyan and Sinclair, 1987; Hardiker, Exton and Barker, 1991). The Adolescent Assessment Service, studied in this research and described in Chapter 5, is an example of this form of service development.

These specialist teams were often in the forefront of changing practices. This can be seen in areas such as:

- working with and listening to parents;
- listening to young people and involving them in decision making;
- using systematic planning processes that were participatory and where all decisions were recorded;
- ensuring that all decisions were reviewed regularly and as often as necessary if circumstances changed.

Indeed when the Department of Health published their second review of research, *Patterns and Outcomes in Child Placement*, they were able to point to a much greater awareness of the importance of child care planning and to new procedures to ensure that this was happening (Department of Health, 1991a). Despite this increase in planning activity, major concerns were expressed about the quality of decision making. As we shall see in the next chapter, the overriding message to come from this substantial body of research was the importance of adequate and accurate evidence on which the making of appropriate decisions could be based. A central component in the gathering and weighing of evidence is that of assessment.

The Children Act 1989

The decade ended with the passage of the Children Act in 1989. It is generally agreed that this is a considered piece of legislation, founded on a solid base of knowledge, informed by research and evaluation of practice (Packman and Jordan, 1991). The Act sets out to achieve a balance between the rights of parents in exercising their responsibilities towards their children, the rights of the child to be consulted and the duty of the state to intervene to promote and protect the welfare of children in need or at risk. The Act not only contains detailed statutory regulations but it establishes clear principles which should underpin all work with children and families, including partnership, participation and taking account of race, religion, language and culture.

By raising the standards of practice through regulation and

guidance, it was hoped that the Children Act would make the experience of being looked after by the local authority less damaging and less stigmatising than previously and, therefore, it would be possible to regard the provision of accommodation as a positive and preventive service; but at the same time the Act strongly reinforces the belief that in most instances children are best placed at home and that there should be the minimum necessary use of statutory orders. So the Act challenges poor practice while building on existing good practice – good practice that was often developed in the specialist child care teams, many of them assessment teams, which were created from the mid 1980s. The Children Act and its accompanying guidelines confirm planning for children as the cornerstone of good child care practice and identifies assessment as a key part of that planning process. What then does this new legal context mean for the way in which child care assessment is currently conceived and practised?

The majority of the fieldwork for this research was carried out after the passage of the Children Act in 1989 but prior to its implementation in October 1991. So although the principles of the new Act were likely to have been taken on board by staff in the Research Authority, changes had still to be made to procedures to take account of the details of the new statutory regulations. However, the more general question of the role of child care assessment under the Children Act will be considered in the final chapter.

The purpose of this introductory chapter is to remind readers of the way in which child care policies and practices have developed as new issues have risen to the top of the agenda in social services – driven there by public concerns as well as by research findings and evaluation studies. The particular philosophy and structure for child care services which developed within the Research Authority is clearly a reflection of this wider picture. Within these broad trends in child care policies and practice, the role of assessment has also been subject to change. Developments in the concept of assessment and its application will be the subject of the next chapter.

Summary points

- This introductory chapter has set the context for the remainder of the study by highlighting some of the major themes in child care policy and practice in the last two decades. By the end of the 1980s there was much consensus among local authorities about a range of issues, including: children's welfare is enhanced if, wherever possible and appropriate, they are supported in their own families; there has been a general preference for foster rather than residential care; there is a need to avoid 'drift' by bringing about speedier decision making; and there has been a sharper distinction between voluntary and compulsory care.

- A recurring theme of child care research in the 1980s has been concern about aspects of the decision making process. This study of assessment in child care is a further contribution to that body of knowledge.
- The research focuses specifically on adolescents, which has been a group of particular concern to social services departments over the past 20 years.
- Particular concern has been expressed about the quality of social work services for children and their families who are black and from minority ethnic groups.
- Attempts have been made to tighten management systems. A range of specialist teams have also been created.
- This review of the past two decades ended with the passing of the Children Act 1989. This legislation and its accompanying guidance were widely welcomed and were consistent with recent child care research messages. Although the bulk of the current research was undertaken prior to implementation of the Act, it addresses issues which are highly pertinent to the establishment of sound child care practice under the Children Act.

2. The concept and practice of assessment: an overview

The term assessment has always been part of the social worker's vocabulary. Today if a social worker talks of 'doing an assessment' they may be referring to assessment under Community Care legislation; assessment of whether a child is 'in need'; a comprehensive assessment as set out in the 'Orange Book' (*Protecting Children: A Guide for Social Workers Undertaking a Comprehensive Assessment*, Department of Health, 1988); assessment for special needs provision under the 1981 Education Act as revised by the 1993 Education Act; or assessment as part of the planning process, as recommended under the Children Act Guidance or completion of the Assessment and Action Records, which are increasingly in use in many authorities, having been revised and relaunched in Spring 1995 (Department of Health, 1991b, 1995).

Yet 15 years ago if a social worker referred to assessment they would probably have meant an assessment in a residential observation and assessment establishment, an O & A centre, as they were known. Despite this shift from one dominant approach to assessment to a range of assessment situations, and from residential to non-residential assessments, the concept and practice of assessment have been subject to only limited systematic analysis, and with no substantial comparative evaluation of the outcomes from different forms of assessment. As a result, and in the current climate of change, there is now widespread confusion about what is meant by the term assessment; nor is there available any coherent range of methodologies for undertaking assessments in different circumstances.

The purpose of this chapter is to examine briefly the changes in the concept and practice of child care assessment over the past 15 years, taking as a starting point the concerns and conclusions of the DHSS Working Party, known as the Tutt Committee, after its chair, Professor Norman Tutt, which reported in 1981 (DHSS, 1981).

An historical account of the role of assessment in social services is not straightforward. There is often major disjunction between developments in conceptual thinking about assessment, in departmental policies, procedures and structures and, in the practice of undertaking assessments. Disentangling these strands is made more difficult by the lack at an authority level of basic monitoring of child care services or of written explanations of changes in social services provision or operational arrangements. This is not necessarily to say that individual departments did not evaluate their services or take well-informed decisions; however, the basis of this information is as likely to be an intuitive critique of service provision and practice, based on day to day experience, as it is knowledge of research studies.

Because of the many facets implicit in the concept of assessment, this overview has not been written chronologically; rather it examines, in turn, different components of assessment starting with a brief examination of O & A centres.

Residential Observation and Assessment Centres

The impetus for the creation of O & A centres was the 1969 Children and Young Persons Act. Among other things, that Act required the establishment of 12 regional planning committees which were to submit plans:

> for the provision and maintenance of homes, to be known as community homes, for the accommodation and the maintenance of children in the care of the relevant authorities [Section 36(1)].

That same part of the Act also required that:

> every regional plan shall contain proposals for the provision of facilities for the observation of the physical and mental conditions of children in the care of the relevant authorities and for the assessment of the most suitable accommodation of those children [Section 36(4)(b)].

There are two things to note here. First, the purpose of this assessment was specifically to determine where the young person should live. Second, there was nothing in the actual wording of the Act which suggested that such observation and assessment services should necessarily be residential. Indeed the White Paper, *Children in Trouble*, which preceded that Act had always envisaged that such services should include a non-residential option (Home Office, 1968).

Yet overwhelmingly the new O & A centres were residential. This can be explained, in part, by the particular location of this requirement within a section of the Act dealing with community homes. More importantly the community homes system grouped together a number of different centres, some of which already included provision for the observation and assessment of children. Indeed, many of the O & A centres were simply created by redesignating former classifying schools, remand homes and reception centres, each of which contained an assessment and observation element, albeit for different purposes and for quite distinct client groups.

In addition to these redesignations, many new purpose-built O & A centres were opened, so that by 1978, when the Tutt Committee was established, about one in 20 children in care were accommodated in these centres, with the numbers increasing every year.

The DHSS Working Party was established because of the growing concern about the relevance, cost and effectiveness of these local authority observation and assessment services. In particular, the Working Party saw one of its key tasks as to clarify what was meant by assessment before going on to look at the present role of O & A centres and to make recommendations about future developments.

Before examining the conclusions of the Tutt Committee in more detail it would be helpful to examine briefly the concerns that were being expressed at that time about the residential O & A centres. This is presented in summary form. This summary, and indeed much of the chapter, draws on several key research reports and reviews (Mind Working Party, 1975; Fuller, 1985; Reinach, Lovelock and Roberts, 1979; DHSS, 1981; Grimshaw and Sumner, 1991):

- **an overemphasis with a medical model**: one that saw diagnosis as something preceding and separate from treatment, rather than recognising that assessment is itself a form of intervention, especially if the child or young person is removed from home for the assessment;
- **an unnatural environment**: assessing children and young people when they are placed in isolated residential establishments may produce invalid information, in so far as it denies both the importance of environmental factors, especially the family, on the young person's problems and the impact, on their subsequent behaviour, of their removal to a strange environment. This would apply particularly to children from minority ethnic groups, who were often placed in an alien cultural environment and came into contact with professionals who, predominantly, were white;

- **bias in placement decisions**: the focus of assessments under the 1969 Act was to determine, in an objective way, where a young person was to live. It was felt that undertaking this in a residential setting, often by residential staff, created an in-built bias towards a recommendation for a further residential placement;
- **ineffectiveness of the outcomes**: there was evidence to suggest that limited use was subsequently made of assessment reports. Further, there were often major problems in implementing placement recommendations due to a lack of appropriate facilities. This in turn led to 'silting up' of the assessment centres, so often what was intended as a short-term placement turned into an inappropriate longer one;
- **general concerns over residential care**: as the numbers of young people in care continued to rise in the 1970s, there was growing concern about the impact of residential care; it was felt to be very expensive; had regimes that encouraged institutionalisation; were often located in rural areas, thereby removing young people from their community and limited their contact with their family;
- **non-participatory**: generally assessment was something that was done *to* young people, not something that took place *with* them and their families.

Given these strong criticisms of both the concept and practice of assessment in the 'traditional' O & A centres, what has been the organisational response?

The organisation of assessment

The model of assessment which operated in the O & As was one which viewed assessment as a technical process, something which was a separate and skilled task and which required the necessary 'expert' staff to undertake it. In contrast the Tutt Committee saw assessment as an integral part of the social work task:

> We should make it clear at the outset that all children who come to the attention of the SSD are assessed as part of social work intervention.

This approach would suggest that it is unnecessary for assessment to be regarded as an identifiable activity. However, there was acknowledgement in the report that assessment was not a unitary activity but that 'the extent and manner...varies'. Although Tutt sets out clearly what the aims of an assessment should be, the report does not suggest when and in what way the extent and manner of assessment should vary. Nor indeed has this question been answered adequately since.

The main recommendation of the Tutt Report, that local authorities should 'promote all possible arrangements for community-based assessments', was fully endorsed by the Department of Health and promoted by them at two regional seminars (DHSS, 1982a; DHSS, 1982b). Indeed the report of those seminars indicated that changes in this direction were already underway in some local authorities (DHSS, 1983). These moves away from the 'traditional' pattern of residential O & A centres were part of the broader changes in child care policies which were outlined in the previous chapter. However, as the impetus for these changes was driven as much from within local authorities as through any central guidance, the organisational responses to the same basic problems were many and varied, and certainly not universal. By the time that Grimshaw and Sumner set out to look in detail at assessment in child care in 1986 they were able to identify six different approaches to assessment: an observation and assessment centre; a regional assessment facility; a children's district centre; community assessment teams; an assessment fostering scheme; and assessment by case-responsible social workers.

Many of the newest organisational arrangements were introduced alongside revised child care policies and were associated with changes in social work practice in child care. As suggested earlier it was often the workers in these new specialist teams that led departments in changing practice.

While the study by Grimshaw and Sumner provides valuable insights into examples of different assessment arrangements, it was not able to provide an overall picture of the way in which, across the country, assessment is located within child care structures. Such a picture is simply not available. What we do know is that local authorities have continued to restructure and reorganise. For most this has meant a sharper division between services for children and families and services for adults as well as increasing specialism within the children's division. In addition, the organisation of children's services has been influenced by the structures that have grown-up to implement the community care legislation with some departments introducing a purchaser/provider split in children's services (see, for example, Gardner, 1992; Platt, 1994). Indeed, as we shall see, the new thinking around assessment for community care has, to varying degrees, impinged upon child care assessment. Also important have been the procedural changes necessary to implement the Children Act.

Despite this, the current picture regarding the organisation of child care assessment would still seem to reflect that outlined by Grimshaw and Sumner, with a range of different organisational arrangements still operating. Whereas that study was able to analyse these different assessment arrangements, it did not set out to compare their operation in practice. That is the purpose of this present study; to build upon this earlier conceptual model and to take it a stage further by comparing the outcomes for the young people who have been subject to different assessment processes.

These newer patterns of assessment reflect more than organisational structures; they embody new thinking on the needs of different groups of children, and on the practice and purpose of assessment. We shall follow each of these strands in more detail.

Assessment of whom?

The underlying philosophy behind the 1969 Children and Young Persons Act was to perceive children's problems as deriving from the same fundamental needs, whether they were offenders or victims of neglect. It then followed that if all 'Children in Trouble' could be viewed, in this sense, as a single group then one model of assessment was applicable to every one.

However, as more and more young people were drawn into the care system, experience demonstrated that this approach was too simplistic and that a range of assessment procedures was necessary. The particular form that these new assessment arrangements took would, in part, be determined by factors within the local authority and in part, by the young person's particular situation.

Adolescents

As we noted previously, during the 1970s and into the 1980s older children dominated the care system, particularly those remanded to care, on criminal care orders or with long care histories. So the thinking around the new assessment arrangements, both in terms of organisation and practice, was also dominated by the need to assess the problems that teenagers were presenting and to find the best way to meet these. Hence many of the new arrangements were geared towards adolescents, where the presenting problem was more likely to be behavioural rather than that of protection. For this particular group there was a clear link between assessment and intervention and a style of working that emphasised time-limited work, which focused specifically on presenting problems (Doel and Marsh, 1992).

Similarly, a more participatory style of assessment was particularly relevant to work with teenagers. This is not only apposite from a civil rights perspective and because the contribution of older children can be particularly pertinent, but also because, in practice, these young people exercise significant control over the implementation of any decisions which flow from the assessment; so assessments undertaken with the active participation of young people are more likely to reflect needs accurately and to be acted upon.

Children at risk

However, the series of highly publicised child death inquiries in the mid eighties brought to the fore the issue of assessment in cases of child protection (Department of Health, 1991c). In addition, the Cleveland Report focused particularly sharply on the difficulty in assessing the probability of sexual abuse (Butler-Sloss, 1988).

Here the need was twofold. First an initial and often urgent need to assess the risk to the child; second the need for an in-depth assessment of the child's long-term needs. Recognising the enormous complexity of child protection issues and the long-term implications for these younger children, in 1987 the Department of Health established a working party to produce materials to raise skills in undertaking comprehensive assessments. That guide, commonly known as the 'Orange Book', sets out a detailed framework for comprehensive assessment to assist in long-term planning in child protection cases (DHSS, 1988). As the introduction to the Orange Book makes clear, the use of the guide should be limited to these instances; it is not intended as a general handbook for all forms of assessment.

Children with special needs

A third group of young people for whom particular assessment procedures have been developed, are children with special needs. The 1981 Education Act introduced the 'statement of special educational needs' which could be drawn up following a multidisciplinary assessment of a child's needs. This assessment should involve social services staff. Following criticism of the 'statementing' process by the Audit Commission, the 1993 Education Act provided for a new Code of Practice on identifying and assessing children with special educational needs. This new code came into effect in Autumn 1994. (HMI/Audit Commission, 1992; DFE, 1994).

So far we have identified three distinct groups of children whose situations warranted very different forms of assessment. What about the assessments that are now taking place to ascertain if a child is 'in need' under the Children Act? Does this represent a further type of assessment appropriate for a particular group of children – or is it the *purpose* of the assessment rather than the client group that distinguishes it from other forms of assessments – a point we shall return to later.

Who assesses?

Allied to questions about organisational structure and different groups of young people is that of who actually undertakes the assessment.

In the traditional O & A centres there was often a multidisciplinary team. Residential staff would have a major input into the assessment and many also had a role in coordination. But they would be assisted by educationalists, psychologists or psychiatrists. Similarly, assessment under the 1981 or 1993 Education Acts is a multidisciplinary activity with significant input from Health Service staff. While the management of child protection cases is governed by interagency procedures, social services clearly has lead responsibility (Department of Health, 1991g). The 'Orange Book' was written specifically for social work staff, although other professionals are likely to be needed to assist with the assessments.

This model of social service staff taking the lead, with assistance from other professionals is now a common pattern for assessment. But this begs the question, which social service staff? Earlier we noted the conclusion of the Tutt Report that 'all children who came to the attention of the social services are assessed as part of social work intervention'. The implication of this is that assessment would be done by area social work staff within their case work responsibilities.

Yet in addition to the separation of initial assessment from long-term case work, many social services departments have moved to more specialist arrangements.

The development of specialist child care teams raises a host of questions about the relationship between area or district social workers (most of whom continue to hold case responsibility) and specialist social workers. Here our concern is the impact on assessment. Two immediate questions come to mind. Is the assessment task fundamentally different depending on whether it is undertaken by an area social worker or by a specialist team? And secondly, when should a case be assessed by the area worker and when should it be referred to specialists? By comparing cases in each of these categories, this research has been designed to address these questions.

A further aspect of the question of who assesses is the role of other professionals. The traditional pattern in the O & As was routinely to refer all young people for assessments by educationalists, psychologists or psychiatrists. Grimshaw and Sumner found that under the newer patterns of assessment, social workers were more likely to refer young people to other professionals on a selective rather than a routine basis. Even when other professionals were involved this could be for purposes other than assessment. For instance, these researchers found that professionals who attended planning or assessment meetings could be there for a variety of reasons:

> Some were invited on the basis that they possessed special knowledge of the child; others had a role as holders of resources...they were assigned particular responsibilities as decision-makers. (Grimshaw and Sumner, 1991, p128)

It will be interesting to see whether the new Guidance in the Children Act on Care Plans for children who are looked after significantly alters the role of other professionals. The Regulations require that each Plan should include arrangements for the child's health and education, and these aspects are two of the dimensions covered in the Assessment and Action Records.

The practice of assessment

It will be clear from the discussion so far that the practice of assessment has undergone significant change during the past 20 or so years. To a considerable extent this is part of the broader changes in child care policies and practices that we have chronicled. It may also be a response to some of the criticisms of actual practice in undertaking assessments that have been reported through research, enquiry and inspection reports. In recounting these criticisms once again, we do so with an awareness of the immense complexity of the social work task. Indeed, the changing nature of the criticisms illustrates how our expectations of social work have become enlarged and more sophisticated; our standards have been set much higher as our understanding has increased.

Looking back to the DHSS Working Party Report, doubts about the dominance of residential assessment were coupled with concerns about the limited skills that social services staff displayed when undertaking assessments:

There is a strong case to be made for the development of a greater degree of expertise among social workers.

Of equal concern was the tendency of 'traditional' assessments to concentrate on searching for the origins of past problems, giving too little attention to future options for further work with children and families.

As we have seen, by the mid 1980s the structure of assessments was much more varied; the trend was towards assessments more closely linked to intervention, shorter, more focused on specific presenting problems, more participatory.

Yet at this time a significant body of research evidence had been accumulated which still cast serious doubt on the capacities of individual social workers to undertake 'effective' assessments. Although lack of time, stress, the feeling of helplessness and passivity generated by over-large case-loads were identified as important, the overwhelming impression of these studies was that:

> too many social workers are not enabled to acquire nor encouraged to use the necessary skills. The result is that the whole basis for planning is shaky. Decisions are made on inadequate evidence and it is not surprising if goals are unclear or if there is a lack of congruence between goals and what is actually done – or not done. (DHSS, 1985)

Similar concerns had been raised by other commentators on assessment, who referred to social workers' relative lack of assessment skills compared to other professions such as doctors, teachers and psychologists:

> Although paediatricians and child psychiatrists may compile a detailed assessment and diagnosis, this would not appear to be common practice amongst social workers and is probably not routine for other professionals such as health visitors, GPs and teachers. It is a particularly serious omission on the part of social workers – which was noted in the DHSS study of children boarded out (1981) – since local authority social workers have a statutory responsibility for investigating cases where a child's development may be being avoidably prevented or impaired and for acting in loco parentis to the children in their care. (Adcock and White, 1985)

However, it was in the management of complex child abuse cases that such findings gave greatest cause for concern. This was highlighted particularly in inspection reports, which pointed to the need for social workers to adopt a much more systematic approach to the assessment task (DHSS, 1982c; DHSS, 1986; Department of Health, 1991c):

> There were significant gaps in the information on most case files and

relevant information was often scattered and recorded in snippets so that it could not be used to build up a complete picture of the child and family. Because of the manner in which information was gathered and recorded it was impossible for social workers to assess the dangers of the situation in a realistic way. This often led to over-optimism. (DHSS, 1986)

The publication of the 'Orange Book', as a response to these concerns in relation to child protection, demonstrates the crucial need for social workers to have access to appropriate and workable methodologies, including paperwork tools, that enables them to approach the task of assessment in a systematic and considered way.

The few other paperwork tools that were available were also for specific groups of young people, for instance that developed by Hoghughi for use at Aycliffe, and the assessment schedules developed by British Agencies for Adoption and Fostering (Hoghughi 1992; BAAF, 1994). None of these are appropriate for assessing adolescents who are at risk of coming into care or experiencing placement breakdowns – here the immediate issues are around short- and medium-term decision making. The Assessment and Action Records are the most significant paperwork tool which is now available for assessing continuing need while evaluating the consequences of state intervention in the life of a child (Department of Health, 1991b, 1995). However, the focus of these assessments is to monitor and plan for the day to day needs of children who are being looked after, and thereby to assist the role of corporate parenting, hence it is recommended that the Records are best used once a year and as a preparation for Statutory Reviews.

The research findings in the 'Pink Book' had been very critical of the lack of decision making and deficiencies in the decision making process. When the second compilation of research findings, *Patterns and Outcomes in Child Placement* was published (Department of Health, 1991a), there was some evidence that concerns regarding the lack of care planning had been taken on board – a number of departments had started to develop active planning systems, decision making was more likely to be shared and to involve young people and their families.

But was there a danger that decision making was becoming too hasty and too shallow, based on limited information? Was there too much concern about the procedures for planning and too little for its content? Had the shift from concern with the past to the present and the future gone too far? The SSI certainly felt this to be the case when they published their conclusions on child care planning, drawn from a distillation of their inspection reports.

> The inspectors' reports included examples of files on children which were lacking in even basic data. (SSI, 1989)

This too was the overarching theme from *Patterns and Outcomes* – where is the evidence? While the criticisms in the 'Pink Book' on lack of decision making may have been addressed, this second research review raised concerns about the knowledge base of decision making. Having found many instances where solid information about a child and family was lacking, the key message of the research is summarised as follows:

> Sound assessment of the problems and strengths of individual children and families must be based on clear, sufficient and well recorded evidence about past and present functioning. Decisions can only be as good as the evidence on which they are based and if evidence is distorted, ignored or not weighed up carefully, the decisions will be flawed. (DH, 1991a)

This message, in itself, is not new; it is the thread that runs throughout all the reports on assessment, going back to the clear statement on practice principles advocated by the Mind Working Party in 1975. What is new is a broader and deeper understanding of what such sentiments mean for practice. Hopefully what was once seen as exceptional practice has now become more commonplace and with the passage of the Children Act should gain even greater recognition. Within this section on the practice of assessment, it is important to consider how this may be influenced by the Children Act.

The Children Act 1989

The theme of assessment can be seen as a thread running through most of the Children Act. Here we pinpoint just three sections of the Act where assessment is particularly crucial and relevant to this study – the formation of individual Care Plans; the significance of ethnicity, culture, religion and language; the provision of services to 'children in need'.

Care Plans

The Guidance on the formation of individual Care Plans identifies assessment as one of the four components of planning – inquiry, consultation, assessment and decision making (Department of Health, Guidance and Regulations Vol. 3, 1991e). In this way the Guidance is highlighting the importance of evidence, gathered in a participatory way, which is then weighed or assessed and used as a basis for decision making. Further, the Guidance makes clear that this will be an ongoing process subject to regular review, reassessment and if necessary to adjustments to the Care Plan.

Ethnicity, culture, religion and language

The Children Act takes an important step forward in introducing a statutory requirement to take account of ethnicity, religion, language and culture in making decisions for or with children and young people (S.22(5)(c)). This brief review of some key issues in the practice of assessment, therefore, would clearly be incomplete without raising the specific area of assessing black and minority ethnic young people and their families (see MacDonald, 1991). Indeed, some of the potential problems confronting predominantly white social workers in assessing black clients are highlighted early on in the Orange Book, quoting from the British Association of Social Workers' guidance (Department of Health, 1988):

> Assessment is not value-free. Social workers must be aware of the cultural, racial, gender, class and religious values they bring to assessment. In a multiracial/multicultural society particular importance must be given to issues of race and culture. (p13)

However, as Ahmad (1990) has emphasised, this does not of course mean that black children, compared with their white peers, should be afforded a lesser degree of protection by white social workers, who may erroneously adopt 'liberal' or 'safe' non-interventionist approaches in the guise of anti-racism (but see also Hardiker and Curnock, 1984).

Few authors have specifically addressed practice issues involved in the assessment of black young people and families. The main exception is Ahmed, who has written especially regarding the situation of Asian women and girls (Ahmed, 1986, 1989). She highlights five main problem areas for white professionals assessing Asian young people and their families. First, there is usually insufficient cultural understanding, so that inaccurate assumptions can be made. This leads into the second point, in that when making an assessment it can be difficult to know what is normal or abnormal within a particular culture. Indeed, white social workers may only have contact with black families with *problems*: a cultural *difference* model may therefore become a cultural *deficit* model.

Thirdly, there tends to be a simplistic emphasis on the part of many white professionals on cultural explanations, in which virtually all problems are attributed to a perceived culture clash between so-called 'Asian' and 'Western' values. Overemphasis on perceived cultural tensions may mask other explanations, for example economic, emotional or psychological factors. Indeed, assessments often give insufficient attention to the social context in which many black families live and the historical factors that have shaped their lives, including migration, slavery, colonialism and the pernicious, pervasive institutional and daily effects of racial discrimination.

Fourthly, preference for cultural explanations means that white professionals can overlook acute problems of racial identity and self-image. Asian children and young people coming to the attention of Social Services can be culturally, racially and emotionally insecure. Children in particular find it difficult to identify with a socially rejected group and embarrassment at school or in the wider community may lead to some rejecting of parents' dress and lifestyle. Young people may over-identify with white culture as a result. Alternatively, greater politicisation of Asian and African-Caribbean youths can occur, who are less likely to accept white racism and workplace exploitation in the way that their parents would have done. Assessments of young people need to take these factors into account.

Services to 'Children in Need'

An important part of the new duties set out in the Children Act 1989 are those contained in Part III relating to family support. Here Section 17 '...gives local authorities a general duty to safe-guard and promote the welfare of children in need and to promote the upbringing of such children by their families, so far as this is consistent with their welfare duty to the child, by providing an appropriate range and level of services' (Department of Health, 1991d, paragraph 2.1).

As Tunstill (1993) has pointed out, the guidance accompanying the Children Act makes only passing reference to the issue of the assessment of children in need. This is despite the complexity of the definition of the overall category 'children in need' as well as decisions in individual cases. The way in which local authorities interpret the category of children in need is likely to be a particularly contentious area, influenced by financial as well as professional considerations. Tunstill argues that this discretionary approach has bedevilled preventive work with children and families in the past.

Concerns emerged in the early 1990s that some agencies were

interpreting 'children in need' very narrowly, as being synonymous with child protection matters or children being looked after. Action from the Department of Health, in writing to Directors of Social Services, emphasised that this was unacceptable. Despite this there is continuing concern about the provision of services to 'children in need'. Both the first and second Children Act Reports contain interim findings from a research study of implementation of Section 17 of the Act (Department of Health, 1993a, 1994). These concluded that progress towards full implementation of Section 17 of the Act has been slow, with the emphasis still concentrated on services for children for whom authorities already have responsibility.

As regards the assessment of 'children in need' the second Children Act Report concludes that 'assessment procedures are many and varied beyond those for abuse and neglect' (p13). This conclusion is partly based on a study by Social Information Systems (SIS) which examined procedures for identifying and managing 'children in need' in four authorities. In noting considerations which need to be addressed by local authorities SIS conclude that:

> Differentiated levels of assessment have to be established relative to the local prioritisation of need and priority of service. These arrangements will need to include
>
> (a) screening for an initial prioritisation of the case and for appropriate redirection to other agencies or services.
> (b) arrangements for more considered assessments (where necessary multi-disciplinary and multi-agency related to the complexity of need and case priority. (SIS, 1993, p93)

We shall return to a fuller discussion on models for assessment in the next chapter.

Standards of good practice in assessment

Working from both the broad principles which underpin all work with children and families and those that relate more specifically to assessment, we can identify from the Children Act certain key elements which we feel establish the standards of good practice in assessment:

- the process of assessment should cause the least possible disturbance to the young people's current caring system;
- any delay in assessment and therefore decision making is likely to prejudice the welfare of the child;
- young people should be encouraged to be actively involved in the assessment process;

- assessments should be based on sound knowledge of family history, but should be forward looking;
- assessment should be undertaken in partnership with parents and family;
- in assessing young people due regard must be given to race, culture, religion and language;
- assessments should include health and education needs;
- agencies should actively provide and share information about processes and resources;
- all participants should have a written record of meetings and decisions;
- agencies require a system for conducting assessments.

Although the data for this research were collected prior to implementation of the Children Act, we shall use these principles of good practice as our framework for later discussion on the role and practice of assessment in the Research Authority.

This exploration of assessment within the Children Act raises again the importance of matching the nature of assessment with its purpose – the next dimension we address in our overview of changes in assessment.

The purpose of assessment

Discussions on the purpose of assessment at the time of the Tutt Committee revolved around the distinction between assessment of needs and assessment of problems. Conceptually that distinction is difficult to sustain. Moreover it was largely a shorthand for distinguishing between types of assessment – contrasting the in-depth, comprehensive assessment that concentrated on the implications of past events for the present, with those assessments which were more focused on finding immediate and medium-term solutions to current presenting problems.

From the analyses by Fuller, and by Grimshaw and Sumner, it is clear that it is more appropriate to think of a variety of forms of assessments. Indeed the new *Working Together* document (Department of Health, 1991g) lists seven different ways in which the term assessment is used with that Report – see Appendix A. Given this diversity, the key question becomes what form of assessment is appropriate for which particular purpose?

This overview has suggested at least seven potentially different situations where an assessment of a particular nature was or is considered appropriate. These are not all mutually exclusive and may overlap, but each has a distinct emphasis.

- **Assessment for placement**: the main purpose of assessment within the former O & A Centres was to identify where within the care system a young person was to live. This is still an important question but is now more likely to be addressed as only one of a larger range of options and issues.
- **Assessment of risk**: while this term can also be used for different purposes it is primarily used in relation to child protection cases. An assessment of risk may need to be undertaken immediately, at the stage of the initial investigation, but also needs to occur when planning for the long-term future of children who have been abused. Here a model of cyclical assessments may be appropriate (see final chapter).
- **Assessment of special educational needs**: this usually refers to the assessment procedure under the 1981 Education Act as amended by the 1993 Education Act and, while primarily about identifying special needs within the education system, it should also take account of the child or young person's care needs within the social and family context. These assessments are usually a lengthy process, with recent research showing an average of around ten months to complete (HMI/Audit Commission, 1992). However, the Code of Practice issued under the 1993 Education Act recommends a maximum period of six months to complete a statement of special educational need (DFE, 1994).
- **Assessment as a gate to resources**: having assessed a young person's needs the emphasis here is likely to be on preventing inappropriate use of particular resources – entry into care or accommodation; entry into residential care; placement in private or voluntary homes or to secure accommodation. While assessments of this kind are primarily concerned with meeting appropriately the young person's needs, they may also be related to the management of budgets or the rationing of resources.
- **Assessment for a 'child in need'**: while certainly not intended to be so, in many authorities at present this is a particular example of gatekeeping and is likely to be about prioritising need. Practice in this area is still developing. It commonly takes the form of a brief initial assessment often using a checklist of factors to test whether someone referred to a social services department is a 'child in need' and therefore is eligible for a service.
- **Assessment for Care Plans**: one could question whether this is a separate purpose for assessment; surely that is also the

purpose of all the other assessments that have been discussed? However, as suggested in the previous section, the inclusion of assessment within the Children Act Guidance as a distinct component in care planning establishes this as assessment of a particular type.

• **Assessment of outcomes**: here the focus is assessing the extent to which decisions have been implemented, and the young person's needs continue to be met. This in turn may lead back to assessment for planning as is intended through the statutory review process. The most systematic format for recording such assessments is the *Assessment and Action Records* (Department of Health, 1991b; 1995).

This list could also have included assessment for community care. While this may be appropriate for some older young people, for instance substance misusers, in the main this form of assessment will be applicable to adults. Nonetheless some of the thinking around the development of principles and practice in assessing for community care may well be transferable to assessment for young people, and so some consideration must be given to that.

Community Care Assessment

The community care reforms were heralded in the White Paper *Caring for People: Community Care in the Next Decade and Beyond* (Department of Health, 1989) and in law became the National Health Service and Community Care Act 1990.

The main aim of the community care reforms was to ' ... enable people to live as normal a life as possible in their own homes or in a homely environment in the community' (p4), with a desire to combat what was felt to be a built-in bias towards residential and nursery home care: a sentiment not dissimilar to the philosophy of the Children Act.

In reading the community care literature with the current research in mind, it is immediately apparent that the assessment process is seen as central and, consequently, given much attention. This is in marked contrast to the situation in mainstream child care work – for example, in the guidance relating to 'children in need'. Thus, the White Paper asserted that one of the main objectives was '...to make proper assessment of need and good case management the cornerstone of high quality care' (p5). It reiterated that this is to ensure a needs-led rather than service-led approach.

The literature on the relatively new area of community care

assessments points to four issues that are relevant to our study of child care assessment. First, there has clearly been much detailed thinking about the purpose and nature of assessment activity and this is reflected in the impressive range of documents that have been produced by SSI specifically on this topic. A second point is the emphasis on a needs-led rather than service-led approach. Thirdly, integrated assessments are stressed, in which individual needs are examined in totality and a range of professionals involved, rather than subjecting clients to repeated assessments. Finally, according to the official literature, intervention should be based very much on the results of the assessment and individuals should be periodically reassessed.

The new measures became operational in April 1993 and given the magnitude of the changes, inevitably it will take time for the new processes to be fully developed. Early experience suggests that there is still a general welcome for the new approach, but that progress away from resource- or service-led to needs-led assessments is still slow – partly because of the constraints on overall resources and partly the inevitable time delay in moving from an existing pattern of service provision (Audit Commission, 1994b).

However there are some concerns that the official guidance on care management encourages a mechanistic and procedural approach, with an overemphasis on process and organisation at the expense of content (Walby, 1994). Moreover many feel that too rigid a separation of the purchaser and provider is not appropriate for children's services, especially if this neglects the relationship between assessment and intervention (Ballard, 1994).

> ... the care manager should also be a 'provider' recognising that assessment and care planning are part of a dynamic and therapeutic interaction requiring all the traditional social work skills. (Walby, 1994, p22)

The definition of assessment

The exploration within this chapter of the many aspects of child care assessment illustrates why the Tutt Committee could find no concise definition of assessment and soon discovered that no simple definition would suffice. Despite this, their report continues by offering the following definition:

> assessment is a continuous process whereby problems are identified and appropriate responses decided upon.

As a broad definition few could disagree with this, although in current terminology it is more likely to be phrased as 'to assess need and identify service provision'. However, such a definition is of little value in identifying assessment as a specific process, albeit one which comes in different forms. Fuller brings some additional specificity with his contention that:

> if assessment has a distinctive application it is to the situation where a social worker makes a conscious attempt to stand back from the quotidian details of managing a particular case in order to evaluate a particular problem in some depth and decide on a course of action. (Fuller, 1985)

Grimshaw and Sumner concluded from their detailed examination of assessment in practice that assessment can be defined as:

> a significant preparation for decision-making, typically occurring at a potentially major point of transition in a child's history.

However, these authors were clear that any practical definition must also be linked to an awareness of the elements of assessment context:

- the transitional points in a child's history;
- the institutional framework;
- the provision of services during assessment;
- the significance of settings in assessment;
- the importance of social and personal relationships;
- the purpose and forms of knowledge-gathering;
- the purpose and form of decision-making.

The continuing prevalence of the term assessment, particularly within the very different frameworks of the Children Act and the implementation of the Community Care legislation, serves to reinforce our contention that *assessment is a term which can only have meaning when it is defined in terms of the purpose, the context and the manner in which it is undertaken*. Here we are reminded of the discussion by Hardiker and colleagues on the definition of prevention in social work:

> The difficulty with the use of the term 'prevention' in child care social work lies not so much in the intrinsic meaning of the word as in the differences of meaning that arise once an object is placed after the verb … to prevent WHAT?' (Hardiker, Exton and Barker, 1991 p43)

This seems to have a similar applicability to the term assessment, although here the necessary addition is *assessment for what purpose*? In the final chapter we shall return again to explore this more fully. However it is clear that despite the very confused picture presented by the term assessment in child care, undertaking assessments is still a fundamental and discrete task within social work with children – *and one that requires specific skills.* Our overview of the concept and practice of assessment leads us to conclude that assessment is more than a process, nor is it simply an activity, it is about a set of skills or competences that need to be applied in particular circumstances. It is hoped that the empirical study of assessment which follows will highlight some of the essentials of this task and the competences needed to fulfil these.

Summary points

- Major changes have occurred in the concept and practice of assessment over the past 20 years. The term currently has different meanings in social work relating to different purposes and this can lead to some confusion.
- Assessment in child care was emphasised by the 1969 Children and Young Persons Act, which led to the setting up of residential Observation and Assessment Centres (O & As). However a number of criticisms were soon levelled against this model of assessment; they tended to adopt a 'medical' model of social work, that was also non-participatory; they constituted unnatural environments for assessment; subsequent residential placements were unduly prioritised; doubts were raised about the use and impact of assessment reports and recommendations; and assessment was seen as separate from mainstream, everyday social work activity with children and their families.
- Exactly who should assess has been questioned. Some specialist teams have been established. Furthermore, different approaches have been adopted regarding the extent to which assessments are multidisciplinary, and whether or not a wide group of professionals should automatically be involved.
- A number of specific practice concerns have been raised. For example, there has been a tendency to dwell on past explanations rather than future options, and for assessments too often to be residentially-based. Research has demonstrated the deficiencies of many social workers' everyday 'assessments', especially in comparison with other professional groups. Concerns have arisen specifically regarding child protection cases.
- Problems have been highlighted when white professionals undertake assessments of the circumstances of children and families who are black and from minority ethnic groups.
- The importance of clarifying the purpose of assessment was recognised. Assessment can, therefore, relate to: placement; the degree of risk; special educational needs; a gate to re-

sources; whether or not the child is 'in need'; care planning; and outcomes. Some of the thinking on assessment in community care and assessment of 'children in need' is introduced. Building upon research findings and the guidance which accompanied the Children Act 1989, key elements were identified of what the authors felt should underpin good assessment practice. These are concerned with: minimal disturbance to the young person's current caring system; the absence of delay; young people's and families' involvement; race, culture, language and religion; sharing of information; adequate recording; and an efficient assessment system.

- By considering different ways in which assessment has been defined, it becomes clear that the term assessment can only have meaning when it is defined in terms of the purpose, the context and the manner in which it is undertaken.
- This overview of the concept and practice of assessment concludes that assessment is more than a process, nor is it simply an activity; it is about a set of skills and competences that need to be applied in particular circumstances.

3. The research study: aims and methods

Aims of the study

The broad aim of this study is to analyse the role which assessment currently plays in social work decision making with adolescent young people and their families. More specifically, by examining several different forms of assessment, both residential and community-based, the study aims to explore the following questions:

- What are the main components of the different forms of assessment for adolescents?
- Which children or young people are allocated to which form of assessment and why?
- Who participates in the assessment and what are the participants' perspectives on the assessment process?
- What is the outcome of these assessments in terms of their impact on young people's circumstances one year later?
- What are the relative costs of the various assessment packages – is there a relationship between costs and outcomes in terms of the child's subsequent care career?

Definitions

Before describing the research methodology employed, it is necessary to set out the key definitions which help to establish the parameters of the study. Later, we shall explain how each of these definitions was operationalised for the purpose of this research.

Assessment

As the previous chapter has made clear, the term assessment has a variety of meanings, even within social services, with yet more variation if we include other agency contexts, such as education or the provision of services to children with disabilities. For the purposes of this research it was necessary for us to establish a working definition of assessment.

Earlier work by Grimshaw and Sumner suggested that the most significant activities associated with assessment can all be regarded as preparation for decision making. Hence any gathering of information, immediate or short-term interventions, ascertaining the views of young people and their families, are all undertaken so that informed decisions can be made about the child's present and future (Grimshaw and Sumner, 1991). Detached from decision making, assessments have been shown to be ineffective. So in designing this study the notion of decision making was seen as central to the definition of assessment.

However, decision making in child care takes many forms, not all of which may require prior assessment activity. The research by Grimshaw and Sumner further suggested that assessment is likely to be associated with decisions around transitional events in a child's care or social services career; for instance, consideration for admission to care or accommodation.

This is less likely to be so in cases that have got 'stuck'; where little progress is being made and the social worker is unsure what steps to take. Here a further assessment by someone new to the case may well be appropriate. With ongoing cases with no significant transitional events, the six-monthly Statutory Review provides a mechanism for considering whether a more specific assessment is required. However, such cases were not included in this research.

Putting together these two aspects – decision making and significant transitional events – leads to the following definition of assessment, and the one employed in this study – *a significant preparation for decision making, typically occurring at a possible point of transition in a child's care career*. Although this definition was originally constructed prior to the implementation of the Children Act 1989, it equates closely to the way in which, within the Guidance, assessment is seen as a part of the child care planning process.

Transitional events

Throughout a young person's contact with social services there may be many events which are of sufficient significance to be regarded as transitional points. These include admission or consideration of admission to care or accommodation; changes of placement, including returns home; changes in legal status or child protection registration; leaving care.

Grimshaw and Sumner's study indicated that for adolescents the most significant transitional events triggering assessment are consideration of admission to care, admission to care and placement breakdown. The occurrence of any one of these three events was one of the criteria defining our sample frame.

Operationalising this definition, for instance by deciding when serious consideration is being given to the admission of a child or young person to accommodation or care, is not necessarily simple. In this study we have followed the definition of 'serious consideration' developed by Packman:

> Serious consideration of a child's admission to care was established if one or more of the following applied: a parent, caretaker or child requested admission to care; a social worker, whether on referral from another agency or as part of his current work with a family discussed the possibility of admission with his senior or team leader or recorded its consideration in the case file. (Packman, 1986, p26)

Similar problems of definition apply to placement breakdowns. Again a definition has been developed and employed in previous research and found to be both appropriate and workable. So the definition we shall adopt is that used by Berridge and Cleaver, which was developed from the Dartington study, *Lost in Care* (Millham and others, 1986). A change of placement will be regarded as a placement breakdown if it is 'a placement ending that was not included in the social work plan, either in the ending itself or in the timing of the termination' (Berridge and Cleaver, 1987, p30). Within our sample we also include those cases where a placement breakdown was threatened and some assessment work was planned in advance of any actual breakdown.

For brevity, throughout this report these three categories of transitional events will be referred to as 'considered for care', 'admitted to care' and 'placement breakdown'.

Forms of assessment

It will be apparent from the definition of assessment set out earlier that child care assessments can be undertaken in a variety of ways. In employing our definition of assessment the first major distinction to be made is between assessments conducted by area staff and those referred to the specialist service. These are characterised as *routine* or *referred*. A Routine assessment is one undertaken by area or district social workers in the course of their everyday case work, although possibly involving contributions from others. A Referred assessment is one that is referred to a specialist assessment service and undertaken within that specialist assessment process.

A further dimension to the form of assessment is the location in which it takes place. The specialist assessment service in this research was able to undertake assessments within Residential Assessment Units, in Assessment Foster Homes or through the Day Assessment Unit while the young person was living at home with family or friends. Similarly when assessments were carried out 'routinely' by the area social worker, the young person could be living in a Residential Unit, with foster carers or at home. However in this instance these resources would not be specialist assessment resources. The two dimensions to the form of assessment are shown in the following manner:

Table 3.1   Forms of assessment

Assessment category	Type of assessment	Location options
Referred	Assessed by specialist worker(s)	Assessment Day Unit Assessment foster home Residential Assessment Unit
Routine	Assessment by area social worker	In the community In a foster home In a residential unit

Inevitably, in practice, the assessment of a young person may involve more than one of these categories.

Outcomes

One of the specific aims of this research is to examine the results of assessment in terms of their impact on young people's subsequent care or social service careers. In other words the outcome of the assessment. Defining and measuring the outcomes from personal social services interventions is a complex task. Considerable progress has been made in unravelling the concept of outcomes in the *Report of an Independent Working Party* established by the Department of Health and led by Parker (Parker and others, 1991). It is not our intention to repeat that comprehensive discussion here; rather we shall use their framework to explain the definition of outcomes which has been used in this study.

Parker and his colleagues suggested that when defining outcomes it is necessary to consider first the answer to these three questions:

(1) For whom is something considered to be an outcome?
(2) Should greater emphasis be given to specific or to general outcomes?
(3) When are outcomes assumed to occur? (p19)

The answers to each of these questions will define the measures of outcome applicable to this study.

The authors define five perspectives from which outcomes may be considered: public outcomes; service outcomes; professional outcomes; family outcomes; and child outcomes. Let us consider these perspectives in relation to this study. An immediate output from an assessment is a plan or series of decisions. In looking at the outcomes from an assessment process, a possible proxy measure is the successful implementation of the original or revised plans – this is, in Parker's terms, *a service outcome*.

However, the implementation of plans is only one dimension to a successful intervention; also important are the manner and means by which plans are achieved and changes brought about. Much of the information on this will derive from social workers, so this can be regarded, again in Parker's terms, as *a professional outcome*. Although this study includes interviews with some young people and families, these are used to illustrate the general findings and are not employed in the general assessment of outcomes. So in this study we are using only two of the perspectives on outcomes, namely service outcomes and professional outcomes.

The second component of outcome definition relates to the *specific* or *general* nature of the outcomes. Using implementation of decisions as a basis for measuring outcomes, provides an outcome that applies only to specific areas. To balance this, we have also included broad-based measures of subsequent changes in the health, social skills, behaviour, relationship with family and the balance of positive and negative features in the overall situation of the young person. These indicate whether the young person, one year later, is in a situation that, in general terms, is better, worse or much the same as that which pertained when the assessment was completed.

The third consideration is the time-scale over which outcomes are to be measured. The research has been designed to gather follow-up data one year after an assessment has been completed. Our measures of outcomes, therefore, relate to that specific point in time.

In summary, the outcome measures used in this research are

derived largely from service and professional perspectives. They infer the success of social service interventions following an assessment through the implementation of care plans and the nature of the social work undertaken. They cover both specific areas of work with young people and broad assessments of their current well-being, and they have been measured one year on.

Methodology

Having established the aims of the research and the definitions employed, we now describe the methodology, starting with discussion of the research site.

The location of the research

The fieldwork for this research was undertaken in a London Borough which shall be referred to simply as the Authority or the Research Authority. This Authority was chosen as a research site for a number of reasons. First, it offered a range of assessment resources, including referral to a specialist assessment service with access to residential units, assessment foster care, day assessment resources and fairly ready access to external specialists from several disciplines. Second, the Authority was sufficiently large to generate, within the necessary time-scale, an adequate number of cases which met the necessary criteria for inclusion in the study. In addition, the diverse ethnic composition of the population provided an opportunity to take into account issues of ethnicity, culture, religion and language. A further attraction of the Authority is its tradition of internal evaluation and engagement with external researchers. Finally, the Authority was relatively well resourced, especially in its allocation to children and families. A detailed description of the local authority will be found in the next chapter.

The focus of this research is comparisons between the outputs and outcomes of different types of assessment. A parallel study examines issues of costs and cost-effectiveness (see Chapter 12). Comparisons between assessment systems within six different local authorities has already been undertaken by Grimshaw and Sumner. In contrast, this research used only one authority, which encompassed a comprehensive range of assessment facilities, thereby enabling the researchers to regard the organisational setting as a relative constant and to concentrate on the comparisons between the assessment types.

However, we did not design the research to be an evaluation of that Authority's service. Rather, using the Authority as a critical case study it is hoped that the research findings can inform a detailed discussion of the issues likely to be faced in assessment of adolescents by all social services departments.

Nonetheless any conclusions drawn from research undertaken within one authority run the risk of being regarded as relevant only to that authority and being disregarded by others. Having completed the study it is our firm belief that the problems posed by adolescents in, or at risk of entering, the care system; the legislative framework for addressing these problems; and the level of knowledge and skill of practitioners, are sufficiently similar across the country to make this research pertinent for all authorities.

Selecting cases

The study was prospective. A group of 75 adolescent young people were to be identified, each of whom had an assessment following the occurrence of one of the three identified transitional events. It was hoped that the total sample could be evenly spread across the three event groups. However, this depends on the actual flow of events experienced by young people in contact with the Authority. More specifically the criteria for including a case in the sample were:

● the young person had experienced a transitional event;
● the case was continuously active, though not necessarily allocated for a full three months following the event;
● an assessment took place.

Each of these criteria requires further explanation. First, this study is primarily concerned with young people over 12 years of age. As we saw in Chapter 2, in many social service departments adolescents are no longer accorded the high priority of a decade ago, so a study focusing specifically on their needs is important. Moreover the remit of the specialist assessment service in the Authority was for 12 year-olds and over. However, in order to test the way in which younger people or sibling groups were assessed, a small sub-group of 10 to 11 year-olds were included in the sample.

Second, as explained when defining 'transitional events', we have deliberately chosen only three key transitional points which are of particular relevance to adolescents; namely, consideration of admission to care, admission to care and placement breakdown. The choice of these particular transitional points and the adolescent age group means that the sample chosen was young people whose presenting problems are more likely to revolve around their behaviour and relationships with family, rather than issues of child protection. This is important in terms of the type of assessment that is likely to be appropriate for these cases and the particular skills offered by the specialist assessment service.

Third, it was decided to include only those cases which were continuously active for three months. This was to allow time for any assessments to take place and to exclude any transient cases from the analysis, such as runaways, emergency overnight stays or remands.

Fourth, it is necessary to operationalise our definition of assessment. It will be remembered that assessment was defined as a significant preparation for decision making. The *minimum* form of preparation which was necessary for inclusion in the study was *the holding of a meeting, at which decisions were made and recorded* (not including supervision).

It is also necessary to pinpoint the assessment period. The starting point was the date of the identified transitional event. The end point was the date at which the Final Assessment Conference or equivalent planning meeting was held. For those cases 'referred' to the Assessment Service, these start and end points were clearly identifiable; for cases assessed by district social workers, 'routine' cases, there was no single procedure which was applicable to all cases, although it was always possible to identify a planning meeting at which decisions based on the assessment were taken. The usual period of assessment was three months, although occasionally this was shorter or longer.

So having clarified the criteria for inclusion, how were sample cases identified?

Identification of the sample

The Authority had a computerised client index system (CIS) and the intention was to use this for the identification of young people admitted to care and for changes in placement from which placement breakdowns could then be identified. However, no formal mechanism existed within the Authority for identifying young people considered for care, so it was necessary for the researchers to establish a monitoring system to undertake this task. Team leaders from each area office and hospital social work teams were asked to complete a monitoring sheet every fortnight, identifying all cases which fitted the given definition of 'considered for care'.

It soon became apparent that the CIS was not a sufficiently comprehensive or reliable source of information and that it would be necessary to extend the specially created monitoring system to identify admissions to care and placement breakdowns. This was done by using the Authority's gatekeepers to resources, the assessment service and community fostering teams, and supplementing this with information from team leaders. While the researchers are confident that they were informed about all admissions to care and most considered for care cases, they may have missed some placement breakdowns, especially those movements within the Authority's children's home or within the private and voluntary residential sector.

Having received a monitoring sheet, the researchers would wait for three months before going back to ascertain if the case was still active and that an assessment had been or was being undertaken. Those that fitted this criteria were included in the sample.

It is possible that more than one monitoring sheet would have been completed on a young person; for instance, if they had experienced more than one event, such as an admission to care followed by a placement breakdown. In this situation, the young person was only included once, and placed in the category which identified the event he or she had experienced first. In this way our sample is made up of 75 different young people, not 75 'events'.

In total during the monitoring year 88 young people fitted the criteria for inclusion in the study. The 75 cases were chosen from this group largely on a chronological basis, while also trying to ensure that the numbers in each of the three 'event' groups were matched. However the number of young people who were notified to us following a breakdown in placement remained disappointingly low. Overall only 22 young people qualified for inclusion in this 'event' category during our 12 month monitoring period.

There are two main reasons for this. Firstly, many of the placement breakdowns notified to us involved young people whom we had already included in the sample. Because we only included them once, this meant that as time went on the number of new cases which were allocated to this event category declined. Secondly, although we found that it was often the same youngsters who accounted for many of the breakdowns in residential care, we were also conscious that some unplanned endings may have been missed by our monitoring system; particularly those which involved transfers between local authority residental establishments, or where young people left a community home, ostensibly for a brief 'time-out' or 'cooling-off' period, but who did not return later, either because they were unwilling to go back, or because staff in the unit were unable or unwilling to take them. It was also rare for us to be informed of breakdowns in older adoles-

cent placements, such as hostels, lodgings and other semi-independent living arrangements, even though numerous research
studies have suggested that such placement breakdowns are common. This may need to be borne in mind when looking at our
findings, since the majority of young people in our breakdown
group were notified to us following a family placement breakdown,
although most had prior experience of both residential and foster
placements during their time in care.

Data collection

Having identified our sample of young people the next stage was
to gather data. Information was obtained from case records and
through interviews with the social worker who was responsible for
the case. The information collected covered the following topics:

child characteristics
- biographical details, family and case histories;
- previous assessments, services and interventions;
- descriptions of their current situations.

assessment process
- type of assessment resource employed;
- the professionals involved;
- the information collected;
- the tools and techniques employed;
- the degree of child and parental involvement;
- the duration of the assessment;
- the number and type of meetings held;
- the content of reports submitted;
- the recommendations and decisions reached.

services received during assessment
- social work input;
- input from others;
- accommodation/placements;
- support services offered and received.

social worker views
- why they selected that particular form of assessment;
- what influenced their decision;
- what they saw as the main purpose of the assessment;
- whom they consulted and why;
- what aspects went well, which were problematic and why;
- their views on the decisions reached.

A similar data collection exercise took place one year later, with the emphasis on outcomes for the young person. Data were gathered on the implementation of plans and changes in the young person's circumstances in the following areas:

- accommodation;
- legal and Child Protection Register status;
- education and/or employment;
- family contact and social networks;
- the extent to which the young person's ethnicity, culture, religion and language had been taken into account;
- health, social skills, behaviour;
- contact with social worker/other professionals;
- support services received.

In addition information was collected on:

- meetings held during the year;
- new decisions or plans made;
- use made of the assessment;
- value of social services intervention;
- overall assessment of the young person's current situation;
- a prognosis for the next five years.

In designing these instruments, the researchers were able to build upon the experiences of others. For instance, many of the questions had been tested previously in the *Child Care Now* study and by Grimshaw and Sumner (Rowe, Hundleby and Garnett, 1989; Grimshaw and Sumner, 1991). The classification of presenting problems, behaviour and health concerns was informed by those used in the Fairfield Lodge Study (Reinach, Lovelock and Roberts, 1979), by the Bridge Consultancy (unpublished) and in the Child and Adolescent Problem Profile used at Aycliffe Adolescent Centre (Hoghughi, 1992).

As well as these two stages of data collection on each of the 75 young people, additional information was gathered from other sources. First, interviews were conducted with a small group of parents and young people in order to ascertain their perspective on the assessment and decision making process in particular and their relationship with social services in general. Second, the decision making process was observed and additional information gathered by attendance by researchers at planning meetings, in particular, at final assessment conferences.

Third, a series of interviews was held with a wide range of people involved in assessment including professionals outside social services, residential staff and foster carers, area staff in social services and divisional management staff. Here the purpose was to focus on their experiences of assessment rather than on particular cases. For example, questions were asked about their understanding of the term assessment and how this matched the concept and practice of assessment within the Authority.

The costs study

It will be recalled that the National Children's Bureau researchers worked in association with colleagues from the Personal Social Services Research Unit (PSSRU), University of Kent (at Canterbury), whose specific brief as social care economists was to gather information on the costs of assessment. More specific details of the approach adopted are contained in Chapter 12. However we shall provide a brief summary here.

The costs work was undertaken following the same four basic rules in cost evaluation as previous PSSRU work: namely that costs should be measured *comprehensively*, including all components of care packages (including for example an element for management costs and indirect activities not involving direct contact with the client); differences in costs should not be ignored but examined and explained; comparisons drawn from such examinations should be made on a like-with-like basis; and finally, as adopted in this research, cost information is of most use and less likely to be misleading when it is considered alongside client-based outcome data (Knapp, 1984, 1993b).

Gathering costs information is a complicated process. Social work or other professional records will not always document accurately whether or not a particular service was received, let alone the extent of use. Similar inaccuracies can also stem from individuals' own accounts, which rely on memory. The PSSRU approach developed over time, which was followed here, is therefore to use a multi-faceted procedure in which data is obtained from a variety of complementary sources.

It was decided that the best way to gather costs information on assessments was for specific questions to be included in the National Children's Bureau researchers' interview schedules. These data were subsequently analysed separately, as well as in association with other related information. For each of the 75 young people, therefore, detailed information was gathered from social workers about use of *all* services during the three-month period following the event which precipitated assessment. This period covers the time in which the assessment activity should have been completed. At follow-up, service use data were collected referring to the four-week period preceding interview.

Where necessary, case files were scrutinised to complement the information provided by social workers. These sources were used particularly to gather data on accommodation and placements, social work and education: as we shall see, the three main contributors to the costs of assessment packages. For services that were used more selectively and, therefore, would have a more peripheral influence on overall costs – such as, for example, adolescent psychiatric services – social workers were asked only whether or not the young person had received that particular service. Three strategies were then used to quantify level of service receipt: contact was made by the PSSRU researcher directly with the providing agency; data from other clients in the study were used where standard levels of care were provided; or, failing these attempts, assumptions were made on the basis of previous work in this area.

Receipt of services and assessment packages were calculated both in total and as weekly averages. Unit costs of providing services, such as social worker input or the cost of a residential service, were obtained from the relevant agency providing the service. These took account of local variations and were calculated so as to approximate the *long-run marginal opportunity cost* of providing each service – that is the *additional* cost of providing for the young person in question (see Allen and Beecham, 1993).

Summary points

- This chapter has outlined the aims of the study and the methods employed. It also establishes the operational definitions employed in the research. For example assessment was defined as 'a significant preparation for decision making, typically occuring at a possible transition point in a child's care career.' The 'transitional events' employed in the study incorporate three different circumstances: consideration of admission to care; admission to care; and placement breakdown.

- We have differentiated between 'Routine' and 'Referred' assessments, depending on whether or not a specialist assessment service is involved. Assessments could occur in the community, foster homes or residential establishments.

- The research was based in an inner London authority, which contained a range of assessment approaches. It also had a diverse ethnic population.

- The study was a prospective one, following-up 75 young people over the age of 12 years for a period of one year.

- Identification of the sample was complex and various administrative arrangements had to be developed with social services. Only cases that were continually active for three months were included in the sample.
- Information gathered at the assessment stage related to child characteristics; the assessment process, services received during assessment; and social worker views on a range of relevant issues. A year later data were gathered on the implementation of assessment plans; changes in the young person's circumstances; as well as more general information.
- Additional material was gathered directly from young people and families themselves; by attending assessment meetings; and from a range of wider professionals involved in the assessment process.
- The concept of outcomes in child care is a complex one. Our research focuses over a 12-month period on the implementation of assessment plans, and changes in young people's situations.
- Cost information was gathered by University of Kent colleagues by inserting specific questions in the Bureau research instruments. Supplementary information was collected where required. Costs were calculated for *all* services used during the three-month assessment period. At the 12-month follow-up, attention focused specifically on the preceding four-week period.

4. The local context

Social services departments are subject to substantial local variation, particularly in the role and organisation of child care assessment. Our contention that the findings of this research have a general relevance notwithstanding, it is important to make clear the particular context in which this study was undertaken. This chapter presents that context through a description of the Authority, the social services department, the assessment service and the child care population.

Pen picture of the Authority

The Authority is a medium-sized inner London Borough, which the 1991 census showed had a resident population of almost 175,000. To this can be added the many thousands of people who come into the borough on a daily basis giving a working population of approximately 530,000 and a day time population that is estimated to be almost one million (OPCS, 1992).

Child population

We can see from Figure 4.1 that the proportion of the population in the Authority under 18 years of age was comparatively low, 15.3 per cent, compared to 21.2 per cent for all inner London and 22.7 per cent for England as a whole. This comparatively low figure applies across all three age bands – 0-4 years, 5-15 years, 16-17 years.

Economic characteristics

Lying as it does in central London the Authority is one of the richest and most prosperous of all London boroughs. Nevertheless like other London boroughs it contains pockets of deprivation and unemployment which increased during the recession. Recent figures (Autumn 1992) show the contrasting levels of unemploy-

Figure 4.1   Children as a proportion of the resident population

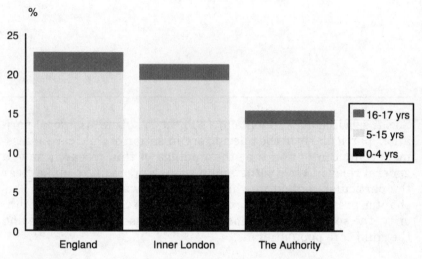

Source: 1991 Census

ment across the borough with a low of 2.5 per cent in one ward, compared to 24.0 per cent unemployment in another. These differences in unemployment are mirrored in the child care figures for these areas.

Housing

Housing tenure reflects the policies of the council, with only 20 per cent of the population living in local authority housing. The figure of 35 per cent in owner-occupation is slightly lower than the average for inner London. The remainder of households are in privately rented or housing association accommodation. The shortage of affordable accommodation creates homelessness among residents of the borough. In addition, the existence of a large number of hotels and bed and breakfast establishments means that the Authority is often accommodating homeless families from other areas. In September 1990 there were an estimated 916 local families homeless and in temporary accommodation and a further 1,550 homeless families from outside in temporary accommodation in the borough.

Ethnicity

Figures from the 1991 census (see Table 4.1 and Figure 4.2) show the ethnic composition of the population of the Authority compared to that for England and Wales and for all inner London boroughs.

Table 4.1   Population by ethnic origin

	England & Wales %	Inner London %	Authority %
White	94.1	74.4	78.6
Black	1.8	13.5	7.6
Asian	3.2	8.1	6.6
Other	1.0	4.1	7.2
	100.0	100.0	100.0

Source: 1991 Census

Figure 4.2   Population by ethnic origin

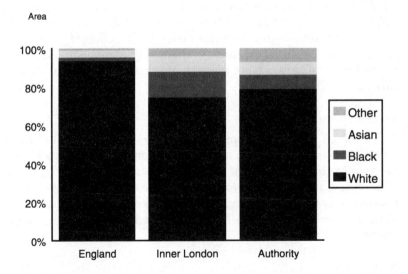

Although the proportion of the population of the Authority that is white is much lower than that for England and Wales, it is only slightly higher than the average for inner London boroughs. Figure 4.2 also shows that compared to the average for inner London (13.5 per cent) there is a low proportion of black residents

(7.6 per cent). The above average number of people who placed themselves in the 'other' category reflects the enormous diversity of the population including significant numbers of people from North Africa and the Middle East. This was illustrated by a caseload census carried out in the Authority in 1990, which identified at least 44 different ethnic groups among clients of the social services department.

Political context

There have been major external changes that have affected all local authorities during recent years. In addition to these, there are internal factors which relate specifically to the Authority, and which influence its policies and operation. Three such areas are highlighted; equal opportunities, the role of the private sector and budgets.

Policy on equal opportunity

Until it become a statutory requirement under the Children Act to take due account of a child's religious persuasion, ethnic origin and cultural and linguistic background, the attitude of the council to equal opportunities meant that staff were unable to give this a high priority. Indications of this were the lack of any equal opportunities statement and the prohibition by the council of any monitoring of the ethnic origins of clients or staff. This made the recruitment of carers from a range of ethnic backgrounds particularly difficult.

Service provision

The Council has actively promoted the role of the local authority as an enabler rather than a direct provider of services, which can be seen in the replacement of the Authority's facilities by the use of private and voluntary resources. Indeed recent decisions by the Council mean that the majority of services, including services to children and families, will be contracted out through Business Units.

Budgets

The budget per head for social services has always been regarded as generous; the Chartered Institute for Public Finance and Accountancy (CIPFA) statistics for actual budgets for 1990/91 show that the department spent over £27 for every person in the population. This compares to an average figure of £10.72 for SSD expenditure per head for all English authorities and £17.20 for all London authorities (CIPFA, 1991).

The proportion of the total budget going to children and families is also comparatively high; in the Authority 24.4 per cent of the SSD budget went to children compared with an average of 17.1 per cent for all English authorities and 22.2 per cent for all London authorities. Given the low child population of the Authority, these figures indicate that the services for children and families are relatively well resourced (CIPFA, 1991).

The Social Services Department

In the year prior to this project starting, the Social Services Department had undergone a major reorganisation. One of the main features of this was the move from generic to specialist teams and the creation of a new Children and Families division (see Figure 4.3). The Assistant Director (Children and Families) was responsible for all child care services. These were delivered through four geographical divisions and the specialist city-wide Adolescent Services.

Figure 4.3   Social Services structure at the commencement of the research

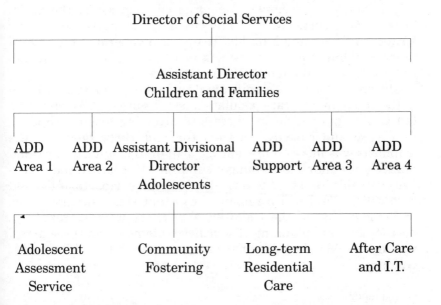

Director of Social Services

Assistant Director
Children and Families

ADD Area 1   ADD Area 2   Assistant Divisional Director Adolescents   ADD Support   ADD Area 3   ADD Area 4

Adolescent Assessment Service   Community Fostering   Long-term Residential Care   After Care and I.T.

The Adolescent Assessment Service (AAS) predated the above reorganisation, having been created in 1984. At this time it was supervised by the Head of Assessment who reported to the Assistant Divisional Director of the Children Specialist Services. The creation of the Children and Families Division in 1988-9 did not significantly change this line-management structure. A more detailed description of the structure, functions, resources and practices of the AAS follows in Chapter 5. Further changes in structure occurred during 1992 to prepare for the introduction of community care. As this was after the fieldwork was completed it did not directly affect the research, although impending change has become a continued source of anxiety in social service departments in recent years.

Child care policy

When our study began in the summer of 1990 the Department was in the process of reviewing its child care policies in preparation for the implementation of the Children Act in the following year. However, as it was felt that in many ways it had already fulfilled many of the central requirements of the Act, the Department's new policy statement, *Policy for Children and Families*, 1991, had few significant changes, leaving much of the 1986 document as the most current statement of policy.

This four-page document was originally agreed by the Social Services Committee in 1986 and circulated to staff in the newly formed Children and Families Teams as a general guide to good practice. It built upon successful implementation of important policy initiatives in the late 1970s and early 1980s.

Clearly visible is the significant drop in the numbers of children in the department's care population (see Figure 4.4). Much of this fall was accounted for by success in diverting teenage children from care and custody. So from the mid 1980s onwards, the emphasis was more on preventing 'drift' into long-term care, and reducing the number of younger children who reached their teenage years in care. Three themes dominated the department's child care policies and which remained constant right through to the implementation of the Children Act. These were permanency, partnership and planning. The policy statements on these areas, written in 1986, do indeed have resonance with the Children Act Guidance.

Permanency

The concept of permanency – securing stable relationships at home and in care – is summarised early on in the Department's policy statement and underlies many of the objectives it contains.

> The caring environment which best meets the child's needs is a permanent parental relationship which is expected to last and is legally protected. It should thus be regarded as the birthright of every child to grow up in a stable family, for it is this that provides the means by which a child may develop the sense of security and identity that derive not solely from the parents but also from the wider familial, cultural and social environment within which the child grows to maturity. (Policy for Children and Families, 1986, p1)

Rather than focusing narrowly on the need to find substitute family placements for children in long-term care, the primary objectives of this policy were the prevention of family breakdown and the preservation of important family and community links. A high priority was therefore attached to early preventive intervention supported by a detailed and thorough assessment of need.

> Children whose needs are not met or who risk losing their families must be identified at the earliest possible time and a detailed and thorough assessment of their physical, emotional, social and educational needs determined. (ibid.)

However, whilst teenagers were specifically mentioned in the policy document as being at particular risk of coming into care, interestingly, no mention was made of the role which the Assessment Service played in this preventive strategy.

> A large number (of teenagers) will be at risk of coming into care because of concern about their behaviour or their ability to cope at home or in school or because of delinquency. In such cases the objective will be to strengthen the position of the young people at home, at school, or at work, in order to prevent reception into care, and to offer community-based alternatives to both care and custody. (ibid. p3)

Partnership

In providing services the emphasis was on complementing the efforts of families and wherever possible 'sharing care' with parents. Indeed, local authority accommodation was presented as just one of a range of positive options by which social services might help prevent family breakdowns.

Although the legal routes by which children come into care were not specifically mentioned, there was a suggestion that, wherever possible, voluntary measures should be used, with care proceedings and wardships only being invoked when a voluntary reception could not adequately safeguard the child's welfare.

In line with the department's aim to promote 'open partnerships' with parents in the delivery of all child care services, a high level of parental involvement in planning, assessment and decision making was seen as essential, as was the promotion of continuing parental contact for children, both by the proximity of placements and the attitude and role of the carers. Children also,

> have the right to be listened to, understood, and their wishes and feelings to be considered. The child also has the right to participate in discussion as far as able, while knowing that final responsibility for decisions rests with adults. (ibid.)

Planning

However, whilst emphasising the positive aspects of short-term admissions for some children and families, the policy document also made it clear that local authority care should only be seen as a means of securing a child's future welfare, rather than as an end in itself. Long-term care was therefore presented as something which should be avoided. Indeed one of the Department's main policy objectives was that 'no child should spend the major part of his or her childhood in care'. In order to achieve this goal, a system of planning, with clearly defined time-limits, was to be introduced:

> Plans for children in care must be made at the earliest possible time, and other than in exceptional circumstances this should be before the child comes into care. (ibid.)

In spite of these objectives, when our study began there were still no formal mechanisms in place across the Authority by which such planning objectives could be implemented and monitored, other than the statutory review process. One such unified system of 'care conferences' was proposed, which would include the Assessment Service meetings (see following chapter), and encompass all children who were either in or on the margins of local authority care. Interestingly, the three main transitional events which it was suggested should trigger off these conferences are similar to those which form the focus of our research study.

Social workers' understanding of policy

At the time when our research began, most of the child care procedures were in the process of being rewritten, most had been out-of-date for some time and the status of some of the procedures were not always clear. There was little evidence of them being used as a procedural tool, although the more recently produced pocket-sized child protection procedure handbook was. Significantly none of the social workers we interviewed mentioned it as a source of guidance in relation to their work with the young people in our study. Instead, social workers tended to rely on the guidance of their team-managers and the knowledge and experience of their colleagues and team-clerks. As one newly appointed social worker commented:

> 'I've not seen any guidelines. I'm still picking up on my training. I'm lucky, I work with a very experienced team. With adolescents I think the procedure is to refer on to the Adolescent Assessment Service. But with younger children I'm not sure of any particular procedures.'

Most social workers we interviewed said they were aware of a policy document, but few had any recollection of having seen it, and were generally unable to tell us what policies it contained, or how these impacted on their work with children and families. Knowledge about departmental policies tended to be picked up more informally, either through attendance at meetings or through observation, and tended to be focused on the Department's placement preferences rather than on any values or principles which should underlie their approach to work with children and families, as the following examples show:

> 'I know that the authority doesn't like children to be placed in children's homes. It seems to be policy to go for family placements wherever possible, except in exceptional circumstances.'

> 'I believe it's policy to go for a family placement in the first instance and a black family for black children, but apart from that I'm not really sure.'

> 'I know that I'm unlikely to get a secure placement in this case as the authority don't like secure, so I'll need to look elsewhere.'

Child care resources

In spite of a declared preference for family placements, the number of foster placements in the Authority has always been relatively low (see following section). For example, despite a fourfold increase in short-term foster placements in the Authority during the 1980s, by 1991 foster care still only accounted for 46 per cent of all child care placements, compared with well over half (55 per cent) in inner London, and 58 per cent for England as a whole.

This factor, combined with a much reduced residential capacity in the Authority, had a number of consequences. Firstly, in the late 80s, increased admissions meant that children for whom a foster placement might have been most appropriate were frequently

being placed in residential care. In addition, the overall shortage
in foster placements in the Authority meant that children were
often being placed some distance away from their families. Indeed
in 1991, no less than three-quarters of the Authority's foster placements were made outside the borough boundaries.

Secondly, an increased pressure on short-term residential resources in the Authority also meant that an increasing number of
children were being placed in private and voluntary placements.
In 1992, for example, the proportion of children placed in private
and voluntary residential resources was 21 per cent, almost equal
to the number of children placed in the Authority's own residential
resources.

Thirdly, increased occupancy in the Authority's smaller group
units substantially reduced their capacity for outreach assessment
and after-care work, and had a significant impact on the preventive role of the Assessment Service (see following chapter).

Finally, a severe shortage of long-term placement options for
older children in the Authority, both in foster and in semi-independent accommodation, meant that young people were increasingly spending longer periods in assessment placements. Such was
the problem that by the early 1980s the decision was made to open
two new residential units for teenagers; one as a short-term admission unit and the other as a bridging unit for young people
awaiting permanent placements.

A brief summary of the Authority's child care resources is listed
below. These are presented under two main age-headings as
mostly this was how services were organised in this particular
authority at the time of the research.

Accommodation resources for children under 12 years of age

Long-term foster placements: 40 places
Short-term foster placements: 40 places
Community home – intermediate length: 10 places (all ages)
Community home – assessment unit: 14 places (under eight years
of age only and families)
Community home – assessment unit: 10 places (7 to 13 year-olds)

Accommodation resoures for young people 12 and over

In addition to two short-stay residential assessment units, of five
and ten beds each, there was a small bridging resource which
provided intermediate care for those young people who were waiting to be placed in long-term foster homes or in semi-independent
accommodation. At the time when the study began there were also

seven Assessment Foster Families, and 19 long-term Community Foster placements. The Authority had no secure accommodation of its own, but like other London authorities had access to Regional Resources, although this department traditionally made little use of this service.

Other child care services

In addition to its own assessment facilities the Department was also well placed geographically to access other specialist assessment resources, particularly in the health service as many of the capital's leading teaching hospitals were within easy reach. Social workers also seemed to have made relatively heavy use of a particular NHS family therapy service, which was located on the patch of one of the borough's largest area offices.

Although there were a number of specialist educational resources in the borough, including an educational programme run under the auspices of the Intermediate Treatment service, recent cuts in the number of on-site facilities, as well as a decline in Head of Years' pastoral capacities, meant that these services were often in great demand.

Children in care in the Authority

Number of children in care

Historical information on the number of children in care on 31 March each year is available from the report *Children in the Care of Local Authorities*, published by the Department of Health. Information for this publication is supplied through the annual statistical returns from each local authority.

In addition the Policy Review Unit of the Authority, for the four years prior to our research, has published performance indicators, including child care data. Information on the numbers of children in the care of the Authority in recent years is contained in both these sources, but unfortunately because of refinement to the computerised system within the Authority there is substantial difference between them (Research Authority, 1992). In this report statistics published by the Department of Health are used for trend data, and the Authority's performance indicators for current data.

As we saw in Chapter 1, the number of children in care in England reached a peak at the end of the 1970s and declined throughout the 1980s. A very similar pattern pertained within the research Authority; the number of children in care was halved

Figure 4.4   Children in care on 31 March – rate per thousand of population under 18

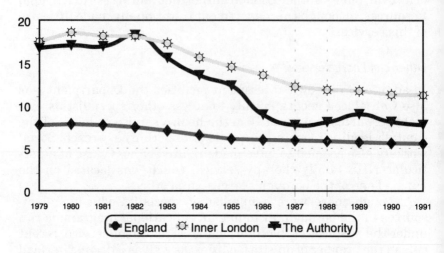

during this period (Department of Health annual returns). However, according to the Authority's performance indicators, the number in care has risen in the past three years and at March 1992 stood at 300 or 11 per 1,000 of the population under 18 years.

Figure 4.4 shows the trend in the rate of children in care in England, in inner London and in the Authority on 31 March for each year.

The rate of children in care in the Authority was more than twice that of England in 1979, but has fallen more sharply, especially in the period 1985 to 1987. (However, it is possible that the Department of Health figure of 7.73 per 1,000 for 1991 is an underestimate and that the more accurate figure is nearer to the 11 per 1,000 in the Authority's report.) While the rate in the Authority is much higher than that of England as a whole, it is lower than the average rate for all inner London authorities.

Variations within the Authority

Within the Authority-wide rate of children in care at 11 per 1,000 for March 1992 there is substantial variation between the four districts from 5 per 1,000 to around 22.3 per 1,000. This variation reflects the diversity in wealth and housing standards within the Authority, noted earlier.

Children admitted to care

Table 4.2 indicates that the number of children admitted to care in England fell in the early 1980s, rose slightly in the period 1985 to 1987, before falling again. The general pattern was similar for the Authority, although there has been a more marked drop in recent years in children admitted to the care of the Authority.

Table 4.2   Number of new episodes during the year up to 31 March

Years	England (000's)	Authority
1980	40.0	233
1981	37.6	240
1982	36.0	240
1983	32.3	222
1984	28.8	191
1985	28.8	192
1986	31.3	215
1987	32.1	162
1988	31.8	118
1989	29.6	130
1990	30.1	105
1991	29.3	93

Source: Department of Health, *Children in the Care of Local Authorities*

As suggested in Chapter 1, this pattern reflects the emphasis on gatekeeping policies during the 1980s, with a halt in the downward trend being partly explained by the 'Beckford effect', whereby social workers tended to be somewhat more cautious in their assessment of risk following the public inquiry into the death of Jasmine Beckford in 1985 (Brent Borough Council, 1985).

Legal status of children in care

As the initial data collection for this study was undertaken prior to the implementation of the Children Act 1989 in October 1991 the information on legal status refers to the legal status that was relevant at that time.

Figures 4.5 and 4.6 show the proportions of children in each legal status category in the Authority and in England. Figure 4.5 presents the data for children in care on 31 March, and Figure 4.6 shows those admitted to the care of the Authority in the year ending on 31 March.

Three differences are apparent between the Authority and the

Figure 4.5   Legal status of children in care on 31 March 1991

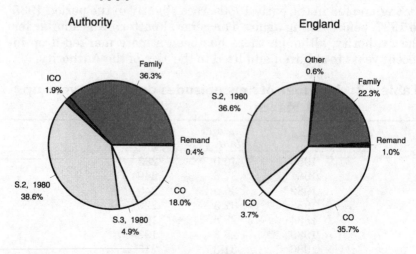

Figure 4.6   Legal status of children admitted to care during the year up to 31 March 1991

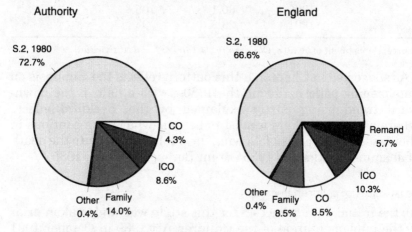

Code for Figures 4.5 and 4.6
S.2, 1980 – Section 2, 1980 Act
S.3, 1980 – Section 3, 1980 Act
Remand – Remanded to Care
Family – Family Proceedings
CO – Care Order
ICO – Interim Care Order
Other

country as a whole: the greater use of voluntary care within the Authority; the very low number of young people who are remanded to care; and the very distinct preference in the Authority to use wardship under family proceedings rather than to go for Care Orders under the 1969 Act.

The first of these confirms the policy of the Authority, mentioned earlier, namely to prefer voluntary to compulsory care. The low number of remands to care reflects the surprisingly limited evidence of offending that we found in our sample cases. The role of the Intermediate Treatment team within the Authority must be a factor here.

Changes in the practice of using wardship will be necessary as a result of provisions of the Children Act. While it is outside the remit of this study it would be interesting to see how this subsequently affected both the numbers and routes into 'being looked after' by this Authority.

The ages of children in care

Reference has been made several times to the predominance of teenagers within the care system and the impact that this had on the development of policies and practices. Figures 4.7A and B show the age distribution of children in care on 31 March 1985 and 1991

Figure 4.7A   The ages of children in care 1985 and 1991: the Authority

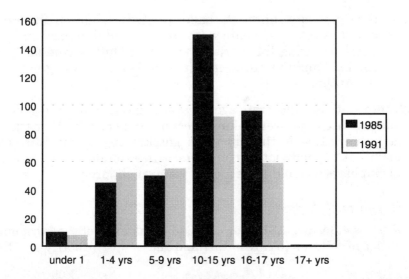

Figure 4.7B   The ages of children in care 1985 and 1991: England

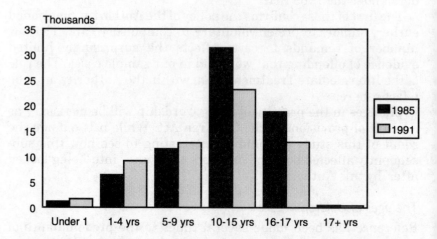

for both the Authority and for the country as a whole. These graphs highlight three points:

- the similarity of the age distribution of children in care in the Authority to that of England, at both points in time;
- the predominance of children over ten years, making up over 70 per cent of all children in 1985 and around 60 per cent in 1991;
- the significant shift in the balance between children under ten and those over ten years, with younger children increasing in number during this period. While this shift is true for both England and the Authority, the shift is marginally greater in the Authority.

These statistics illustrate again the changes in child care policies and practices that were taking effect from the mid 1980s; particularly noticeable is the impact of gatekeeping policies directed mainly at 'beyond control' teenagers, with a simultaneous increase in emphasis on child protection of younger children.

Placement of children

Figures 4.8A and 4.8B show a broad breakdown of the accommodation of children in care in England and in the Authority over the

**Figure 4.8A   Placement of children, England,
1981–1991**

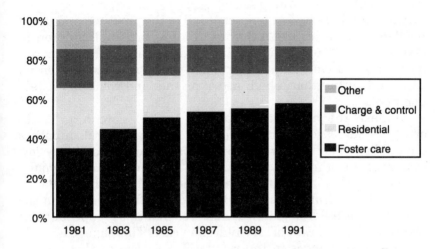

**Figure 4.8B   Placement of children in the Authority
1981–1991**

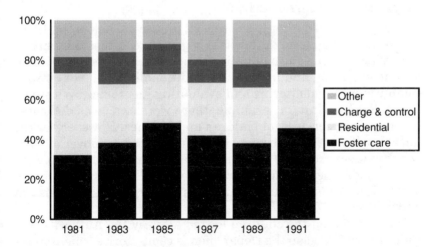

past ten years. The pattern of change in the Authority is less even
than that for the country as a whole. This may be due in part to
the inaccuracies and inconsistencies in the data collection by the
Authority that has been mentioned. The high proportion of young

people placed in the 'other' category further suggests some caution in interpreting these two figures. Two factors here are the use of bed and breakfast for older teenagers and a comparatively high use of residential boarding schools.

Although there was a significant fall in the provision and use of residential care in the Authority, the proportion of children in residential care remained much the same. Indeed the Authority now has a relatively high proportion of young people in residential care, and within that a high use of private and voluntary establishments.

Similarly the proportion of children in foster care in the Authority has increased over the decade, although overall numbers have fallen. The Authority's use of foster care is relatively low compared to other London boroughs with many, older young people in particular, being placed outside the borough boundary.

Also of note from Figure 4.8B, is the significant decline in the proportion of children placed at home, so that this group makes up less than four per cent of all children in care. This change is likely to be due to changes in the regulations governing these placements, and to active policies to discharge the large number of wardships in anticipation of the Children Act.

Monitoring and evaluation

As we mentioned earlier in the report, the second half of the 1980s was a time when local authorities began to recognise the importance of monitoring and evaluating their services. This Department was no exception and indeed has traditionally had a very strong commitment to monitoring and evaluating its practice. Within its Policy Review Unit, for example, there were two posts dedicated to monitoring services for children and families. However, for the duration of the research there was a significant turnover of staff. A subsequent freeze in recruitment also meant that there were long periods when these posts remained unfilled. As a result management information during our research period was inconsistent and patchy.

Information on the children looked after by the Authority was routinely recorded on the Department's computerised client index system. This was inputted into the system at area level by clerks in the children and families teams, either on receiving information directly from social workers or by retrieving it from records kept on individual case-files. However commitment to the maintenance of an accurate and up-to-date computerised record was known to be variable throughout the Department and so confidence in the information held on the system has been low.

The Authority has also been a popular site for academic child care researchers, and indeed shortly after our research began, a special standing conference was organised in collaboration with an academic institution, to discuss main areas of work with adolescents in the Authority. This standing conference subsequently resulted in a useful publication (Dennington and Pitts, 1991).

This chapter has provided an overview of the Authority and its child care population. We turn now, in the next chapter, to a more detailed description of the Adolescent Assessment Service, a major focal point for this research.

Summary points

- We have described the Authority in which the research was based – a medium sized, inner London borough. It was generally prosperous but with pockets of deprivation. There was a relatively low child population and proportionately fewer children in care than the average for other central London boroughs.

- The Authority has a highly diverse population; over 21 per cent of the population is not white, more than one third of whom see themselves as other than black or Asian. Despite this variety, until quite recently the Authority had not paid particular attention to equal opportunities issues.

- The Authority had spent generously on Social Services, including those specifically for children and families. It had deliberately encouraged a mixed economy of care and made significant use of the private and voluntary sectors.

- The Authority had developed in 1984 an Adolescent Assessment Service, which played an important coordinating role.

- Overall, changing trends within the Authority in the numbers of children in care and their characteristics and placement, reflects that of the country as a whole, although with some features peculiar to the Authority.

5. The Adolescent Assessment Service

In this chapter we explain in more detail the operation of the Adolescent Assessment Service of the research Authority. However, it must be remembered that it is only those young people within the 'referred' group in our sample who will have been assessed by this Service. The 'routine' group will have been assessed by the district social worker.

In earlier chapters we noted the developments in child care policy in many social services departments in the mid 1980s which led to a change in emphasis from residential to community-based services, with particular emphasis on strengthening services for adolescents. The creation of the Adolescent Assessment Service (AAS) in the Authority was very much part of this broader pattern.

The AAS became operational in November 1984, following a decision to reorganise the service previously provided by the Observation and Assessment Residential Unit. As the name implies, the Adolescent Assessment Service was designed to cater for young people of secondary school age.

The structure of the Adolescent Assessment Service

The structure of the AAS during most of the research period was as outlined in Figure 5.1. The Service was responsible for two short-stay assessment residential units, a small medium-term bridging unit, and a Day Assessment Unit. In addition, the Assessment Service coordinated the services provided by the assessment foster carers, a part time educational psychologist and the intermediate treatment worker, although within the matrix approach, these staff were line-managed elsewhere.

In 1989 the Social Services Committee agreed to the establishment of an assessment service for those under 12, and one post was created to develop this service. As with the adolescent service the emphasis here was on preventive work rather than child pro-

Figure 5.1 Structure of the Adolescent Assessment Service

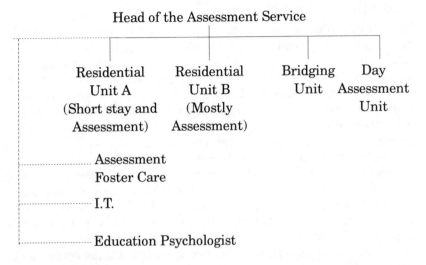

Head of the Assessment Service

Residential Unit A (Short stay and Assessment)

Residential Unit B (Mostly Assessment)

Bridging Unit

Day Assessment Unit

Assessment Foster Care

I.T.

Education Psychologist

tection. However, in practice it was difficult to impose a strict age demarcation, especially with sibling groups, so in 1992 it was decided to merge the two services into one united Assessment Service for all ages. However, the Service described here is that which was current in 1991 during the first data collection stage of this research.

The functions of the Service

From examining the work of the AAS and from interviews with staff it is possible to establish a set of six functions which the Service fulfilled to a greater or lesser extent.

Prevention of admissions to care

In the mid 1980s many social service departments developed new policies and services specifically targeted at reducing the number of teenagers who were admitted to care inappropriately. Typically, these were young people where the major concern was their behaviour, being 'beyond parental control', rather than child protection. The Authority was no exception and the AAS was created as a part of their preventive strategy. However, the AAS did not operate as the sole 'gatekeepers to care', for instance it did not consider all possible admissions to care as was the practice in many other authorities (Bunyan and Sinclair, 1987; Bilson and Thorpe, 1987; Cliffe with Berridge, 1991).

Gatekeepers to short-term placements

The intention of departmental procedures was that there should be two gates to care placements; a short-term gate operated by the AAS and a Placement Panel to approve medium- or long-term placements. The AAS was to act as gatekeeper to some short-term placements; the assessment foster carers, two short-term residential units, regional resources and secure accommodation. Social workers could access other units both within the Authority or elsewhere either directly or through the Placement Panel.

However, it has been acknowledged that these gates did not always operate as intended and some short-term placements were made directly without reference to the AAS. Moreover, because of its role as a gate keeper social workers could access places in short-term residential care through the AAS but without necessarily signing on for an assessment. Clearly then the AAS had functions other than assessment, and this was a source of some confusion to area staff.

Provision of assessment packages

The Service was able to offer, uniquely within the department, access to a range of departmental assessment services; residential assessment, assessment foster care, community-based assessment and the use of the Day Assessment Unit (DAU). Depending on the particular needs of any one young person, a package of services could be offered and supported by the Assessment Service.

Apart from the support of one IT worker and the teachers in the DAU, at the time of the research there was no automatic or organisational arrangements for referral to other professionals. Access to other specialist assessments such as child psychiatry or educational psychology could be arranged through the AAS, but this was not a required route. District staff could and did refer directly to these services without consulting the AAS.

Forum for group decision making

One of the changes in child care practice noted earlier was the significant reduction in the power of social workers to take major decisions on their own without recourse to some form of procedure, whether referral to more senior management or to specially constituted meetings or panels. The AAS provided a collective forum which acted in this way. However, this particular arrangement was not primarily about management accountability nor about monitoring practice, rather it stemmed from the belief that shared decision making leads to better quality decision making.

> 'One of the things the AAS is very good at is bringing people together – a range of professionals – for example, a young person may have an EWO but there may be very little communication. We work with the EWO, the school, the young person and bring them together ... we seem more aware of the need to network especially with education and other people in social services.' (AAS staff member)

Coordinator of case information

Experience shows that for many young people being considered for care there is already a sizable group of professional people already involved (Packman with Randall and Jacques, 1986). Furthermore the AAS itself offers experience from a wide range of social service perspectives. So a further function of the AAS was to bring together all these views and pieces of known information, thereby enabling a more holistic assessment to be made.

Coordinator of resource material

It has often been noted that the knowledge of individual workers or teams regarding appropriate resources is very limited. AAS accepted responsibility for maintaining up-to-date information on the facilities and quality of care offered by different residential establishments, whether local authority, regional, or private and voluntary. Recognition of the importance of this function is provided by the Warner Report, which recommends the compilation of a national directory of residential child care facilities (Warner, 1992).

Having considered the functions that the AAS did perform, it is perhaps worth making clear that there were certain functions which it did not have. Firstly, the AAS did not have any monitoring function, either in terms of monitoring entries into care or placements, nor for monitoring overall standards of practice. Secondly, the AAS was not a compulsory service. District staff had discretion about approaching the Service for an assessment. As we shall see this had implications for the nature of the assessment that was undertaken. Thirdly, at the time when we were conducting the research the gate to short-term resources via the AAS was not always used, thereby limiting its functions as a gatekeeper to care.

Procedures

Referrals to the Service

Referrals to the AAS come from District Teams, Hospital Social Work Teams, Educational Welfare Service, I.T. and Police. District social workers were the most significant source, followed by hospital social workers, who were comparatively active in work with adolescents.

Referrals were made in order to discuss a complex problem, request an emergency or short-term admission to residential care or to seek help with an assessment. Referrals are received by a member of the Joint Assessment Meeting (JAM) (later to become IAG – Intake and Assessment Group). Members of JAM provided office hours cover on a rota basis with out-of-duty cover provided by the emergency duty team or the manager of the Service.

If the referral was urgent or a crisis, a member of the JAM would meet with the district social worker, the young person and family in order to consider all possible alternatives to resolve the immediate crisis. Non-urgent referrals would be brought to the weekly meeting of JAM, where if it was agreed that an assessment was required, the most appropriate resource would be allocated. Urgent cases which had had an initial response were also discussed at JAM to consider if continuing work was required.

Planning meetings

As soon as possible after acceptance of a referral a planning meeting would be called by the Assessment Service worker, who would also chair the meeting and ensure that minutes were taken and distributed. The purpose of the meeting was to decide on the immediate course of action, to think about what reports would be required for the assessment and to allocate tasks. Planning meetings involved the young person, their family, the case responsible social worker and any other relevant professionals. Three weeks later a review meeting with the same participants and chair would be held to review progress and a Final Assessment Conference (FAC) was held following the six-week assessment period. The participants and chair were as before. The purpose of this meeting was to consider the assessment reports, to use these in order to identify the young person's needs and to recommend ways of meeting those needs.

The Assessment Service continued to remain involved, as a general rule, for a further six weeks in order to assist in implementing the decisions taken at the FAC. If the young person remained in an assessment facility, or members of the Assessment Service were continuing to do work, then review meetings would be held every six weeks.

Principles of operation

While the AAS operated within the children and families policy of the Authority, there were other principles which related specifically to its work; six are highlighted below.

Case responsibility: A social worker from a district team should continue to hold case responsibility. Several benefits flow from such an arrangement; the work of the assessment team can be clearly seen as over and above that of the district team; the child and family will have ongoing social work support that will continue after the assessment period; the child and family can gain access to other departmental services.

Partnership and participation: In all its work, the AAS worked closely with the child and the family. This is most clearly evident in the involvement of young people and their families in assessment meetings. In this and other principles of operation the AAS staff believed that they were anticipating both the principles and specific operational regulations of the Children Act 1989.

> 'Working with families, involving them in decision making, encouraging them to be at all meetings, being up front with them – that has had quite an impact ... we have always done this since the start of the AAS and with the Children Act others are catching up on us. The spirit of the Act moves this on – giving more emphasis to partnership and involving people.' (AAS staff member)

Time-limited work: Although some of the resources within the AAS can be deployed for considerable periods, the actual process of assessment is regarded as essentially short-term. In most cases the intention is that a Final Assessment Conference will be held within six weeks of a referral for assessment, with a further six-week period for implementation.

Retaining the young person in a known environment: It is well established that child care assessments are best carried out with as little disruption to the young person's existing caring and social networks as is consistent with their well-being. This was a principle endorsed by the AAS and greatly assisted by the range of assessment options available to the team. However, in practice, the lack of facilities, especially assessment foster places within the locality, mitigated against applying this principle in all cases.

Multidisciplinary assessment: Young people coming to the attention of social services are likely to benefit from assessments from a range of professionals. While non-social services staff within the AAS were limited to teachers in the DAU, in conducting assessments the team aimed to bring together all relevant professionals to facilitate a multidisciplinary approach.

Team work: The style in which the AAS worked was firmly based on the principle of team work: multidisciplinary, both between residential and field staff and between AAS and district staff. Joint working provided families with continuity as well as the opportunity to explore their problems with the fresh perspective that can be brought by another worker.

Elements of the Service

A major strength of the AAS was the range of different forms of assessment that could be offered. The elements of the Service, which are outlined below, had remained essentially the same since its inception in 1984.

Residential assessment

The Service managed two residential assessment units and one small bridging unit, with a total of 18 places. One of the residential units has several emergency beds, used by some of the many homeless or runaway young people who end up in central London. So during a six-month period over three-quarters of those admitted stayed less than a week and only 28 per cent were assessed by the AAS. The second residential assessment unit, which was smaller, was located in a block of flats in a residential area. Here the residents tended to be slightly younger, and the atmosphere more settled and controlled than that in the more central location.

Assessment fostering

Seven families had been recruited specifically as assessment foster parents. These families were required to fulfil additional criteria to that of community foster families and, in return, receive an enhanced rate of allowances. The assessment foster carers:

- must agree to one member being available at home full time, both to meet the needs of the young people and to be able to attend regular meetings;
- must be able to take young people at very short notice, and must be prepared to accept any young person that the services wished to place, irrespective of age, sex or ethnicity;
- must have a spare room for a teenager;
- must live within ten miles of the Authority;

- were required to make regular recordings about all aspects of the placement including the young person's behaviour, family contact and wider relationships;
- were expected to attend any assessment or other planning meeting and to make written reports to those meetings;
- were expected to undergo training and to attend a support group regularly.

In recognition of the difficult task they were agreeing to undertake, assessment foster carers underwent considerable training, and received a high level of support from specialist link workers.

> 'We were faced with quite a good training set up ... the training I felt was very realistic and was very well done. When we did come to face the situations we had very good link workers, two excellent link workers who stuck with us through difficult things ... actually the scheme would fall down, the foster parents would not feel supported or able to cope without the extra support that we've had from our link workers.' (Foster carer)

When the Assessment Foster Carer scheme was set up, there was general agreement that it would only succeed if it could demonstrate that assessment foster carers were prepared to take, and were able to sustain in placement, the most difficult of young people. Seven years into the service this would appear to be so. Data gathered during the research demonstrated that within our sample, the presenting problems of young people placed with assessment foster families were at least as complex and severe as those placed in the Authority's residential assessment units.

The greatest problems faced by the Assessment Foster Care service relates to difficulty in recruitment and blockage in the system due to a lack of suitable placements to which young people can move following their assessment. Not only did this cause difficulties for the young people, it creates problems for the system. Are these families still doing 'assessment'; should they still be paid the enhanced rate; how can this be reconciled to community foster carers not receiving the additional allowance?

In addition to the general problem of recruitment, there was the specific problem that none of those families recruited at the time actually lived within the Authority. This was a significant factor in the choices that the Service could offer to young people.

Day Assessment Unit (DAU)

The primary role of the DAU was to work with a family and young person to prevent a breakdown in the home situation. This would be undertaken through outreach work alone or with the young person attending the Day Unit Programme. The provision of education through the Programme was important in building a working relationship with the young person and family; however this was seen as a means to achieve the primary objective of preventing family breakdown rather than as the main rationale for the service.

> 'The role of the DAU is very clearly in the prevention of a breakdown in the home situation – that is where we pitch our service – it is not about providing education although we use education as a way of engaging young people and their families. If someone was referred just because of non-attendance and there doesn't seem to be any home problems, then we don't offer a place.' (AAS staff member)

The staff was multidisciplinary; social work staff undertaking the work with the young person and the family, while the teachers and therapist provided the daily programme. At the time of the study the post of part time educational psychologist had been vacant for three years.

Attendance at the Day Unit was intended to be short-term with young people being helped back into mainstream schools or special units. However, few moved on speedily following the six-week assessment; the average stay was around four months. Some young people had been on the Programme for upwards of a year – often waiting the completion of a full educational assessment.

Outreach assessment

Again the primary aim of this service was, wherever possible and appropriate, to prevent the admission of young people to care. As with other parts of the service, case responsibility was held by the district social worker, with the assessment staff offering immediate additional support to the family and young person. Ideally all cases being assessed would be allocated to a social worker, but the preventive nature of outreach work gave it a low priority in case allocation. Hence in practice, the role of the case responsible worker was often fairly nominal.

Outreach work was conducted by the staff from the DAU or from residential units. The amount of outreach work had been lower than hoped: there was a lack of awareness by district staff that such a service was offered by AAS, resulting in few referrals that had not already reached crisis point; also a reduction in the size of residential units so that fewer residential staff are available for such work.

'We could be used in more of a preventive way – so often we are used in crisis – everyone is working under pressure and miss the opportunity to put the input in early; if they could it might prevent something more serious occurring later. In districts, cases don't get allocated until things have gone quite far down the line.' (AAS staff member)

Having spent some time in establishing clearly the context in which this study of assessment was conducted, it is now time to introduce the empirical data.

Summary points

- The functions of the AAS were identified as: prevention of admission of adolescents to care; providing a range of assessment services; acting as gatekeeper to certain short-term placements; coordinator of case information; forum for group decision making; and coordinator of resource information. However, it did not have any monitoring functions, nor was it a compulsory service.
- AAS received referrals, often in emergency situations, from a wide range of social work and other professionals. The normal pattern was for an early planning meeting to be organised. This was followed three weeks later by a review meeting, and a final assessment conference after the six-week assessment period.
- The main principles underlying the work of AAS were that: a social worker from an area team should continue to hold case responsibility; young people and their families should actively be involved in the assessment process; wherever possible, the young person should remain in a familiar environment; assessments should be multidisciplinary; and teamwork should be encouraged.
- Assessments could be undertaken in the community, residential and foster homes, a day assessment unit and Intermediate Treatment centres. Psychological assessment could also be facilitated.

6. The characteristics of the young people

The young people in the sample

The process for identifying the 75 young people in our sample was reported in Chapter 3. Here we describe the characteristics of those young people. As one of the main aims of our research was to find out which types of young people were allocated to different forms of assessment and why, our analysis begins with a description of the young people concerned, their previous involvement with social services and other agencies, as well as the circumstances which led to their consideration for care, admission or placement breakdown. Figure 6.1 shows how the 75 young people who qualified for inclusion in our study were distributed amongst these three main event groups.

Figure 6.1   Young people in study by type of event

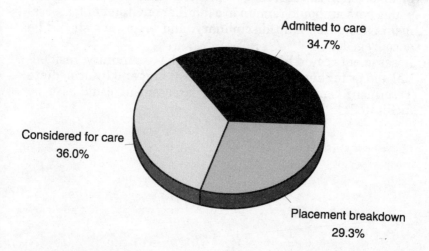

Admitted to care
34.7%

Considered for care
36.0%

Placement breakdown
29.3%

Age and sex

Figure 6.2 depicts the age and sex distribution of the sample at the start of the assessment period. Although this included children as young as 10 and 11 years of age, more than two-thirds of our study group were between 14 and 16 years old when they were notified to our project, whilst 20 per cent of the total sample were already over school leaving age at the time when the event took place.

Figure 6.2   Age and sex of young people

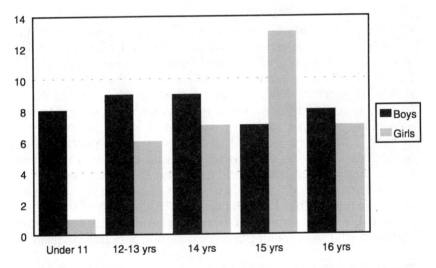

There were some interesting age differences between the three main event groups. For example, whereas the 'considered' and 'breakdown' groups contained youngsters across the whole teenage range, the 'admitted' group consisted mainly of older teenagers. More than four out of five of the 'admitted' were 14 years of age or over, compared with fewer than two out of three in the other two event groups.

There were also some interesting sex differences between the event groups. As is the pattern in the care system nationally, boys outnumbered girls slightly, accounting for 55 per cent of the overall sample. However the boys tended to be somewhat younger than the girls, particularly at the point of being considered for care. Indeed, more than a third of the boys in this event category were aged 13 or under, whereas girls did not seem to provoke similar concerns until they were at least 14 or 15 years of age.

Legal status

At the time of the event, none of the 27 young people in the 'considered for care' group were subject to any Court orders. Of the 'admitted to care' group, all but five of the 26 were admitted into voluntary care; three young people entered on place of safety orders, all of which became voluntary care [Section 2, 1980 Act]; one interim Care Order became a full Care Order and in one case the local authority was given charge and control in a wardship case. Of the 'placement breakdown' group only seven out of 22 were on Care Orders; most were pre-Children Act wardship cases.

Ethnicity, religion and language

The ethnic diversity of the Authority's under 18 population provided us with an opportunity to look at how each of the dimensions of ethnicity, culture, religion and language were approached in this Authority's assessments. As Table 6.1 shows, nearly two-thirds, 63 per cent, of the youngsters in our sample were black and from a number of different minority ethnic groups, each with their own history, culture and linguistic and religious heritage. Some of their families had settled in London some decades ago and formed part of a well established community. Others were more recent migrants to Britain, and had often fled here to escape civil and political unrest in their own countries. In addition, this Authority like many other London boroughs in the early 1990s became responsible for a significant number of unaccompanied refugee children, who were seeking temporary asylum in Britain from war

Table 6.1   Ethnic origin of young people in the study

	Considered for care	Admitted to care	Placement breakdown	Total
White	15	8	5	28
African	5	4	1	10
African Caribbean	1	3	5	9
Arab/North African	3	4	2	9
Indian/Bangladeshi	2	2	0	4
Mixed parentage	1	5	9	15
Total	27	26	22	75

(In this table we have employed the classifications used in the 1991 census. Children of Turkish, Greek and Cypriot origin are coded as White. The term Arab applies to those of other Middle Eastern origin such as Iraq, Saudi Arabia and Kuwait. By North African we refer to those countries which lie north of the Sahara, such as Morocco, Algeria and Tunisia. The term mixed parentage refers to those children with one black and one white parent.)

torn Ethiopia and Eritrea (British Refugee Council, 1990; Eaton, 1994). Eight of these youngsters were either admitted or considered for care during our first round of data collection, accounting for more than 10 per cent of our total sample.

However, it was young people of mixed parentage who made up the largest minority ethnic group in our study, a population that is beginning to attract greater attention (Tizard and Phoenix, 1993; Smith and Berridge, 1994). Overall nearly one in five of our sample had one black and one white parent and as we can see from Table 6.1 that more than half of the children of mixed parentage were notified to us following a placement breakdown, accounting for 40 per cent of our 'breakdown' group. The reasons for this are difficult to determine not least because of the lack of census and child care data on children of mixed parentage in the Authority. However, several other studies have also pointed to the disproportionately high numbers of mixed parentage children in care (Batta and Mawby, 1981; Bebbington and Miles, 1989; Rowe, Hundleby and Garnett, 1989).

Nor do we have any adequate explanation why so many of the mixed parentage youngsters were notified to us following a breakdown in placement. Research studies on the placement outcomes of black children in care are both scarce and contradictory (see Smith and Berridge, 1994), and are not strictly comparable for the purposes of our study (the studies by Fratter and others, 1991, and Charles, Rashid and Thoburn, 1992, for example, both examine the outcomes of permanent family placements). However, it has been suggested that dissimilarity in the ethnic backgrounds of young person and carer may be one contributory factor. Unfortunately we were not able to test this hypothesis within our study sample. The number of placement breakdowns was too small, the range of different religious, linguistic and cultural traditions too great to draw any reliable comparisons. However we should note that as many young black people in our 'placement breakdown' group left family placements where the carers were white, as left family placements where the carer was black.

Within the broad ethnic groupings, there were significant differences in young people's cultural, religious and linguistic backgrounds. Whilst the majority of young people were said by social workers to be Christians, of various denominations, Muslims accounted for one in five of our study sample, including young people of African, Asian and Middle Eastern descent. There were also a small number of young people who practised the Hindu and Jewish faiths. Whilst most social workers were able to tell us what religion was practised at home, few had felt this to be of sufficient importance to record on file.

Similarly, whilst most of the young people of African, Asian and Middle Eastern origin, and indeed many of their parents, had been born and educated in this country, for nearly a third of them English was not their first language. Yet, even though social workers were aware that another language was spoken at home, this information was also absent from social work records. As one social worker said of a young Bengali woman who had been considered for care and who, it seems, often acted as interpreter for her parents who spoke very little English, 'I never knew what this language was as she always spoke English to me'.

Special needs

Fifteen young people in our sample, 20 per cent of the total, were reported to have special needs at the time of the event, which required specialist medical or educational support. Ten had been statemented as having special educational needs, of which half were reported to have severe or mild learning difficulties. The other half were classified as having emotionally or behavioural difficulties (EBD). All of these young people were enrolled at special schools. The remaining five in this group were reported to have a recurrent or chronic health condition, which required specialist medical supervision. None of the young people in the study were said by the social worker to have any severe physical or sensory disabilities.

Family background and disruption

Only a minority of the young people in our sample came from households where both parents were present. In fact fewer than one in five, 19 per cent, had both parents living at home at the time of the event. The majority, 43 per cent, were from lone parent households, most headed by lone mothers, although a quarter of the single parents were men. Of the rest 23 per cent were said to come from reconstituted families, where one parent was living with a new partner or spouse.

There were some interesting differences between the various ethnic groups in this respect. Whereas the majority of young black Caribbean and white people were reported to come from lone parent households, this applied to only one of the Asian young people in our sample. Furthermore, all of the young people of mixed parentage lived in households where only one parent was present.

Eleven young people, 15 per cent of our sample, had no adult carers. Included amongst this group were the eight unaccompanied refugee children whose parents' whereabouts were unknown. Although some were said to be imprisoned, and a few were feared to be dead, it was often difficult for social workers to verify this information as most of these youngsters were reluctant to give more than the barest details about their family background, for fear of jeopardising the safety of their relatives back home. The remaining three young people had either lost contact with their parents after several years in care, or had been admitted to care as a result of their parents' death or desertion.

Although detailed family histories were often missing from the young people's files, it was evident from earlier referrals and reports that many of them had lived through other major family disruptions, in addition to parental break-ups, divorce and remarriage. Indeed most of the young people in our sample had spent at least part of their childhood living away from their parents, either in local authority care, with relatives or family friends, and in a few cases in private fostering arrangements. Some of these separations were due to parental ill-health, others because of housing and employment problems. Nor was it unknown for the young people to initiate changes for themselves. Movement to other family members – older siblings, separated parents – was a common response to relationship problems at home.

These background patterns have been identified in other studies of young people being looked after (for example, Millham and others, 1986; Fisher and others, 1986; Farmer and Parker, 1991; Triseliotis and others, 1994). Some families had been separated by migration, with children remaining in the care of their extended families until their parents had secured employment and accommodation in this country. Separations from siblings also happened with considerable frequency. More than one in five, 21 per cent, had a brother or sister living elsewhere in the care system at the time of the event.

Stress factors

Social workers were asked to select, from a list, up to three life events or stress factors in the child's or family's background which they felt to be most significant at the time of the event. This list was based on one used by the Bridge Consultancy which is an amended version of a classification scheme proposed by Rutter, Schaffer and Sturge (Fitzgerald, 1990). The most often mentioned factor was the lack of a local family network which was able to offer emotional or practical support. This was said to apply to more than a third, 35 per cent, of the young people in our sample, although in an additional 10 per cent of cases relationships with existing family networks were said to be very poor.

The link between deprivation and admission to care has been graphically demonstrated by Bebbington and Miles (1989). Yet this was highlighted by social workers as a significant stress factor in only 10 per cent of cases; severe financial difficulties were said to affect only 16 per cent of families, in spite of the fact that the majority were dependent on state benefits for income, with nearly two-thirds of parents, 64 per cent, said to be unemployed at the time of the event.

The second most commonly mentioned stress factor was a history of inadequate or inconsistent parenting which was felt to apply to one in three of the young people. The third most important factor was migration or recent changes in accommodation, affecting 29 per cent of young people and their families, although just over one-third of these were unaccompanied refugee children. Poor or inadequate accommodation was mentioned in 16 per cent of cases, many of whom were in temporary accommodation or who were seeking rehousing.

Surprisingly perhaps, considering how many black and Asian youngsters there were in our sample, fewer than 10 per cent were felt to have been victims of persecution or adverse discrimination. However social workers often confessed that their knowledge of the young person's family background and history was insufficient. This might also explain the low levels of physical and mental ill-health reported amongst parents and other family members which, at 10 per cent, is somewhat lower than that recorded in other relevant studies (Packman with Randall and Jacques, 1986; Rowe and others, 1989).

Education and employment status

Although most of the young people in our study were under school leaving age at the time when the event took place, few were regular attenders. In fact, persistent non-attendance was reported as a presenting problem for more than two-thirds (68 per cent) of the school age children in our study, of whom more than a quarter had been out of full time education for over a year. Table 6.2 gives the education and employment status of the total sample at the time of the event.

Table 6.2   Education and employment status

	Number	%
Under school leaving age	60	81
Unemployed	10	13
Over school leaving age at school/FE	3	4
Youth Training Scheme	1	1
Employed	1	1
	75	100

About half of the 60 school age youngsters in our sample, 51 per cent, were enrolled with local mainstream schools. Of the rest, 13 per cent were attending full time special day or boarding schools outside the borough, including one young man who was at a residential EBD school. Sixteen per cent were being schooled on a part time basis, either at home or in a special tuition centre, although the number of teaching hours that these children received varied, from five half-days per week within some specialist centres, to no more than a few hours per week home tuition.

One in five however were not enrolled with any school or alternative educational programme. Although some of these were unaccompanied refugee children who had only recently arrived in this country, more than half of this number were young people with histories of educational problems and poor school attendance, who had either been unofficially excluded from school pending a Statement of educational needs, or who following a formal exclusion were experiencing difficulties in finding another school which was willing to take them. Overall, more than a quarter of the sample, 28 per cent, had either already received a Statement of special educational need, under the 1981 Education Act, or were currently undergoing the assessment process at the time when the event took place. One in four had Statements pending and had been waiting some months for the process to begin. One young man in our sample had been waiting two years for a Statement during which time he had received no educational provision at all. Indeed it was only when he came to the attention of social services following a string of petty offences that alternative part time arrangements were finally made for his education. This delay in assessing for special educational needs has been highlighted by the Audit Commission and HMI in a highly critical report and changes to the process were made in the 1993 Education Act through the publication of a new Code of Practice for assessing special educational needs (Audit Commission and HMI, 1992; DFE, 1994).

Altogether 12 young people, almost one in six of our study group, were officially excluded from school at the time of the event, and for three-quarters of them this exclusion was permanent. Poor attendance coupled with disruptive behaviour were the most common reasons given for these exclusions, although since social services were not always involved at the time when these exclusions took place the precise circumstances surrounding these events were not always clear. Most of these youngsters had subsequently been enrolled on some form of part time educational programme, although many were not attending these schemes regularly. One in three, however, had been excluded from school with no alternative educational arrangements being made. As these tended to be older youngsters who had been excluded in their final year at school, social workers were generally pessimistic about securing an alternative place for them before they reached school leaving age, particularly as the precious few specialist schemes in operation in the borough were in such great demand. Indeed some felt that the education department had been deliberately slow in responding to the needs of these older adolescents, as with the passage of time they would no longer be legally required to make any form of provision. Whatever the reasons, few of these older teenagers were said to be working towards any formal qualifications at the time of the event; specifically only a quarter of 14 to 16 year-olds were said to be studying for any GCSEs.

This summary of the current educational status of this group highlights major deficiencies in the education system, which in turn tends to propel young people towards social services or the juvenile justice system. There is now a considerable body of evidence to suggest that these problems have significantly increased since the Education Reform Act 1988. Despite some recognition of this, with the publication by DFE in 1994 of six circulars, *Pupils with Problems*, it seems unlikely that the new market forces within the education system will help to meet the needs of 'unwanted' pupils, like those vulnerable young people in our sample (DFE, 1994; Blyth and Milner, 1993; Oxford Review of Education, 1994).

The results of such inadequate educational provision are only too evident in the older age group. Of the 15 school leavers in our study, only three were continuing their education, one at a special school for children with learning difficulties and the other two at Colleges of Further Education. Fewer than a quarter of these older teenagers had actually attended school up to their official school leaving date, most having left at least six months before, half of them as a result of formal exclusions. None of these young people were said to have passed any GCSEs prior to leaving school, although disconcertingly in more than a third of cases social workers either did not know if any examinations had been taken, or had not thought it sufficiently important to record on file.

Only one of these school leavers was in full time employment, whilst another was engaged on an employment training scheme. Overall, more than half of these school leavers were unemployed at the time when the event took place, although few were in receipt of any form of state benefit.

Referrals to social services

The young people in our study came to the attention of social services in a number of different ways. Of the 53 youngsters who were either considered for or admitted to care, 32 per cent were referred by their parent or relatives. A further quarter came from the young people themselves, 17 per cent from schools or other education professional, 8 per cent from hospitals, and 6 per cent from the police. The remaining 12 per cent of referrals came from other voluntary agencies who were already involved with the young person or their families at the time when the event took place. For example most of the unaccompanied refugee children in our sample were referred by a London-based voluntary organisation which offered advice and assistance to asylum seekers from other countries. Amongst the 22 young people in our placement breakdown group, slightly more referrals at the time of original involvement – 45 per cent – came from parents, with significantly fewer, 9 per cent, coming from the young people themselves.

Reasons for referrals

The reasons for seeking social service assistance also varied within this group of 53 cases. Where referrals came from parents or carers their main complaint was their inability to control their son's or daughter's behaviour. High on their list of concerns was their youngster's persistent non-school attendance, which in turn had led to other problems at home as attempts to get them back into school had failed, and relationships within the family had become fraught. Either they were at home all day which led to serious conflicts within the family, or they were out on the streets and felt to be at risk of crime, drugs, sexual exploitation and abuse. As we shall see in Chapter 12, significant behavioural problems reported at the time of the event, particularly self-injury, tended to be associated with more complex and costly assessments.

Offending behaviour amongst this group of young people was, nevertheless, relatively low, although again this was found to be a cost-raising factor for the assessment period. Although more than a quarter (27 per cent) had been cautioned or found guilty of at least one offence in the 12 months prior to this referral, most of these were for relatively minor offences, such as begging and shop-lifting for small sums. Indeed, none of the young people in our sample were admitted to care on remand or criminal care orders; and more serious offences, such as taking and driving away and burglary, were relatively rare amongst this group. A similar number, whilst not in trouble with the police, were said by parents to be stealing from home or from relatives who feared that this may be to fund a drug habit, although with the exception of one case, these suspicions were rarely supported by any hard evidence.

Concerns about offending were generally confined to the boys in our group. With girls, parents were far more likely to express concerns about their 'moral' welfare. Complaints about staying out late, and the sort of company they kept, particularly with older boys, were common, as was the fear that they were sexually active and at risk of becoming pregnant – and as other studies have shown this is a serious concern (Farmer and Parker, 1991; Garnett, 1992). As some of these girls often went missing from home overnight they were also felt to be putting themselves at considerable risk of exploitation and abuse. Running away from home was reported to be a serious problem for almost a quarter (23 per cent) of those who were considered for or admitted to care. And at the time of their referral, eight youngsters had been reported to the police by their parents as missing.

Concerns about young people's health was also expressed by some parents. Four youngsters who were diagnosed as suffering from diabetes were failing to take their medication regularly and consequently experienced repeated admissions to hospital. Three young women were referred to social services following serious attempts at suicide and parents were concerned that they underwent a full psychiatric assessment. The majority of health concerns expressed by parents, however, related to possible drug, alcohol or solvent misuse. At the time of referral this was said to apply to nearly one in three of those considered for or admitted to care.

Whatever the complaints, it was clear that these problems had been going on for some time; as we shall see later, many had previously been referred to social services, often more than once. Parents were therefore often at breaking-point and sometimes arrived at the office with their son's or daughter's bags already packed – very reminiscent of the 'last straw' effect described by Fisher and others, and the conclusion from a recent study that the level of tolerance of parents determined whether young people with problems were admitted to care or supervised at home (Fisher and others, 1986; Triseliotis and others, 1994).

Where referrals came from young people, the emphasis was more on the tensions and conflicts at home. Some complained that they were being unfairly scapegoated by their families, whilst two alleged that they had been physically abused by their parents or older siblings during rows and were fearful of returning home. Others had spent some time living with friends or relatives because of arguments with their parents, but these relationships had subsequently broken down. Four young people had been 'kicked out' by their parents and presented themselves to social services after a period of 'living rough'. For many this pattern of moving around continued after admission to care and as other studies have shown is likely to dominate life after care (Stein and Carey, 1986; Kirby, 1994).

Referrals from other agencies, such as schools, GPs and hospitals, tended to follow disclosures by young people that they had been physically or sexually abused by relatives. Other professionals expressed more general concerns about the young people's welfare at home. For example, two young people were referred to social services by educational psychologists as it was felt that their home situation, rather than any special educational needs, were at the root of their truancy and underachievement; another was referred by the head of a residential EBD school as he was concerned about the capacity of the parents of one of his pupils to care for him and felt reluctant to discharge him home in spite of a marked improvement in his behaviour and educational performance. (This reluctance to discharge from residential schools has been revealed in another study of residential EBD schools, see Grimshaw with Berridge, 1994.) Most of the referrals to hospital social work teams followed attempts at self-injury or suicide and most notably involved young women.

In addition to the unaccompanied refugee children in our sample there were also a handful of other young people who for a variety of reasons had no one immediately available to care for them. Two young people, for example, were admitted to care following their mother's death, whilst a further three were offered accommodation whilst their parents sought treatment for alcohol or drug dependency.

Previous involvement with social services

We should point out that only a third, 32 per cent, of these young-sters were new referrals to the Department (less than one in five, 18 per cent, if one excludes the unaccompanied refugees in our sample). The majority, 68 per cent, had been referred to social services before, nearly half of them, 45 per cent, within the previous 12 months. Table 6.3 gives the number of previous referrals made and compares these for the 'considered' and 'admitted' groups.

Table 6.3 Number of previous referrals to social services

	Considered for care (n=27)	Admitted to care (n=26)	Total (n=53)
	%	%	%
None	41	23	32
One	30	15	23
Two	19	19	19
Three or more	10	42	26

As we can see the majority of both groups were already known to social services prior to this referral. However, in contrast to Packman's study (1986), it was the 'admitted' youngsters who were more likely to have been previously involved, more than a third of them, 42 per cent, on at least three separate occasions. The degree and type of involvement varied considerably. Although many of these young people were referred for the first time in their teens, just over a quarter, 26 per cent, had been known for six years or longer.

Some of those young people had been the subject of child protection referrals. Indeed, more than a fifth, 21 per cent, had at some point in the past been on the Department's child protection register as a result of earlier abuse or neglect. One in five of these youngsters had also been admitted previously to care, many of them, 17 per cent, on at least two previous occasions. Others had first come into contact with the Department through the work of the juvenile justice team. Just over a fifth of the sample had been in contact with this team as a result of earlier offending behaviour.

Placement breakdown

Amongst the placement breakdown group of 22, more than half

had been in care for longer than a year, although only a quarter of placements had lasted this long. The majority of these were family placements, 77 per cent, including a small number who were placed at home under family proceedings. Interestingly most of these young people had experience of both foster and residential care in the period prior to this breakdown, showing the often interdependence of alternative types of placement (Berridge, 1985; Rowe, Hundleby and Garnett, 1989). Roughly half of the placement breakdowns were said to have been initiated by the young people themselves, either by requesting a move or by simply walking out of the placement and refusing to return. The other half were said to have ended following requests from carers for their removal. Although only a quarter of young people in this group had experienced breakdowns in residential care, it is significant that four out of five of these placements ended at the request of unit staff.

As with the considered and admitted groups, the most common complaints about the young people which were made by carers concerned poor school attendance and their difficult and challenging behaviour. Unauthorised absences from placements were common. More than half were said to have 'run away' from these placements at least once in the period prior to the breakdown, whilst the whereabouts of two young women were reported to have been 'unknown' for at least two months at the time they were referred to our research project. Interestingly though, when social workers were asked the primary reason for the placement breakdowns, the majority put this down to the unsuitability of these young people's care placements, confirming that placement endings can be a complex phenomenon (Rowe, Hundleby and Garnett, 1989). Table 6.4 shows, for the 75 cases, the number of times that social workers recorded these presenting problems as having been reported by anyone at the time of the event. For instance, from the checklist of given problems, in 27 of the 75 cases the social worker recorded stealing or being destructive at home as having been identified as an issue in the case.

Other agency involvement

In addition to social services involvement, more than two-thirds of the young people in our study were also said to have been in contact with at least one other agency in the ten years prior to this event. Overall, about half were reported to have been involved with the Education Welfare Service, although in view of the number with a poor school attendance record it is surprising that this figure was not in fact higher. The next largest group were those who had been involved with the Education Psychological Service. This applied to a third of our sample, of whom most had been referred for a Statement of educational needs.

Table 6.4   Presenting problems

Home / Placement	*Total*
Control issues	28
Stealing or being destructive at home	27
Running away	24
Relationship problems	28
Abuse/neglect	9
Education	
Attendance	41
Performance	17
Behaviour	11
Physical / Mental Health	
Drug/solvent misuse	12
Alcohol misuse	5
Under developed	3
Diabetic (mismanaged)	4
Self-injury	4
Suicide attempt	3
Poor hygiene/physical condition	8
Anorexia	2
Offending	
Cautioned/found guilty offence in last 12 months	20
Perpetrator of sexual abuse	2
Prostitution/soliciting	1

Interestingly, as many as one in five of the total, 21 per cent, had previous contact with child or adolescent psychiatric services, of which five were still actively involved at the time when the event took place. Three of these were young women who had been admitted to hospital following serious suicide attempts. The other two were undergoing psychiatric assessments in support of the department's application to the High Court for parental access to be terminated. The rest had been referred for a psychiatric assessment in the past, either on the recommendation of social services or following a referral from a child guidance clinic.

A slightly smaller proportion, 19 per cent, had also been involved with the local Family Service Unit at some time in the previous ten years. Three young people were still actively involved with Unit staff at the time of their consideration for care and were transferred over to social services at the point when an admission to care seemed imminent.

Some of these young people were also known to the police as a result of earlier offending behaviour, although this tended to be limited to the older teenage boys in our group. In total more than a quarter, 27 per cent, had been cautioned or found guilty of at least one criminal offence in the previous 12 months, half of whom were technically in care at the time when the offence took place.

Previous assessments

In view of their previous involvement with social services and other specialist agencies within the education and health sector, we were not surprised to find that some of these young people had already been subject to some form of assessment procedure. What was surprising, however, was how many. Overall more than two-thirds were reported to have undergone a formal assessment prior to this event, including about half of those who were considered or admitted to care and all but one of those in the placement break-down group. More than a quarter, for example, had either already been statemented under the 1981 Education Act, or the statement process was ongoing at the time of their consideration, admission or placement breakdown.

In addition, one in five were reported to have undergone some form of psychiatric assessment, and as we saw above, some of these young people were still actively involved with psychiatric services. Most were seen at community outpatient clinics following referrals from social services, child guidance or education. Just under a third, however, were assessed residentially either on a hospital ward, following attempts at suicide or self-injury or following a referral to a regional resource for a comprehensive assessment.

More significantly, perhaps, more than a third of the total were said to have already undergone an assessment within the Department's Assessment Service. This applied to about half of the admitted and placement breakdown groups and about one in five of those who were considered for care.

Although each file contained a report divider to allow for easy access to these and other reports, detailed records about the process and conduct of these assessments were frequently missing from their files. In fact, in only a third of cases where an assessment was said to have taken place, were all of the relevant reports available.

Many of these assessments had not been successfully completed, either because the young person or their family were unwilling to engage in the process for very long, or because of breakdowns in assessment placements. Fewer than half of those previously referred to the Assessment Service successfully completed their assessments. Those most likely to have been completed were the Statements of educational need, although these could often take a very long time. However, parents and young people seem to have been highly motivated and generally participated fully in the process, perhaps because a tangible service was likely to result from this intervention.

Overall, in 27 out of 75 cases there was no record of any previous assessment having been attempted, although in 15 cases these were either pending or had at some point been planned. Of the remaining 12 for whom no record of a previous assessment could be found, eight were accounted for by our unaccompanied refugee children. When we looked at the remaining youngsters about whom nothing was known prior to their referral to social services, we found that they were all young Muslim women in their mid-to-late teens who had been admitted to care following allegations of physical or sexual abuse.

The sample as a group

One of the most consistent messages that has come from child care research studies in the past decade, is the need to carefully disentangle the very heterogenous population of children and young people who seek help from social services. Only then can we understand how best to respond to the range of needs of any particular group. In this chapter we have described in some detail the characteristics of our sample of 75 young people. But it may be useful to present these young people. as an identifiable group, hopefully without doing any injustice to their individual difficulties.

The criteria whereby the group was selected provide the first definitive features – they were adolescents, all at a point of crisis, which brought forth social work support for a period of at least three months and which resulted in assessment and formal decision making. For most, that crisis related to concerns about their behaviour or relationship problems. Child protection or offending were rarely primary factors. These problems were reflected in the lack of very limited schooling that most were receiving and in a tendency to move around between family and friends, or within the care system, as relationships deteriorated.

The assessment and decision making processes which this

study now describes were responding to the needs represented by the broad characteristics of this group, and it is in that light that they are best understood and evaluated.

Summary points

- Two-thirds of our study sample were aged between 14 and 16 years of age, a fifth being over school leaving age. There were slightly more boys than girls.

- Almost two-thirds of the young people were from minority ethnic groups; the largest grouping being children of mixed parentage. Eight of the 75 had come to England as unaccompanied refugees, their parents' whereabouts were unknown. Our study population embraced a variety of religious beliefs – while most were said to be Christians, one in five was Muslim.

- A fifth of the sample were said to have 'special needs', requiring medical or educational support. Ten had Statements of special educational needs, all of whom were enrolled at special schools.

- Most young people had experienced highly disrupted lives, including changes of carers and earlier separation from home. Social workers also highlighted their experience of poverty and inconsistent parenting.

- Educational experiences were unsatisfactory in many respects. Two-thirds of our sample were said to have been persistent school non-attenders. Indeed, a quarter had not been receiving full time education for at least one year. One in five school age pupils were not enrolled with any school or alternative educational programme. Only a quarter of the older pupils were said to be studying for any GCSEs. Those not attending school had frequently posed problems for carers and this had often prompted referral.

- More than half the school leavers were unemployed. Disconcertingly, few were receiving any state benefits.

- Parents of the sample had frequently contacted Social Services requesting help in dealing with unruly behaviour, although offending seemed not to be a major issue. Parents feared drug, alcohol or solvent abuse and were concerned about the vulnerability and moral welfare of girls. Parents had often experienced these problems for some time and were frequently felt to be at breaking-point.

- A quarter of young people had initiated contact with Social Services, complaining of severe conflict or rejection at home. Four had been 'sleeping rough' in the interim.

- Placement breakdowns, mostly in foster care, had been in-
stituted in roughly equal numbers by carers and young people.
However, social workers felt the main reason for placements
ending was their unsuitability.
- Most young people and their families were known to Social
Services prior to referral. As a group, they also had considerable involvement with other services. One in five had previous
contact with child or adolescent psychiatric services. Three
young women had attempted suicide.
- Overall, more than two-thirds had previously undergone a formal assessment, half of which were with the Adolescent Assessment Service. However, not all of these were satisfactorily
completed. Information on file about previous assessments
was often incomplete.

7. The decision to assess

Introduction

So far, we have looked at the characteristics and care histories of the young people in our study and the sorts of problems they presented at the time when they were considered for care, admitted to care or experienced a placement breakdown. In this chapter we describe how each of the young people were assigned to either the Referred or the Routine group. We look at what arrangements were made for assessing their needs; where these assessments took place; and what other agency professionals were involved in the assessment process. More specifically, we consider which young people were allocated to which forms of assessment, and why.

Before looking at these findings, however, we begin by considering the time-frames within which many of these 'events' occurred, for, as the subsequent sections show, this had a significant bearing on the type of assessment that followed. Also, it is worth remembering that the operational definition of assessment which was used in this study links assessment to the occurrence of an 'event', so the cases in the sample are likely to have an element of crisis.

Emergency admissions and placement breakdowns

Although most of the young people in our study were already known to social services, and more than a third of cases were 'active' at the time of the event, social workers were, nevertheless, often ill-prepared for admissions and placement breakdowns. For many of those in our 'admitted' group, the admission to care took place shortly after a referral was made to social services, half within 24 hours and another quarter within a week. Likewise social workers were often unaware that a placement was failing until the situation had reached crisis point, or were only informed of the breakdown after it had actually occurred. As a result, few of the admissions and placement changes which these young people experienced could be said to have been well planned.

Similar findings have been reported in other child care studies. For example, *Lost in Care* and *Who Needs Care?* both reported high proportions of emergency admissions and hastily made placements. They linked this to social workers' lack of preparation and planning and their ambivalence towards admissions to care (Packman with Randall and Jacques, 1986; Millham and others, 1986). Similarly the *Child Care Now* study, found that three out of four admissions were described by social workers as 'emergencies' even though more than half of the children involved were already known to social services (Rowe, Hundleby and Garnett, 1989).

Some of the reasons for this apparent lack of foresight and planning in our study cases are summarised below. This exploration soon moves beyond the specifics of case planning to broader concerns which in many ways characterise the context in which social work with adolescents is currently undertaken.

Firstly, compared with younger children and child protection referrals, adolescents in need, in the districts at least, were accorded a much lower priority on social work case-loads. Unless a young person or their family was in major crisis, their case was unlikely to be dealt with beyond the duty room. Consequently, once allocated, social workers rarely had time to employ any preventive strategies which might avert an emergency admission to care. In fact, the majority of young people in our 'admitted' group were allocated a social worker only after their admission to care had taken place.

Secondly, departmental procedures restricted the allocation of child protection cases to social workers with at least two years' post-qualifying experience. This meant that these older, more troublesome, adolescents were likely to be dealt with by less experienced staff, who, being new to the department, were also less familiar with the range of community resources on offer.

'This was the first case I took on in this department. Although Mum had referred to us before, the family had only ever been dealt with on duty, and it seems that they were never followed up. Basically when I got hold of the case Mum was climbing the walls. She was completely besieged and said she couldn't look after the boys any more. One of them was in trouble with the police and the other hadn't been in school for two years. The final straw came when one of them threatened her and her daughter with a knife. I was hoping to get some sort of day resource, but I found the whole youth work system really confusing. I was just phoning up every project I could think of. No one seemed to be able to come up with anything straight away. We were running out of options.' (Social worker)

'I'm not criticising my social worker. I think the main problem was that she was part time. I just couldn't get hold of her when I needed to. I was a single parent with three other small children and a husband who was trying to take my children away from me. I was in court every week. I just couldn't cope. I had a lot of worries and was under a lot of stress. [son] has learning difficulties and you need a lot of patience and humility to care for him as he is very demanding ... he was bitter, angry, resentful and jealous and I just wasn't able to cope. I know it sounds a bit of a cheek as it was me who asked if he could go into care in the first place but I just feel that they could've done more.' (Parent)

Thirdly, the age of this group and the sorts of problems they presented often made it difficult for social workers to negotiate with parents around alternative ways of dealing with difficult behaviour, particularly where this was their second or third referral to social services in a matter of months. Social workers often had little option but to remove the young person from home, as by this stage many of the suggested alternatives had already been tried by parents with little noticeable effect.

'I just told them I'd had enough. I couldn't cope. I'd tried everything. She was well into drugs and God knows what else. I told them I wasn't going to go to any more meetings. I'd done what I could. My whole life seemed to revolve around meetings, the police, hospitals, etc. I didn't know what else I could do. I wanted her to be safe. Not happy but safe. So I told them, 'she's your responsibility now'. I didn't know what else I could do.' (Parent)

At the same time, social workers' lack of confidence in the ability of the care system to effect any lasting positive change in the young person's behaviour made them reluctant to make any plans in the event of an admission to care or placement breakdown. The pressure on short term placements also precluded against preparing a place as a contingency option.

Fourthly, poor communication between social workers, residential staff, foster teams, and other professionals involved with the young person and their families meant that social workers were often unaware of any serious problems at home or in placement until a major crisis had developed.

'Getting a clear picture of what was going on at (residential unit) was really difficult. We'd get a phone call from the night shift who'd say they couldn't cope and were desperate for her to leave. This was generally first thing in the morning when they were obviously very tired. When the new shift came on they'd give us a completely different story, saying that things were OK and that they could cope after all.' (Social worker)

'I knew more about what was going on in the foster placement than my social worker did. In fact there was a time when Mr and Mrs R. (foster carers) were phoning me daily to tell me about S. It used to drive me mad. I also found it very difficult to take all their criticism of her. I was very unhappy about this. We were communicating directly about what was best for her when it was social services who should have been involved.' (Parent)

Although some of these communication problems were no doubt due to the pressure of work on other cases, they were certainly not helped by the department's recent structural reorganisation, as relationships between key staff seemed to be constantly disrupted and broken as staff moved into new posts. In addition, shortly after our research project began a job 'freeze' was announced. This led to tensions between social workers and managers, especially where area offices already had a large number of unfilled field-worker posts. This precipitated a period of industrial action by social workers, who refused to take on any cases of social workers who had left the department. As a result, some young people in care were without an allocated social worker for several months during the course of our research. In fact, nearly one in four of the young people in our placement breakdown group (23 per cent), had no allocated social worker at the time when their placement break-down occurred.

'When I took on the case neither he, the parents nor the foster carers had any contact with social services for some time. Not surprisingly when I tried to get work going nobody was very interested. Basically the problem stemmed from the fact that the case wasn't allocated until later on when it was too late. It's all a bit of a mystery about why the placement ended the way it did.' (Social worker)

However, the particular situation pertaining in this Authority at the time of the fieldwork is by no means unique. Working in a context of restructuring, reorganisation and unfilled posts can al-most be regarded as the norm for staff in today's social services departments.

Fifthly, poor communication between social services and certain minority ethnic communities also meant that some young people were unlikely to come to the attention of social services until the situation at home had reached crisis proportions. This was par-ticularly evident in the case of young people from Asian and North African Muslim communities, who represented more than a third of the 'admitted' group, and who, with the exception of the unac companied refugee teenagers in our sample, were more likely to be admitted to care with little or no history of previous social services involvement. A number of factors contributed to this. For example, some families were unaware of what support services might be available to them through social services, whilst others were reluctant to get involved with the department as they were fearful of what this might entail.

'It was clear that the problems that she and her family had been experiencing had been going on for some time and that they needed a lot of support and advice. But they didn't know what social services was. It took a long time to explain to them what our procedures were and to convince them that we would respect their views as regards their daughter's care.' (Social worker)

Few of the social workers in our study (the majority of whom were white Europeans) said they had any prior experience of working with Muslim young people and their families and lacked both the time and the confidence to work with them in a proactive way. This led to tensions and misunderstandings.

'The parents' inability to compromise over certain things, such as their daughter's dress, social life, and particularly boyfriends, made it hard for us to do any meaningful work with them. We were very ignorant though. In fact it was only later, when she'd been in care for some time, that we began to understand their reticence about this. Given their cultural background it was clear that we had totally unrealistic expectations of them.' (Social worker)

'Right from the beginning neither parents were willing to engage in any dialogue with me. In fact they wouldn't let me into their home. They seemed to believe that social services were simply there to remove Muslim children from their families for re-education. This made my position very difficult.' (Social worker)

Social workers reported that there were no Muslim foster carers or residential staff working in the Authority, which also made it difficult for them to make contingency arrangements for these young people in the event of a placement being needed. Indeed, many of the department's short-term placements were regarded by social workers, and families, as unsuitable for Muslim children and young people.

Finally, whilst it is possible that some admissions and placement breakdowns could have been averted by earlier or more intensive social work intervention, by the time they had reached older adolescence some of the young people in our study proved

stant to any form of parental or agency control. In-
of them had already exhausted many of the avail-
s social workers were often at a loss about what to do
ample, one 16 year-old who was being considered for
care, been known to the department for at least two years.
During that time he had been excluded from his residential EBD
school because of behavioural problems, had experienced at least
three foster placement breakdowns, and had run away from a
therapeutic community which had been recommended for him following a psychiatric assessment. Nor was he able to remain at
home, as neither his parents nor his extended family were able to
tolerate his behaviour for very long. He often went missing for
weeks at a time and on this occasion had ended up sleeping rough
on the streets. Although his social worker was sceptical that social
services would be able to effect any change in his behaviour he was,
nevertheless, homeless, vulnerable and at risk.

> 'I felt that this was our last chance to help him. He was rapidly ap-
> proaching his seventeenth birthday, and soon there wouldn't be any
> options available to him. As it was, no departmental resource was
> willing to entertain him. He had such a bad reputation. I wasn't look-
> ing for a care package, just a roof over his head. He was very depressed.
> In fact I was concerned that he may be suicidal. I just felt that getting
> him admitted to care was the only way that he'd get the sort of help
> that he needed.' (Social worker)

Whatever the reasons, the dramatic circumstances surrounding
many of the admissions to care and placement breakdowns in our
study meant that social workers were often more concerned with
finding a resource which could accommodate a young person at
short notice, than they were with organising an 'assessment of
need'. The impact of this and other factors on the type of assessment undertaken is the subject of the next section.

Routine or Referred Assessment?

When an assessment was required following one of the 'events', the
social worker first had to decide whether to undertake the assessment themselves (with or without the contribution of other agency
professionals), or whether they would refer to the Adolescent Assessment Service; Routine and Referred assessments respectively.
When the social worker referred a case to the Assessment Service,
a further decision was made regarding the appropriateness of the
referral and whether the AAS would undertake the assessment. In
addition, in a small number of cases, the Assessment Service was
already working with a young person when the event occurred and

here the option was whether they continued with the case or referred it elsewhere. This process is presented diagrammatically as Figure 7.1.

The options available to the social worker

Social workers in this Authority had a number of specialist assessment facilities at their disposal: the department's own Adolescent Assessment Service, which offered community-based, foster and

Figure 7.1 Assessment decision path

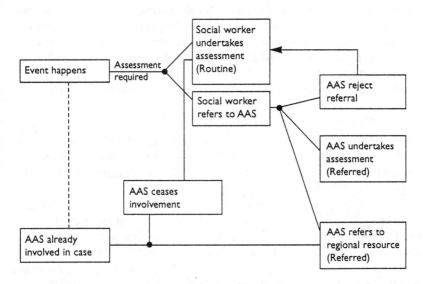

residential assessments; placements in the London Boroughs' Children's Regional Resources (which were capable of undertaking assessments in both secure and non-secure residential settings); as well as a range of other private and voluntary agencies in and around the capital which offered residential and non-residential assessment packages.

Although there were no explicit departmental rules about which form of specialist assessment facility should be used, social workers' discretion was effectively limited by a number of managerial constraints. For example, before making a referral to a private or voluntary assessment resource, social workers would normally have to seek approval from senior management both in terms of professional appropriateness and funding. The higher the cost of the proposed package or placement, the further up the management structure the decision would be taken.

Access to secure assessment facilities was also strictly monitored and controlled. Applications for secure orders could only be made with the agreement of the Assistant Director. This would only be given after full consideration of the possible alternatives at a 'risk of secure' case conference.

Social workers could exercise more individual discretion in their decision about whether or not to refer cases to the AAS for an assessment. However, this too was subject to some limitations because, in addition to its assessment function, the AAS was also gatekeeper to most of the short-term teenage placements in the Authority. Any social worker seeking to place a young person in one of the Service's residential units, assessment foster homes or short-term private/voluntary resources, including bed and breakfast accommodation, was therefore obliged to seek prior approval from the AAS, whether an assessment was required or not.

How many young people were referred?

Overall, more than two-thirds of our study group (53 young people) were referred to the AAS or other specialist assessment service around the time of their consideration for care, admission to care or placement breakdown.

The majority of these referrals (86 per cent) were made by district social workers, often within hours or days of the event occurring. Nine per cent of referrals were made by hospital-based social workers. Only five per cent were made by other agencies such as Education or Health. The majority of these came from Education Welfare Officers and the Authority's Schools Psychological Service with which the AAS had good professional links.

A further seven young people (9 per cent) were already involved with the AAS at the time when the event occurred, and were included in the study following a breakdown in their Assessment Service placement.

These decision paths, together with the numerical distribution of our sample into the Routine and Referred categories are shown in Figure 7.2.

The decision to refer

Not all of these referrals resulted in a formal assessment; only 12 social workers said they had referred to the AAS specifically for assistance with an assessment. Some said that they had been trying, unsuccessfully, to undertake a formal assessment with a

Figure 7.2   Distribution of the sample into Routine and Referred categories

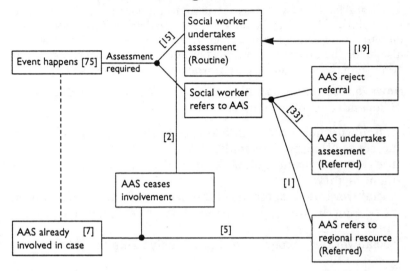

family and young person for some time, and hoped that the AAS might be able to provide a fresher and more objective perspective on the case.

> 'In spite of our long-term involvement with him and his family, no-one had ever really got to the bottom of his problems. The DAU had done some valuable work with him in the past and so I thought they might be in a better position than other places to undertake an assessment as he was already known to the Service.' (Social worker)

> 'Although I really didn't want to move him, home supervision hadn't really worked. I was very keen to find out how he functioned in another family setting and so I contacted the Assessment Service as I knew it had some very experienced foster parents. (Social worker)

Others felt that, as non-statutory workers, the AAS staff might have more success in getting young people and their families to engage in a formal assessment.

> 'At her last placement review, which she didn't attend as she'd gone missing from the residential unit, the DAU was recommended to us. It has a good reputation for being able to engage young people and it was felt that she was unlikely to cooperate with the department unless she could live in the community.' (Social worker)

The opportunity to do joint work on complex cases was also an important factor in the decision to refer young people to the AAS for an assessment, as the size of case-loads in some of the district-teams, we were informed, often made this quite difficult.

> 'It's useful for social workers to have someone else involved in the case, particularly when they haven't got much experience in dealing with difficult adolescents. It helps them to see things in a different way. It also helps the family to see things differently, when there's someone other than the statutory worker involved.' (Team Manager)

However for many social workers the decision to refer to the AAS depended on other factors:

- the role of the AAS as a gatekeeper to short-term placements;
- access to other professionals;
- the lack of awareness of AAS, especially of the outreach assessment facility;
- social workers' judgement of the need for further information regarding the young person and who was best placed to provide this;
- social workers' experience of previously using the AAS.

Access to short-term placements

As pointed out earlier, one of the functions of the AAS was to act as gatekeeper to short-term placements. Not surprisingly, many of the referrals to the AAS which were made during the course of our study came from social workers in search of an emergency bed. Overall, less than one in four young people were said to have been referred there for the purposes of an assessment. Instead, in the majority of cases the departmental procedures left social workers with little choice but to contact the AAS to get access to short-term teenage placements.

> 'We needed an emergency foster placement and this was the only way to get access to one quickly.' (Social worker)

> 'I didn't have any choice but to go through the AAS. We needed a respite placement and this was the only way to get access to one. We weren't looking for a formal assessment, just a short-stay bed until things had settled down at home.' (Social worker)

> 'I didn't make the referral. This was done by the duty team whilst I was on leave, presumably because it's the only way to get access to a placement.' (Social worker)

However, as noted in Chapter 5, in practice the AAS was not the only route into short-term teenage placements. On occasion, social workers did access resources directly. In our study this occurred in four 'placement breakdown' cases where young people were already known to foster carers or residential units (for example, through previous holiday placements), and where a short-term 'bridging' resource was required. Nor was the AAS the sole 'gatekeeper to care'. Although the majority of young people in our 'admitted' group were referred to the AAS, this was not compulsory. For example, one young person in our sample was placed with a relative foster carer on her admission to care, without reference to the AAS.

Given the high proportion of emergency admissions and placement breakdowns in our sample, it is perhaps not surprising that so many young people should be referred to the AAS for the purpose of securing a short-term bed. What was noticeable, however, was how few social workers were able to give other reasons for contacting the Service, more often than not due to limited knowledge of the Service.

'I generally use it when I need a placement for an adolescent in an unplanned emergency.'

'I've only ever used it for advice on finding placements.'

'I've never used it. In fact I didn't know until recently that it existed.'

'I tend to use it as an advisory service for placements, or if I need a placement quickly for a troublesome adolescent. I don't think I'd refer anything complex, like a child abuse case. Nor would I use them for home-based assessments. They don't do them do they?'

'I've never used it before. I've never needed to as there's only one other adolescent on my case-load. I would though if I was looking for an emergency placement.'

Figure 7.3 displays the reasons that social workers gave for referring to the AAS.

Staff in the AAS had a somewhat different perspective on referrals from social workers. For instance, much help and advice was given by telephone that would not constitute a referral. Also, while district staff may be requesting a placement, AAS staff may feel that the changes in the circumstances of the young person leading to that request may warrant some assessment of the current needs. AAS staff at times found it frustrating that referrals would come when the opportunity for outreach work had all but gone. Indeed some staff felt that some district workers tended to exaggerate problems in the case in order to secure a placement for a young person.

Figure 7.3   Reasons for referring to the AAS

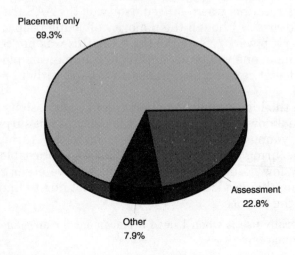

Placement only
69.3%

Assessment
22.8%

Other
7.9%

Social workers' access to other agency professionals

Another important factor which influenced the decision about referral to a specialist assessment service, was the need for an interdisciplinary assessment and the degree of access which social workers had to other agency professionals. Social workers in district offices often experienced difficulty in getting help from health and education specialists, so some referred to the AAS because they felt this would give them better access to these health and education professionals.

The likelihood of this happening was related to the proximity of other agency resources to social work teams. For example, social workers who had frequent and regular contact with other agency professionals, such as the Special Needs Team, rarely referred young people to the AAS or other specialist assessment services for an assessment. (Indeed some of these specialist team members said they had never used the AAS before, and were not aware of what the AAS was!) Social workers in district offices which had specialist health or educational resources on patch, also said that they were more likely to use these services for a community assessment rather than the AAS, although the shortage of staff in some of these resources meant that young people and their families could be waiting many weeks to be seen.

The need for further information

Social workers were clear that they were more likely to seek help in the form of an assessment when they felt the need for further information before making major decisions on a case and, likewise, this was an important criterion in the AAS decision to undertake an assessment. This need for information was in turn related to the extent of social work and other professional involvement in the case prior to the 'event' taking place. As we saw in the previous chapter, nearly two-thirds of the young people in our study were already involved with social services at the time when the 'event' took place, more than a quarter of them for six months or longer. However, not all of these cases were necessarily 'active' or allocated at this time. Twenty per cent of these 'open' cases were either being dealt with on a duty basis, or were held by social workers based in other organisations, such as the local Family Service Unit. Those cases which had been allocated for some time were, however, much less likely to be referred to the AAS for an assessment. Some social workers had already completed their assessments by the time that these 'events' occurred, or at least felt that they had enough information upon which to base their plans for these young people.

'I'd already completed an in-depth assessment of his needs whilst he was in the foster placement. By the time the placement ended we'd already made plans for him to move into a therapeutic community. When I referred to the AAS I wasn't looking for another assessment. Just a bridging placement for a few weeks.' (Social worker)

'I knew exactly what I wanted (a long-term foster placement), but they (the AAS) insisted on doing a six-week assessment anyway. I told them that I knew all that I needed to know and that an assessment wasn't really necessary. I just thought this was going to delay plans for her further.' (Social worker)

Some social workers feared that they would lose overall control of a case once a young person was referred on to one of these specialist services. One social worker declared that she never had, and never would refer any of her cases on to the AAS for an assessment.

'I find the suggestion that I would quite offensive as I'm very capable of conducting an assessment myself.' (Social worker)

Some young people were involved with a range of other agency professionals at the time when the 'event' took place. Many of the 'considered for care' group were in the process of undergoing other assessment procedures (such as psychiatric assessments, the statementing process, or an assessment of risk under the local child protection procedures) at the time when they were notified to our project. The introduction of yet another assessment procedure, which involved an additional set of professionals was therefore often regarded by social workers as inappropriate and unnecessary. The majority of social workers who referred 'considered for care' cases to the AAS were seeking information and advice about possible placement options, should an admission to care become necessary.

Social workers' prior experience of using the AAS

Interestingly, for most of the social workers in our sample this was their first experience of making an AAS referral. Although this may seem surprising given its six-year history of operation, many social workers were relatively new to the department; 45 per cent, for example, had worked there for under a year, whilst others said they had rarely dealt with adolescent referrals prior to the Department's reorganisation into specialist adult and children services teams. Their understanding of the way the Service operated and the assessment function it served (and particularly its capacity to undertake outreach assessments) was therefore limited. Indeed, in spite of its name, when asked what assessment resources they were aware of within the Department, few social workers mentioned the Adolescent Assessment Service itself!

> 'This was the first occasion I'd used the Service for an outreach assessment after four years in the Department. It was a very useful experience for me. Now that I know a bit more about how the Service works I'll use them more often. It does seem terrible though that I'm only just beginning to find out what is available after four years here.' (Social worker)

Whilst it is difficult to know whether more young people would have been referred to the AAS for an assessment had social workers been better informed, their perceptions and experience of the AAS must have played some part in their decision to refer.

Significantly, most of those in our sample who did refer to the AAS for an assessment had either used the Service before for this purpose, or had made the referral on the recommendation of a team member who had done so. As a result, these types of referrals tended to come from the same district teams and were often made with a particular assessment resource in mind.

Interestingly, only one social worker specifically requested a residential assessment. Of the other 11, five were seeking DAU or outreach assessments, whilst the remainder were hoping to secure an assessment foster placement.

Referrals to regional resources

As shown in Figure 7.2 six young people were referred, in the course of our study, to regional resources for the purposes of an assessment. All but one of these young people were already involved with the AAS, and were referred to these Regional Resources following a breakdown in their Assessment Service placement.

In all six cases the main reason given for making the referral was because staff in the department's own residential units felt unable to cope with the young person's difficult behaviour, and it was hoped that the more structured regime of a residential O & A centre would be better able to identify their needs. Some of these young people had committed serious offences whilst they were in care, whilst others were regarded to be at risk because of their persistent running away. Two young people were 'missing' at the time when the referral was made, and in both cases a 'secure' placement was recommended.

All of this group, apart from one young person who was referred to a Regional Resource at the point of her admission to care, were already known to the AAS, although none of them had been in placement long enough for a formal assessment to be completed. Having exhausted the department's assessment resources, a Regional Resource placement was often felt to be the only option left.

> 'It wasn't really my choice for her to go to (Regional Resource). It says something about a girl if she's been in there. But there was basically nowhere else for her to go. The assessment foster placement didn't last long and our residential units simply couldn't cope with her persistent absconding and offending behaviour.' (Social worker)

However, they were by no means the only young people in our study who presented difficult and challenging behaviour. Indeed, some young people had already been down this route by the time that they were notified to our project. By this stage the placement options had become increasingly limited. Depending on the young person's age, the alternatives were then seen as either another (expensive) agency placement (possibly in a secure setting), a return home, or bed and breakfast accommodation. As we shall see when we consider the outcomes for the group, for older teenagers these options seem to be almost interchangeable.

The response of the AAS

Once a referral had been made to the AAS, it was then up to the Service to decide what level of response was required. At this stage there could be lengthy case discussions between district and AAS staff about the possible ways forward. Often it was necessary to move quickly to find places for young people who were referred on the point of admission to care or following a breakdown in placement; the question was whether they should instigate the full assessment process and, if not, what other type of service (if any) should be offered.

Although there were no hard and fast rules – in the form of written procedures – determining which cases should undergo an AAS assessment, there was general agreement amongst Service staff about the types of young people for whom this was considered to be most appropriate, namely:

- young people who were at risk of admission to care or custody;
- 'emergency' admissions, where little was known about the young person and/or their family;
- long-term cases where social workers were unsure about how to move forward.

'If it's already clear what the young person's needs are, we wouldn't be saying let's do an assessment so that we can confirm what we already know. So one of the criteria must be that you need to find out more, as opposed to simply pulling all the information together.' (AAS staff member)

Of course, it was not always possible to make this sort of decision at the point of referral, particularly where social workers had only recently been allocated to work with a young person. The decision to undertake an assessment was, therefore, often deferred until a meeting had been held where information could be shared between all of the relevant professionals.

'Sometimes we find out that there's already an extraordinary amount of information available on these young people. As there's no point in re-running that, we might simply offer them the option of joint work with the young person and their family, or perhaps just offer them a short-term bed.

Often what is happening though is that a new case is referred to us just at the point of admission. Rather than make a decision then and there about assessment, we might wait for a week or so until we've got a clearer idea of what direction the case is going in. If a case looks like it's obviously not going to be turned around quickly, or if we were particularly concerned about the young person, then we would go ahead and institute the assessment process.' (AAS staff member)

The sorts of arrangements that were made when the Service undertook a piece of work with these young people also varied. Although the process of assessment was governed by specific principles and procedures (as outlined in Chapters 5 and 8), the objective of the AAS was to provide a flexible service, which could accommodate both the individual needs of the young person, and those of the allocated social worker. Assessments might be undertaken by the Service staff alone, or jointly with the young person's social worker. Alternatively, if the social worker wished to undertake the assessment work themselves, the Service might simply act in a coordinating capacity, and/or help to organise and chair a planning meeting between all of the relevant individuals.

> 'It may be that the area teams are saying that they don't know what to do, or that they need help to do it in a different way, because you can't do everything one-to-one with the whole family turning up at the office. In this case one of our staff might take on a long involved piece of work with the family and young person. Or it may be that the area worker does it. Either because they want to or because they have been involved for some time. Or we may decide to do it jointly. It's not something I think we should impose upon people. We try to work much more in collaboration with social workers.' (AAS staff member)

However, this view was not shared by all AAS staff members. Indeed, because the AAS controlled access to most of the short-term teenage placements in the Authority, some AAS staff felt that social workers had no choice but to accept the Service's decision about whether or not to instigate the assessment process.

> 'Because we have a structured approach, it allows us to say, if you want this resource then you have to comply with our process. What this offers social workers is the chance to step back from a case and to create some space and time to look at the situation afresh. It takes the pressure off, although the assessment process itself can present it's own pressures as well!' (AAS staff member)

The outcome of referrals to the AAS

Of the 53 young people who were referred to the AAS, at the time of their consideration for care, admission to care, or placement breakdown, nearly two-thirds (34 young people) were offered a Service assessment. In addition, five of the seven young people who were already being accommodated by the AAS at the time of their placement breakdown were referred to one of the capital's Regional Resources for the purposes of an assessment. These 39 young people make up the Referred group in our study, representing just over half of the total (see Figure 7.2).

In the 21 cases where the AAS did not undertake an assessment, responsibility for assessment and decision making remained with the district social worker, who would undertake these tasks as part of their routine case work with the young person. However the AAS could offer services other than assessment to this group of young people.

Ten were offered short-term 'bridging' placements, either in AAS resources or in private/voluntary accommodation, while the social worker made an assessment and a plan for the future. In three cases it was felt important to defer the assessment process in order to give young people time to settle in their placements. In four instances the AAS offered to undertake a piece of joint work with the young person's social worker in order to help them prevent an admission to care.

Three young people had been offered assessments by the AAS but in the event these were never instigated. In two cases this was because parents were unhappy with the Service's accommodation plans. In the other case, the plan to undertake an outreach assessment with a young person was reappraised by the AAS after he was charged with a number of offences.

In four cases the AAS was unable to offer any service at all. Three of these referrals concerned 16 year-old males who were referred to the AAS for emergency accommodation as they were homeless, vulnerable and had no financial means of support. Rather than admit these young people into care, the AAS suggested that social workers try alternative hostel accommodation, and in the short-term arrange for them to stay in bed and breakfast accommodation supported by monies from the 'Section 1' budget.

One social worker was very unhappy with this decision and felt that had the young person been younger or female, the request for an admission to care would have received a lot more support.

> 'He seems to have crossed the boundary for reception into care. Even though his needs are the same as they were three or four years ago the options are shrinking. If he'd been a girl I doubt whether the department would have responded the way that it did, and it certainly wouldn't have supported him living rough the way he is. He's one of the most marginalised adolescents that this department has been working with.' (Social worker)

Finally, one young person was notified to us following a breakdown in her assessment foster placement. This young person returned home and neither she nor her parents were willing to engage in any more work with the AAS.

These 21 cases, plus the 15 who were not referred to the AAS, make up the Routine group in our study; a total of 36 young people (see Figure 7.2).

The Referred and Routine groups

The type of assessment process undertaken is a key variable in this study. Here we briefly compare the characteristics of each of these sub-groups; first in terms of personal characteristics – sex, age and ethnic origin – and then in terms of the 'event' which preceded their assessment.

Sex: As we saw in the previous chapter, the overall sample group included more young men (41) than young women (34). The female group was divided equally between assessment types, while slightly more young men were assessed by the AAS, as shown in Figure 7.4.

Age: Table 7.1 shows the age distribution of each sub-group. It can be seen that all ages are substantially represented for both assessment types, but with a definite tendency for the oldest age group to be more prevalent within the Routine category. This age

Figure 7.4   Assessment type by sex

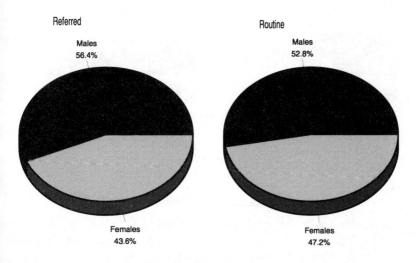

distribution strongly reflects the type of event, with Referred assessments being used much more frequently for 'admitted to care' cases, which are least likely to be found in the oldest age group.

Table 7.1   Age by type of assessment

	Under 13	13–14 years	15 years	16 years	Total
Referred	5	16	13	5	39
Routine	7	12	7	10	36

Ethnic origin: We have already noted the very diverse ethnicity of the sample group; as Figure 7.5 illustrates, this diversity is distributed in a very similar pattern between the two assessment types, with just over one third of each group classified as white.

Type of event: Although our sample was split fairly evenly between Referred and Routine assessments, there were major differences within these sub-groups in the distribution of cases by type of event. Table 7.2 summarises how this distribution resulted from the decisions that have been described earlier in the chapter.

Figure 7.5   Assessment type by ethnic group

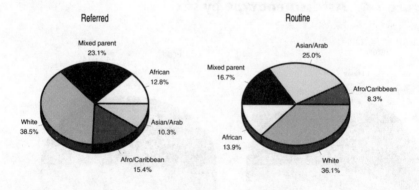

In particular, only three of the 'admitted to care' cases were assessed by social workers, compared to 23 whose assessments were undertaken with reference to a specialist assessment service. Where the event was 'considered for care' or 'placement breakdown' social workers were twice as likely to undertake the assessment themselves. In fact, only a third of the 'considered for care' cases underwent a Referred assessment in spite of them being the

main target group for AAS intervention. The reasons for this have
already been considered.

Table 7.2   Outcome of referrals to the AAS

	Considered for care (n=27)	Admitted to care (n=26)	Placement breakdown (n=22)
Referred group (n=39)			
AAS assessment instigated	9	22	2
Referred to Regional Resource	–	1	5
Routine group (n=36)			
Other service offered by AAS	4	2	8
No service offered by AAS	4	–	3
Not referred to AAS	10	1	4

The breakdown of cases by 'event' and type of assessment is illustrated further in Figure 7.6, demonstrating again that the flow of
work to the department and the AAS did not, in practice, enable
the sample to be fully symmetrical.

The objectives of assessment

We turn now to examine whether the objectives that the social
workers hoped to achieve through the assessment varied by type

**Figure 7.6   Distribution of cases by assessment type
              and event**

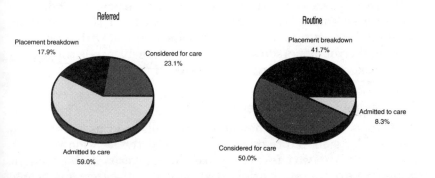

Referred

Placement breakdown
17.9%

Considered for care
23.1%

Admitted to care
59.0%

Routine

Placement breakdown
41.7%

Admitted to care
8.3%

Considered for care
50.0%

of assessment. However social workers could only identify their objectives when they accepted an assessment had taken place. This was not always the case.

While all the sample met *our* assessment criteria, in 15 instances social workers did not regard the work that they, or the AAS, planned to undertake with the young person and/or their family as constituting an 'assessment' at all. (Social workers' definitions of assessment are considered in the following chapter.) Twelve of these young people fell into our Routine category, making up more than a third of this assessment type and three were Referred. As information on the objectives of the assessment was based on social workers' evaluations, it has been necessary to exclude these cases from our analysis. Table 7.3 gives details of the main objectives of assessment for those 60 young people for whom an assessment (according to social workers' definitions) was said to have been planned.

Table 7.3 The objective of assessment by type of assessment (n=60)

	Referred (35)	Routine (25)	Total (60)
'Risk assessment'	–	3	3
Education/employment needs	3	3	6
Behavioural problems	3	1	4
Capacity of parents/carers to care/control	14	9	23
Long-term placement needs	9	5	14
Other	–	2	2
More than one of these	6	2	8

The pattern of objectives is similar for the two sub-groups. For both types of assessment the most important reason for undertaking an assessment was to judge the capacity of the parents or carers to look after and control the young person, with an assessment of the young person's long-term placement needs the second most cited reason – again for both types of assessment.

The venue for assessment

There was a further dimension to any planned assessment on which a decision had to be made – namely, the location in which the assessment was to take place. In categorising assessment types we have therefore drawn distinctions between young people according to whether they were assessed:

- at home, or in some other *community* location (such as the DAU, the young person's school, a clinic, or bed and breakfast accommodation);
- in *foster* homes (including both 'assessment' and 'ordinary' foster placements);
- in *residential* placements (whether this was an 'assessment' unit or other community home).

Allocation to these categories was, however, not always clear cut. We have already mentioned that some young people experienced more than one 'event' during the course of our three month assessment period. Similarly, they might experience different types and venues for assessment. For instance, if an assessment placement broke down, the assessment may not be completed or may continue in another placement, which may be an assessment placement or a non-specialist placement. In such instances, cases were classified according to where the young person had spent most of their time prior to the final assessment conference or other decision making meeting. Figure 7.7 shows the different venues used according to the type of assessment. The very different pattern in the venues was closely linked to the different types of event that preceded the assessment, as shown in Table 7.4.

Not surprisingly, given the different spread of 'events' between these two assessment types, the patterns of placements also varied considerably. This variation is an important factor in the cost of assessment, which will be discussed in detail in Chapter 12. Al-

Figure 7.7   Assessment type by venue

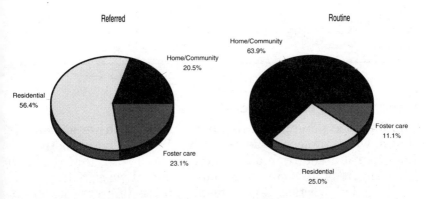

Referred

Home/Community
20.5%

Residential
56.4%

Foster care
23.1%

Routine

Home/Community
63.9%

Foster care
11.1%

Residential
25.0%

most two-thirds of the Routine assessments (64 per cent), were undertaken whilst the young person was living in the community, compared to less than a quarter (21 per cent) of those undertaken by the AAS or other specialist assessment service. Of those who were Referred, more than half were assessed residentially. Only nine young people were assessed in one of the Service's specialist assessment foster homes, often following a period of days, and sometimes weeks, spent in another resource waiting for an assessment foster home to become available.

Where foster care was the preferred placement the most common reasons given were the age and vulnerability of the young people concerned. However, there were concerns about the location of many of these assessment foster placements, *all* of which were outside of the borough. Where residential placements were made, social workers stressed the advantages of their proximity to home, school and relatives. Indeed, a preference for residential care was often expressed by young people. The choice of venue was, however, more often than not, based on availability rather than any notions about what would make an ideal assessment placement for a particular young person. In fewer than half of the 75 cases did social workers say they had any choice about the location of the assessment.

Table 7.4   The venue for assessment by 'event' type

	Considered for care	Admitted to care	Placement breakdown	Totals
'Referred'				
Outreach/DAU	7	–	1	8
Assessment foster	2	7	–	9
Residential	–	16	6	22
'Routine'				
Community	18	1	4	23
Foster	–	1	3	4
Residential	–	1	8	9

Other agency involvement

The final decision around the assessment which we examine is that of which professionals to involve. We have noted, both from the literature and from our interviews with staff, that the term 'assessment' is interpreted in many different ways, both conceptually and in practice. One element in these different interpretations is the necessary depth or breadth of an assessment. This in turn revolves, in part, around the arrangements for interdisciplinary working. So which professionals from other agencies were directly involved in the assessment of these 75 young people?

In 49 cases other agencies were directly involved in the assessment and planning process, either through attendance at meetings, preparation of reports, or both. In 26 cases no other agency was said to have contributed directly. Table 7.5 records the instances of direct involvement by others, although the nature of their contributions varied considerably. Some cases involved more than one other professional and so the total is greater than 75. In this Table the category 'Other Education' includes Education Welfare Officers, teachers, special unit staff and school pastoral staff.

Table 7.5   Other agencies directly involved in assessments, by type of assessment

	Referred	Routine	Total
Profession			
Educational Psychologist	4	5	9
Psychiatrist	5	3	8
Clinical Psychologist	3	1	4
Health Professional	7	6	13
Family Therapist	4	4	8
Other Education	15	9	24
No involvement by other agencies	9	17	26
Total	47	45	92

Interestingly, this pattern of interdisciplinary assessment did not differ greatly between the Referred and Routine cases, although because of the DAU the number of other education professionals involved was greater for those cases which were assessed by the AAS. Whether the AAS could provide access to key experts was a key question for many staff and one to which we shall return later.

Overall less than half of these young people's assessments involved direct contributions from education professionals, in spite of poor attendance and performance at school being one of the main presenting problems at the time of the precipitating 'event', and only a third of them involved contributions from health professionals. The degree to which education and health issues were addressed during the assessment process is considered in more detail in the following chapter.

This analysis of the sub-groups, Routine and Referred, shows major differences in the type of assessment undertaken according to the precipitatory event – most 'admitted to care' cases were Referred for assessment while proportionally more 'considered for care' and 'placement breakdowns' were Routine assessments. This pattern is correspondingly reflected in the age distribution and the venue for assessment – most Referred assessments were residential while most Routine assessments took place when the young person was living in the community.

However, despite these marked differences, the social workers' objective in initiating an assessment and the use of other professionals was remarkably similar for both groups.

Summary points

- As other studies have also revealed, social workers were frequently ill-prepared when admissions to care or placement breakdowns occurred. This was related to the low priority allocated to adolescent cases; the relative inexperience of the social workers involved; the intractability of many situations and pessimism about what social services had to offer; poor communication between social work professionals; and lack of social workers' involvement in, and awareness of, certain minority ethnic communities.

- Consequently, social workers were often seeking accommodation at short notice rather than specifically an assessment of need.

- A variety of alternative arrangements existed for assessments. However a number of management and other constraints influenced which approach could be chosen.

- More than two-thirds of our sample were referred to the Adolescent Assessment Service, usually by social workers. AAS could respond in different ways, including suggesting various forms of joint work. However, nearly two-thirds of these referrals were offered a Service assessment.

- Six young people were referred to Regional Resources, as local residential facilities were unable to deal with their behaviour.

- There was a slightly increased tendency for males to experience Referred assessments. The oldest age group experienced Routine assessments more frequently. 'Admissions to care' were more likely to be Referred cases, and 'considered for care' and placement breakdowns Routine. There was no difference in type of assessment experienced according to ethnic group.

- In 15 of our cases, social workers did not consider that an assessment was being undertaken. For the rest the main objective was to judge parents' capacity to look after and control the young person.

- Almost two-thirds of Routine assessments were undertaken while the young person remained living at home, in contrast to a quarter of those that were Referred. More than half the latter were assessed residentially, and only nine young people in assessment foster homes.
- In two-thirds of cases, other agencies were directly involved in the assessment and planning process. Referred and Routine assessments were similar in this respect.

8. The assessment process

Introduction

In this chapter we compare in detail how social workers and staff from the Assessment Service approached the task of assessing the needs of the young people in our study. We begin by comparing the frameworks for assessment in its Routine and Referred forms. We then examine what effect, if any, these differences had on assessment practice, in terms of three key child care principles – involving young people, working in partnership with parents and taking due account of the young person's racial and cultural background.

The material for this chapter has come from a number of different sources: interviews with field social workers, assessment staff, some young people and their parents; case records and assessment reports; and observations of assessment meetings.

The frameworks for assessment compared

In Chapter 2 we argued that one of the key elements to setting good standards of practice in assessment work with young people is the existence of an explicit system or framework through which assessments are conducted. We begin our analysis, therefore, by considering how far this condition was met within the two forms of assessment under study. Our comparison of assessment frameworks focuses on the following five themes:

- the concept of assessment;
- principles in undertaking assessment;
- the procedures for assessment;
- decision making meetings;
- the tools for assessment.

The concept of assessment

It will be recalled that a main criterion for inclusion in this study was that some form of assessment had occurred at the time of a young person's consideration for care, admission or placement breakdown, the minimum form of which was represented by the holding of a meeting at which decisions were made and recorded. However, this did not mean that social workers, or the Assessment Service for that matter, necessarily shared our definition of when an assessment was taking place. Indeed, as we saw in the previous chapter, in some cases social workers did not regard the work they had been doing with young people and their families as constituting an 'assessment' at all. We were therefore interested to find out what social workers did understand by this term, particularly in view of the emphasis which has been placed on assessment in the guidance and regulations which accompany the Children Act 1989.

Previous National Children's Bureau studies have noted how the term assessment has taken on a much broader definition than hitherto in social services departments. In their exploratory study of assessment systems in six different local authorities, Grimshaw and Sumner found, amongst managers at least,

> a clear tendency towards viewing assessment as part of a more general intervention, in which there was an emphasis on planning for the future, and on reducing the possibility of the child's passage into, or through, the care system. Assessment was seen as a task essentially for fieldworkers to perform and the role of the specialist facilities lay in supporting their endeavours and helping to achieve broad community care objectives. (Grimshaw and Sumner, 1991, p211)

As one manager in that study commented,

> (Assessment) should be part and parcel of work going on, of change happening, and it needs to involve all parties involved with the family and to involve parents in decisions ... A social worker ought to be able to make a formal assessment in an area office with a review meeting. Formal assessment is available to anyone. (ibid, p52)

How far was this concept of assessment shared by social workers and managers in our authority? Although no attempts were made to define assessment in any departmental documentation, most of the senior managers with whom we spoke tended to share the above view. Furthermore, whilst the role of 'specialist' and 'expert' was recognised as important, assessment was generally regarded as a task for area-based social workers which would typically take place 'in the community' before any decisions were made about whether or not to accommodate a young person.

Social workers' definitions of assessment varied widely. Some defined it in terms of its specific applications, such as in child protection work, mental health, or under the provisions of the 1981 Education Act. For them the term assessment was associated with a specific process of information gathering and analysis, which would typically be undertaken by specialists outside the social services department. Others offered a more open-ended definition. For these social workers, assessment was not necessarily associated with a particular process, or application, but was seen more as a continual process of monitoring and evaluation in which they were engaged throughout the life of a 'case'.

The majority of social workers, however, were less categorical about what the term assessment meant, and tended to regard both definitions as having some legitimate value. They tended to use such terms as 'formal' and 'informal', 'specialist' and 'non-specialist' assessments, in order to distinguish between these two types.

However it was defined, assessment was commonly associated with identifying needs or problems, the purpose of which was to find the appropriate resource or solution.

'Assessment is a very broad term. Every social worker will do it differently so it's hard to put your finger on something and say that is assessment. My definition is that you have a problem that needs changing and you work towards that change.' (Social worker)

'For me assessment means taking an all round look at a child looking at the home background, health, education needs, etc., and pulling all this information together to decide what should be done next.' (Social worker)

Again, there was no attempt to define assessment in any of the Assessment Service documentation, but the AAS staff were more precise about what they meant by the term. They were also more likely to share our definition of when an assessment was taking place, although they felt that it involved considerably more than just a meeting at which decisions were made and recorded.

'Within the AAS we have a much tighter definition of assessment, which really excludes the assessments which go on forever, although we accept that people doing medium- and long-term pieces of work may be continuously making decisions. For us assessment is seen as a time-limited, process-led piece of work, which usually occurs at the point when we first come into contact with a young person and their family.' (AAS staff member)

'It seems to me that what we're talking about is a process, which is more than a straightforward piece of work where an area worker might come to us with a problem on a case and we solve it for them. It's about looking deeper into a case, getting a more rounded view of what they're about. It's about using our resources in a time-limited way, involving all of the relevant people, and arriving at a conclusion about how best to move forward.' (AAS staff member)

As revealed above, the process of 'bringing people together' for the purpose of drawing up child Care Plans was regarded by AAS staff as one of their most important functions.

> 'Although area-based fieldworkers could do this, it rarely happens. When it does, it's normally at a child protection conference. Everyone gets invited to these, but it's not a planning meeting really; it's got a different function completely. In the AAS we have a specific process which involves three meetings which take place over a fixed period of time. Just having those meetings can have a significant impact on a case. It also means that we can monitor the progress of the assessment much more closely.' (AAS staff member)

Assessment was not just about meetings, however. Just as fieldworkers were involved in both assessment and service provision for their clients, so too was the AAS. The assessment process was, therefore, defined in much more dynamic terms, with intervention and treatment forming an essential part of the planning process.

> 'It does not seem helpful to assess it as you see it without trying to influence things; it may require some profound intervention from us. So on Day 1 there may be certain presenting problems but, having done this, this and this as part of the assessment, at the end of the eight-week assessment period the problems may seem quite different. Taking action during the assessment process can therefore often alter the final view of what services should be offered.' (AAS staff member)

Thus, whilst district fieldworkers and the AAS agreed that assessment was a dynamic process which involved information gathering, intervention and decision making, what set the AAS staff's definition of assessment apart from that of their district colleagues, was that it involved a specific process which was both structured and time-limited.

Principles in undertaking assessment

At the time of our study, there were no specific policies or guidelines governing the conduct of assessment within the department's Children and Families Division. The department's general policy statement did stress the importance of undertaking, at the earliest possible time, a 'detailed and thorough multidisciplinary assessment of the physical, emotional, social and educational needs of children and young people whose needs were not being met or who were at risk of losing their families'. It also made reference to a number of key principles which were supposed to underpin *all* work with children and families, including assessment – these were discussed in Chapter 4. However, few of the social workers we spoke to had any recollection of having seen this document. As a result most were unaware of what these principles were, or how they might be translated into practice when assessing the needs of children and young people.

> 'I'm not aware of any departmental policies or guidelines on assessment as such. I know the AAS have a document, which I've got. I'm sure there must be an overall policy on assessment, but I couldn't tell you what it is.' (Social worker)

In fact, many social workers said that they would welcome the production of such a document as they felt that the department's approach to assessment was rather uncoordinated and piecemeal. (Since the completion of this study, the department has produced such a comprehensive document, outlining new policies and procedures in line with the requirements of the Children Act, 1989.)

> 'There probably is a lot of stuff around on assessment in the department if you ask for it, like the 'Orange Book' for example, but as far as I know there isn't a specific document of our own.' (Social worker)

As we saw earlier, the AAS, whilst operating within the department's broad Children and Families Policy, also endorsed a number of other key principles in its approach to the assessment and planning process, and these are summarised in Chapter 5. Although these principles of operation were not made explicit in AAS documentation, the 12-page guide to the Service did contain some helpful material. The section on 'principles for assessment report writing', for example, contained the following useful points.

- Young people and their family should be fully involved in the assessment process. This means having copies of all reports, and being invited to attend all meetings.
- Young people should be encouraged to write their own reports or at least have their views represented at the Final Assessment Conference. A person will be named at the Planning Meeting to facilitate this piece of work.
- Observations and assessment must be clearly separated.
- Reports should be accurate and precise in observed detail. Sources of information should be specified and evidence provided to substantiate Assessments.
- Language in the report should be accessible to all members of the Final Assessment Conference. It should also be non-sexist, non-racist and jargon kept to a minimum.
- The objective of the Assessment report is to provide an overall picture of the young person's needs.
- Any person with significant contact with the young person will be asked to contribute a report for the Final Assessment Conference.

- Reports should have lasting value, not just the justification of the next placement.
- Recommendations for future placement will be made at the Final Assessment Conference.
- All reports should be circulated prior to the Final Assessment Conference.

Of course the existence of policy statements and codes of practice does not, in itself, guarantee that such principles will be represented in social work practice (Packman with Randall and Jacques, 1986; Hardiker, Exton and Barker, 1991; Department of Health, 1991a; Gardner, 1992). In fact, less than a fifth of the social workers we interviewed confirmed that they had seen a copy of the AAS document, although most of them were aware of its existence. However, as the AAS team was a relatively small and cohesive group, these principles of operation tended to be well known within the Service itself, and it was common for JAM (Joint Assessment Meeting) members to inform social workers and others of these principles at the beginning of the Assessment Planning Meeting.

The procedures for assessment

The procedures for assessment were also clearly defined within AAS documentation, as discussed in Chapter 5. In addition to information on the system for referrals, the Service's guide also gave details on the frequency and timing of assessment meetings, who was to be invited, as well as the roles and responsibilities of all assessment participants. As a general rule, all assessment meetings were supposed to be minuted, with copies circulated to each of the participants. However, due to shortages of administrative staff, this task was often left to the Chair. As a result, the practice of recording and distributing the minutes of meetings within the AAS was variable, according to the amount of time each Chair was able to devote to this task.

Apart from the Department of Health's 'Orange Book', and the DES/Department of Health guidance accompanying the 1981 Education Act (Circular No. 22/89), we were not aware of any written procedures on the conduct of assessment within the department's Children and Families Division. For example, there was no documentation to assist social workers and others with the presentation of cases to the department's Placement Panel, which was somewhat surprising given the importance of these particular decision making meetings. Nor was it clear whether young people and/or their families were to be invited to attend. Although we were told by some social workers that it was not departmental policy to invite young people or their parents to Placement Panels, we could find no written evidence of this. In fact, the department's policy statement would seem to suggest just the reverse:

> To have a sense of worth and confidence in the future a child has the right to be listened to and understood. The local authority is required by law to ascertain the wishes and feelings of the child and to take these into account before reaching a decision regarding the child. All children have the right to participate in the discussions as far as they are able, while knowing that the final responsibility for the decision rests with the adults.

Consequently it was not unknown for young people to make their own representations to these Placement Panels, as two of the young people in our study did.

Decision making meetings

We were also struck by the proliferation of different forums in which child care plans were being made and discussed in this department. For example, in addition to the three AAS meetings, which would normally take place during the course of a Referred assessment (see Chapter 5), we identified at least seven other types of meetings where child care decisions were being made. Although some of these meetings were clearly performing an important gatekeeping function, such as 'risk of secure' conferences, 'risk of custody' conferences, 'placement panels' and 'special needs panels', the purpose of others (known variously as 'professional meetings', 'strategy meetings' or just plain 'planning meetings') was rather less well-defined. In addition to this, there were also the routine 'placement reviews', 'child protection reviews' and statutory 'in care reviews' which were taking place at regular intervals throughout the progress of a case.

Unsurprisingly, social workers (and presumably their clients) were often confused about the function and interrelationship of these various planning and review meetings, and about the status of the recommendations and decisions reached. Indeed, it was sometimes difficult to determine which of these meetings, for the purposes of our assessment study, should be regarded as the decision making forum, as it was not unknown for young people to be the subject of at least three different types of planning meetings during the course of our research assessment period. There were also a number of cases where, for a variety of reasons, the assessment process did not complete its course and the young person's

Final Assessment Conference did not take place as planned. (This is discussed in more detail in Chapter 9.) Where either of these situations occurred, we decided to select as the final decision making meeting the last formal meeting which took place during the three months following a young person's consideration for care, admission or placement breakdown, at which plans were made and recorded. Table 8.1 compares the type of final decision making meeting for our study group of 75 under the Referred and Routine systems of assessment.

The different patterns between the two groups reflects the specific procedure and more explicit reference to assessment for the Referred group. The more interesting question is whether the actual purpose and achievements of these meetings is more similar than the nomenclature implies? We shall test this later when we examine the outcomes for the young people from their assessment.

The tools for assessment

The methods by which social workers collect and assemble infor-

Table 8.1   Type of final decision making meeting by assessment system

	Referred	Routine
Final Assessment Conference	26	–
Assessment Planning Meeting	3	–
Child Protection Conference	–	6
Placement Panel	2	6
Placement Review	4	2
Other planning meeting*	4	22
	39	36

* This included 'pre-court meetings', 'professional meetings', 'planning meetings' and 'emergency planning meetings'.

mation for assessment may vary according to the purpose of the assessment, the particular needs of the clients as well as the social worker's individual skills and preferences. There is therefore no prescribed list of techniques or tools that should always be used in an assessment. Having said that, the existence of guidance, proforma, and paperwork tools can help social workers to approach the task in a more focused and systematic way. The Assessment and Action Records, devised by Dartington Social Research Unit, represents a major step forward in the development of assessment tools; these are recommended for use as part of the Reviewing process, as their primary purpose is to monitor whether the care provided to 'looked after' children does meet their needs (Department of Health, 1991b, 1995).

To assist social workers, foster carers and residential key-workers with this task, the AAS documentation contained a basic outline of what an assessment report should contain, as well as some helpful tips about how to help young people to participate in the assessment process. This included a blank copy of a 'flowchart of moves', similar to the one in the *Guide to Comprehensive Assessment*, as a suggested tool for summarising important changes in the young person's life (Department of Health, 1988). In addition to this, the department's Community Fostering section had produced a simple guide to assessment fostering, which was specifically aimed at young people. This, too, contained some exercises for young people to complete as part of the assessment process.

Within each young person's file there were standard proforma available for the recording of important biographical data, such as their family and household composition, school, occupation, agency network as well as details about 'significant others'. The department had also produced a useful summary sheet to help social workers record and analyse information obtained during their initial interviews with young people and their families, although we did not find any evidence that these had been used.

Beyond the provision of these basic tools there were no other departmental guides to assist social workers and others through the process of assembling and analysing information for the purposes of an assessment. We were therefore interested to find out what methods social workers had employed and whether there were any particular approaches or tools which they had found useful.

As most of the young people in our study were already known to social services, one potential source of information was the social work file. However, few social workers stated that they had found previous social work records to be particularly helpful. Either their previous records were said to be too old to be of any significant value, or the information within them was not readily accessible.

'I didn't find the previous files to be particularly helpful in this case, but then I've only had chance to take a brief look at them, so there is probably a lot of information that I've missed. It is difficult to get hold of their previous history though. Information seems to be dissipated through a number of different volumes, and some of the files are so old that they are just falling apart.' (Social worker)

One social worker remarked that as far as possible he avoided reading what other people had written before he met with young people, as he felt this might contaminate his judgement about how to approach the case. Indeed, the view that one should not read young people's files before beginning work on a case was at one time quite a popular one, particularly in residential care; and interestingly this social worker had, prior to this post, worked for many years in a residential O & A unit. This approach was not shared by the majority of social workers. On the contrary, many of them complained that records were not detailed enough. In fact, some of the cases that we encountered had been so poorly recorded that it was difficult to get any sense of what had been happening from the files. As one social worker commented,

'This family was originally worked with by another team and only came to us when the mother changed address. Although the children had been living at home under our care and control for more than a year, when we picked up the files there was no record of what had been happening; no reviews, nothing. We had no idea of what had plunged Mum into such a depression and no idea of what was supposed to have been planned for the children. The records were that bad.' (Social worker)

Although the standard of record-keeping varied considerably, it seemed to be most problematic in those cases which, although active, had not been allocated a social worker for some time. It also meant that there was often no-one with recent knowledge of the young person and their family within the department with whom the newly allocated social worker could discuss details of the case.

'Once I was allocated to this case, her new placement was pretty well established. I was concerned that no-one could really help me, in terms of giving me an insight into why her foster placement broke down when it did. There was absolutely nothing on file about this, and Community Fostering haven't been very forthcoming with any more information.' (Social worker)

Others complained that they had little time to read through all the relevant records, particularly when the young person's involvement with social services stretched over several years.

'To do my job properly and to meet his needs I should have been able to do a potted history from the five volumes on him – but I haven't had time to read them. I'd liked to have had a clearer picture about him from the beginning, but there'd been no allocated worker for some time.' (Social worker)

The files which social workers regarded as most helpful were those that contained brief summaries of the child's and family history, either in the form of a flow chart or in written form, as well as a report of what work had been done to date. However, in spite of the fact that many of these young people were already well known to social services and other agencies, such summaries were rare, and tended only to be present in those cases where an AAS assessment had been successfully completed, or where the case had recently gone to Court. Where assessments had not been completed, the work that had been done was rarely, if ever, summarised on file. It was also disconcerting to discover that, of the 13 young people in our study who either had been or were still subject to a Statement of educational need at the time of the 'event', only six of these Statements were actually in the social worker's file.

Not surprisingly, the primary sources of information for assessment purposes were reported to be the parents and the young people themselves. Few social workers mentioned any particular techniques or paper work tools which they had used to help focus their discussions with young people and their families. Two said that they had used selected parts of the 'Orange Book' to compile family histories with young people and/or their parents. Another said that she had employed techniques such as role-play to help young people communicate their difficulties to others. The same worker had also made use of diaries as a way of helping young people to record their wishes and feelings. The majority of social workers, however, said that they had not used any paperwork tools, although some of them did comment that they would have liked to, if they had more time.

> 'I didn't really get the opportunity to use any in this case as I wasn't allocated for some time. But if I had, I probably would have used some of the stuff from 'Windows to Our Children'. You have to find all of this stuff yourself though. It's not something that's readily available in the area offices.' (Social worker)

Apart from discussion, the other main method which was used for collecting information for assessment purposes was said to be 'observation'. But few of the social workers we interviewed had been able to spend much time observing young people and/or their families, and so for this they relied very much on their professional colleagues.

Under the Referred forms of assessment, the person(s) responsible for observing young people's functioning and behaviour would normally be identified at the Assessment Planning Meeting. Although this task might sometimes be shared between different professionals, the responsibility for this usually lay with the young person's keyworker, which might be an assessment foster carer, residential worker or outreach worker. One assessment foster carer explained this task as follows:

'Well, we have to keep regular notes for everybody … a sort of diary. We don't write down everything that's happened each day … just things that seem important. This acts as a reminder when we come to writing the final report. Sometimes when we're asked to do an assessment, different criteria come up. Mostly though (the assessment) is about whether a young person can live in a family situation because at other times they've shown that they can't manage it. So one of the main questions is whether they can live in a family? For example, can they manage family rules? How do they manage eating and conversation when we're all together as a family? How do they manage their own space and time? Do they get to school and back without any other distractions impinging on that timetable? How do they manage their weekends? How do they respond to us, and their peer group? What are they like after visiting their parents? Do they want to visit their parents?

The other thing is that all the time they're here we're talking about the possibilities for their future, 'cos they know that these placements are only for a few weeks. We tell them that at the beginning. How do they feel about going back to their families? Do they want to be in a long-term foster home or do they want to move into a residential unit or a group home? We're talking to them all the time about how they see the future and what they want.' (Assessment foster carer)

These observations would then be written up in the form of a report and shared with all of the relevant participants at the Final Assessment Conference.

In order to provide a rounded picture of the young person and achieve consistency in report writing, the AAS documentation also contained some brief guidelines on what areas keyworkers were expected to cover in their assessment reports. This included:

- *Background*: How had the referral come about? What tasks were agreed at the Planning Meeting? Flow chart of the young person's past.
- *Placement*: What happened, brief account of the overall placement? Attitudes of the young person to the placement and the assessment.
- *Family*: What contacts were there? Telephone? Visits? Family sessions? Who was present? What was observed? How was the young person after family contact?
- *Relationship with friends, other adults and report writer*: What has been observed? Do they seek/demand attention? Are they withdrawn/suspicious/keen to make close contacts? Do they

resent authority/defy adults? Do they have a group of friends, just one, younger, or the opposite sex?

- *Young person*: Pen portrait/description? How can this young person be engaged? What are the best methods of handling behaviour? Level of maturity/immaturity? Fears and fantasies? Self-esteem, social skills and talents? What do you think they are good at? How do they deal with money? How do they use their time? What do they want for the future? What are the issues/ difficulties for the young person in the context of the current situation?
- *Education / work*: Attitudes to? Difficulties talked about? Good things? Future?
- *Summary of needs*: What order of tackling them is most important?

With Routine assessments, it was much more difficult to identify how these various tasks were agreed and allocated. Not only were assessments far less likely to be preceded by a formal planning meeting, but when meetings did take place they were often not minuted. It should also be borne in mind that the majority of these Routine assessments involved young people who were living at home, or in some other community location. The opportunities for observing young people were therefore much more limited than those undertaken by the AAS, which in addition to assessment foster and residential placements, also had a 'community' resource in the form of the Day Assessment Unit.

The process by which social workers were informed of other professionals' findings was also much more ad hoc in the Routinely assessed cases. Although some agencies and carers did prepare assessment reports, this was not standard practice and only tended to be done in those cases which were due to be presented at court. Where information was sought by social workers from other professionals or carers, this tended to be communicated verbally, either in person at a formal planning meeting, or more commonly, over the telephone.

Whatever the arrangements, few social workers seemed to be aware of how these other professionals approached the assessment task. Once a referral had been accepted by another professional or agency, social workers appeared to have little knowledge of, or indeed, take much interest in, what these assessments entailed. Thus, whilst social workers were usually able to tell us whether or not a young person and/or family had been seen by another professional, such as a family therapist, psychiatrist, or educational psychologist, they were generally unaware of how often they were

seen, how long sessions lasted, or what asses
proaches these other professionals employed. T
picture to that reported by Fenyo and Knapp
the costs of assessment (Fenyo and Knapp
knowledge and understanding also extended to ...
assessment workers such as assessment foster carers anu .
tial workers.

JJ notes interview

> 'One of the things that we often have problems with is when the social
> worker doesn't treat us as a professional, you know with a small 'p'. We
> felt that it was because we didn't have a degree or qualification, that
> people weren't being open with us, weren't giving us the necessary
> information that would have helped us, or the young person. But now
> I think its very often that social workers don't actually know what
> we're about ....We're continually having to educate all the new social
> workers about our role and assessment fostering. Even though a
> booklet's been made up they often don't read it. We've tried to set up
> meetings so they can find out more about what we do. But they never
> turn up. I mean, what can we do? The fieldworkers must either have
> too much on their plates and can't cope with any more, or they just can't
> be interested.' (Assessment foster carer)

This analysis of the framework for assessment suggests that
while staff, whether area-based social workers or specialists, all
had a general understanding of what they meant by assessment,
nevertheless there was a great lack of clarity around the concept.
Most workers saw assessment as part of the overall social work
task and therefore something that all social workers could be expected to undertake; however, few were able to delineate what
specific tasks or skills were actually involved.

Young people and the assessment process

'Young people should be encouraged to be actively involved in the
assessment process'. This statement is one of the essential
elements of good practice in assessment which we identified in
Chapter 3 and is a central theme of the Children Act 1989. While
the Guidance and Regulations which accompany the Children Act
do not specify how participation might be achieved through the
assessment process, it is implied by the following legal requirements. Firstly, the duty to ascertain the wishes and feelings of the
child and to take these into account before any Care Plans or court
decisions are made. Secondly, the duty to invite children and
young people to attend and participate in reviews and other planning meetings, as far as the authority considers appropriate –
which includes making whatever arrangements are necessary to

their attendance. Thirdly, the duty to notify children and
ng people of the decisions that have been reached at planning
d review meetings. And finally, the duty to inform children and
young people of what services and resources are available to them
(Department of Health, 1991e).

Although the Children Act was not yet in force when the assessments of our sample group of young people took place, the moral arguments for involving children and young people in the assessment process had already been well rehearsed (for example, see Mind Working Party, 1975; Freeman, 1984). Indeed, both child care professionals and researchers had for some time been pointing to the practical advantages of children's participation, in that it:

- provides more accurate information about children and young people;
- promotes greater objectivity amongst professional staff;
- engenders a greater commitment on all sides to the plans and decisions reached, thus making it more likely that these will be achieved successfully;
- increases young people's confidence and self-esteem and helps to strengthen their problem solving skills for the future.

(For an overview of research on young people's participation in decision making see Gardner, 1992; Hodgson, 1991; Thoburn, Lewis and Shemmings, 1993; The Who Cares? Trust and the National Consumer Council, 1993; The Dolphin Project, 1993; The Children's Society, 1994.) The principle of involving young people in their assessment underpins the completion of the new Assessment and Action Records: indeed the Records relating to young people aged 10 to 14, and 15 and over, are all written with the assumption that the young person is the respondent, for example, 'Do you have a suitable place to do your homework?' (Department of Health, 1995).

So how were young people in our study involved in their assessment? We shall consider this under three broad headings:

- being informed about the assessment process;
- meeting with their social worker;
- attending planning meetings.

Before we look at our findings on this, a note about the source of our data. Participation was just one of a range of issues which we aimed to cover in this research, so our analysis is based, for the most part, on information relating to process. Secondly, our information has come either from social workers or from our observation of meetings, with additional comments from ten young people whom we interviewed.

Information about assessment

Those few research studies that have been undertaken into child care assessment in social services, have all pointed to the fact that young people are often not given adequate information about the purpose and content of assessments. In a follow-up study of 79 young people who had been placed in an O & A centre, the majority of young people interviewed said that they did not know why they had been placed there – in most cases because no one had thought to tell them (Reinach, Lovelock and Roberts, 1979). Similar findings were reported in a later study of four residential O & A centres. Although the authors emphasised that the practice of informing young people could vary from one residential establishment to another, nevertheless they did report that:

> The information given to children seemed to follow no systematic plan in any centre. It varied according to the individual staff involved in the assessment, the social worker, the child's case, the certainty or otherwise of obtaining the recommended placement, changes in the child's home background and events taking place in the centre itself. (Walker and Xanthos, 1982)

Such findings were not limited to English authorities. In a study of inter-professional decision making in Scotland, Buist and Mapstone found that, whilst those children who were assessed in residential centres were marginally better informed about the process than those who underwent domiciliary assessments, neither group had much understanding of what the term assessment meant or what it entailed. Although they found that children placed in residential O & A centres often used the word 'assessment', only a quarter of them realised that this involved any 'observation', and that they were being watched during their stay. Moreover, less than half of the young people questioned appeared to be aware that a meeting was to take place at which they would be discussed (Buist and Mapstone, 1985).

One would expect things to have changed from these earlier studies. So we were interested to discover who was responsible for informing young people about the assessment process and whether there were any significant differences in practice between the Referred and Routine systems.

Although most of the social workers we spoke to said that they had explained the purpose of their own interventions to young people, the responsibility for explaining the input of others was generally felt to lie with the individual professionals and agencies concerned, often because social workers themselves were unclear about the procedures of other agencies. As a result many social workers were unable to tell us whether or not young people had been fully informed about the assessment process.

> 'I explained what my part in the assessment was, but I don't know whether the Assessment Service did any more. I wasn't allocated to the case when he was first admitted to care, and as he didn't attend his planning meeting it's difficult to know exactly how much he's taken in.' (Social worker – Referred assessment)

Within the AAS, young people were usually informed about the assessment process during the Assessment Planning Meeting (APM). If young people did not attend this meeting, then the young person's keyworker was expected to explain the process to them. In any event, young people would normally be sent minutes of the APM, although detailed information about the assessment process might not necessarily be contained within them.

Encouragingly, most of the young people we spoke to who were subject to a Referred assessment recalled being informed about why an assessment was being done, how long it would take, and who else was going to be involved.

> '... yes they come round and tell you what is going to happen and things like that, so I usually know what's going to happen – there are not many surprises.' (Young person)

Some young people were quite clear about what their carers and social workers were trying to do and why, but others found it difficult to make sense of what they had been told or to understand what it meant to them.

> 'They said at the meeting that they'd be doing this assessment report thing on me .... But I didn't really know what it was all for. They did tell me but I didn't really understand. All I knew was that they wanted me to go home.' (Young person)

This is perhaps not surprising when one considers that most of these young people's meetings took place shortly after some sort of crisis or traumatic event, and when many were still adjusting to living in a completely new environment. Indeed, one would expect young people to be fairly confused and disorientated at this stage and therefore be unable to make sense of all of the information that was given to them, particularly if this was their first experience of attending a formal planning meeting.

Nor was it always clear to them what were the respective roles of all the different professionals involved. Although most of them were able to distinguish between the responsibilities of their key-worker as opposed to their social worker they were less clear about the roles of other professional agencies. As one young woman who was admitted to care during the course of a child protection investigation explained:

> 'At first I thought they were all from the same team. And then after a while they'd start telling me different things. Like this child protection woman (from the police) was coming to see me in the foster home and she would tell me that she would press charges against my dad, what to do and that. And the social worker was trying to get me to go back to my family. That's when I realised that they were a completely different group.' (Young person)

Understandably, most of the young people we spoke to were more concerned with the outcomes of the assessment, than they were with the assessment process itself. Some of them regarded the assessment period as a complete waste of time, as, from their point of view, it only served to delay plans for them further.

> 'I just don't see the point in all this talking, talking, and meetings. I told them what I wanted from the beginning, a semi-independence place away from here. They said they need time to make plans for the future, but when's the future to them lot?' (Young person)

In fact, the most common complaint that young people made was that they had not been told just how long it might take to secure more permanent arrangements for their care, whether this be at home, in semi-independence, in residential or in foster care.

> 'They said, right, you'll be here for a six-week assessment and then we'll all decide about where you should go next. But I've been here two months now and I'm still no further on. All we have is loads of meetings where we all talk. They said I could go into semi-independence, but nothing ever seems to get done.' (Young person)

> 'I was supposed to be there (in the assessment foster home) for six weeks, and then I thought I would be moving into a new foster home, 'cos they were assessment foster parents and that's only for a short period. But after the six weeks was over and I was still going to meetings I knew that I was going to be there for a long time. They were supposed to be moving me, but I ended up just staying there for a long time.' (Young person)

We were also interested to find out whether young people felt that they had any choice about where they were placed during the assessment period. The majority of young people we interviewed said they had not been given any say in this matter, despite the fact that social workers placed the young person's view high on their list of criteria when choosing a placement. Few of the young people regarded placement choice as something that was open to discussion.

'I didn't think of asking them why I was going to that foster home. I don't know why. I just thought they make the decisions for you, and they just put me there and told me I had to go there. It was an emergency, I think that's why.' (Young person)

'I don't know why I went into that children's home rather than anywhere else. I think it was because it was the only place that had any space.' (Young person)

However, three of the young people we interviewed did say that they had been given the option of either a foster or a residential placement. Interestingly all three had opted for residential care. Two of these young people had been in care before and had not been happy in their previous foster placements, although the same concern was expressed by another young person, who had no previous experience of foster care.

'When I was in care before I was with foster parents, and I didn't like it, so I went home. When my social worker asked me why, I couldn't explain it. I just didn't like (foster carer). She was too snoopy, she phoned up my friends and that, I didn't like that. I was meant to be there a few weeks, but I only slept there about four times ... I went back to my Mum's the rest of the time. Because of that first experience, what happened then, I just didn't take to the idea of fostering. So when I came into care again they said I could come to (residential unit) instead.' (Young person)

'I had a choice about here (residential unit) or foster parents. And I said I didn't want to go to foster parents .... In this place I'm surrounded by friends I can talk to. But in foster homes they haven't got time 'cos they're too busy looking after their own kids. I've been in foster homes before. There was only one I liked, but she wanted to adopt me. I didn't want to be, so they had to let me go. That's why I didn't want to go into a foster home – 'cos they want to adopt you.' (Young person)

'It was my idea to come here. Like 'cos I needed somewhere to go and I didn't want to go in a foster home 'cos I didn't want to feel like I was being adopted. So they said fine so I came here ... I didn't know anything about it, but before I came, me and my Mum looked around the place.' (Young person)

The location of their placement was also something which concerned the young people, especially as all of the assessment foster placements were outside the borough, unlike the residential units.

'When I was living with (foster carers) it was just too far away. It was boring living out there. My school is just down the road from here (residential unit). I don't like being too far away.' (Young person)

When asked in general about who had decided whether they should come into care or not, all of the young people we spoke to had said that this decision had been taken by others, namely their social workers and/or their parents or carers.

'My Mum and my social worker said it might be better for me to come into care for a little while and so we had a meeting to talk about it and they said I could come here for eight weeks and then go home, and so I said alright.' (Young person)

In spite of their lack of involvement in these decisions, the majority of young people that we spoke to, nevertheless, said that they were satisfied with the arrangements that had been made.

'At first I didn't think I was going to like it there (at the assessment foster home). But when they told me there was another girl there my age I didn't feel so bad. I liked it there, it was OK. They were really nice and understanding, and me and this other girl got on really well. She (foster carer) was a bit strict sometimes, but she was nice.' (Young person)

Being away from home also had its attractions!

'It didn't bother me going into (residential unit), 'cos I already knew someone from school who was living there. It was also much better than being at home. I could go out when I wanted to and there was no hassle from my parents. In fact I got on much better with my family whilst I was there.' (Young person)

'The staff here sit down and talk to you properly, they trust you. Like if you want to go out to a friend's party or something, they'll let you go and give you the money to get a cab back.' (Young person)

However, as Fisher and others commented in their study *In and Out of Care*, this attraction of care to young people should not be thought of in absolute terms. Rather,

it is the fact that care contrasts positively with the negative experiences at home which makes it, in relative terms, an attractive option.' (Fisher and others, 1986, p71)

This was evident in some of the comments made during the course of our interviews and, as we shall discuss in Chapter 11, was an important factor in the subsequent outcome for some of the young people, when the relative attractions of care seem to subside.

> 'Even though I've been happy here and I'm glad to have my own privacy and that, I still think the proper place for a child is with their parents.' (Young person)

> 'I'm happy with a lot of things here. There ain't nothing I ain't happy about – except that I haven't got my family around me. I can see them as much as I like, but it's not the same.' (Young person)

Social worker contact with young people during the assessment

In his report *Planning in Social Work and Children's Participation*, Hodgson suggests that 'an open and participatory approach to problem solving with children depends, more than anything else, on the quality of contact between the worker and the child' (Hodgson, 1991, 1995). The survey of children in care conducted by The Who Cares? Trust also points to the very high value which young people place on actually working with the social worker:

> By far the highest number (74 in foster care and 150 in residential care) described the good things about their social worker in terms of their relationship with them: can talk to her/him, there when I need him/her, listens, understands, easy to talk to/discuss problems with, explains things to me ... She sorts out all the things you can't handle or cope with. (The Who Cares? Trust and National Consumer Council, 1993)

Previous research findings suggest that, while social workers generally hold most of the responsibility for decision making in child care, they lack the necessary time and skills to undertake direct work with children and young people (DHSS, 1985).

> There was little evidence to suggest that social workers were much involved in direct contact with children .... The child's primary carers, foster parents and residential staff were seen to have greater opportunities. Where skills beyond this were required, the social worker generally referred the case to an acknowledged specialist in child development, health or education. (Vernon and Fruin, 1986)

> Many social workers feel that they should make a point of seeing foster children on their own at least sometimes. Nearly two-thirds of our social workers reported that they had seen the child alone in the past year ... (but) 'seeing alone' was often very brief and passed unnoticed by child and foster parents. (Rowe and others, 1984)

At two years, nearly half the children were receiving visits from social workers at less than monthly intervals. (Millham and others, 1986)

We were interested therefore to see if these findings represented current practice by recording the level of contact that social workers in our study had with young people during the assessment period.

Although most of the young people in our study were already known to social services, many of the field social workers who were involved in their assessments had not known them for very long. Moreover, five young people (7 per cent), were not allocated a social worker until at least a month after their consideration for care, admission or placement breakdown, whilst four young people (5 per cent) had no allocated social worker during the three months which we had allowed for assessments to be completed.

So what opportunities did field social workers have to get to know these young people better? We asked social workers to tell us how often they were able to see young people alone during the 12 weeks following this initial 'event' – that is, outside of formal planning meetings and excluding those occasions when their parents, carers or other professionals were present.

Although the amount of contact often varied over the period, overall there was surprisingly little face-to-face contact between young people and their social workers. Fewer than a quarter of young people (23 per cent) were seen by social workers on their own as much as weekly during the assessment period, and a similar proportion fortnightly. This meant that more than half of our study group (55 per cent) were only seen alone a maximum of four times in the three months following their consideration for care, admission or placement breakdown. Of these, three young people only saw their social workers in formal meetings; four were only ever seen in the company of their parents or carers. Three young people never got to meet their social worker at all prior to their Final Assessment Conference, as they were only allocated one within days of this meeting taking place.

Not surprisingly, of our three main 'event' groups it was young people who were admitted to care who had most frequent contact with their social workers. However, even amongst this group the proportion of young people who saw their social workers alone as much as once a week or more, was still less than a third (31 per cent).

Of course, it was not always easy for social workers to see young people alone. Some young people were still living at home with their families; others were in out-of-borough placements where some young people were travelling several miles across town to school each day. Social workers either had to arrange visits during school lunch-breaks or after office hours, which was not always convenient for the young people or their social workers.

'She (social worker) used to come and see me in the foster home about twice a week, and then after three weeks that stopped. Then I didn't see her unless I phoned her or she phoned me. Sometimes this was alright as I didn't always need to see her and so I could tell her on the phone how I was and how I was coping, but other times when I really wanted to talk to her I couldn't get hold of her, 'cos it would be in the evening after I'd finished college, and then by the time I did get to see her I'd forget what I wanted to say.' (Young person)

Indeed, some young people were said to be spending so much time out of their foster or residential placements, that it was difficult for anyone to get any direct work done!

'The unit where (young person) was staying was very close to where her Nan lived, and so she spent quite a lot of time after school and at weekends with her. She also had a part time Saturday job. Then there was her music club which meant that she was often out in the evenings. In fact she was spending so much time away from the unit, at school, at work, at her Nan's and with her friends in the neighbourhood, that we had to ask her to make a commitment to be in the unit at least two evenings a week, so that we could get an assessment done!' (Social worker)

Some social workers also commented on how difficult it was to develop a relationship with some of these youngsters, as they had been let down by adults many times before.

'When I took on the case, my first job was to break the news to him that his foster parents didn't want him to live there anymore. He was very upset and angry, and understandably blamed me for it all. This made it very difficult for me to do any direct work with him as he was so distrustful of adults. I'd ring up and go down to the unit to see him at least twice a week, but he just didn't want to see me. I do feel as though I'm making some progress though. He calls me now, which is a bit of a breakthrough. However I don't expect to achieve very much with him. He seems to have had such a bad deal. I just want to keep things at a slow pace to allow him time to develop trust and confidence in us again.' (Social worker)

More than a third of the young people in our study also experienced breakdowns in their accommodation arrangements during the course of their assessments. This meant that social workers were often spending more time on organising alternative placements than on direct work with the young person.

'I was planning to see him every week when he first went into the unit. But I never really got the time to do this. I just seemed to spend all of my time dealing with his behavioural problems and placement changes. We just couldn't get him to sit still for long enough. In fact he never really engaged with anyone during the first two or three months. That was the main problem. Getting enough time to stabilise him and engage him and his family in the time which we had available.' (Social worker)

Given the demands that were being made on social workers' time, it is perhaps understandable that they should find it difficult to undertake much substantial direct work with these young people. However, the impression given was that many social workers simply did not regard this as a high priority for them or something that they, as fieldworkers, should be working on. For instance, within the Referred group, the task of engaging young people in the assessment process was said by the majority of social workers to be the responsibility of the young person's relevant keyworker, be it an assessment foster carer, residential worker or outreach worker.

'It was my job to undertake a family history and to find out more about the background to his parents' marital conflict – why they had such difficulty communicating with each other – what had happened in the past and how this had impacted on (young person). The role of the assessment foster carers was to assess how he functioned in a family setting, to find out what he wanted, what his relationships with his parents and friends were, and whether he had any specific behavioural problems. They're much more expert at this sort of stuff than I am.' (Social worker – Referred assessment)

Indeed, the assumption often was that once a young person was referred for an assessment, all of the direct work with them would be undertaken by these other professionals, thus freeing up social workers' time to work more closely with young people's families and carers. As one team manager explained,

'It was our understanding when we made the referral to the AAS that all of the work with (young person) would be done by them, and that our role was simply to monitor this and get more details on the family's situation …. We didn't think it would be appropriate for us to get involved in any direct work with (young person). We assumed there'd be more than enough people involved with him at this time.' (Team Manager)

Although one of the main purposes of the Assessment Planning Meeting was to clarify the roles of the various professionals involved, in practice the responsibility for undertaking direct work with young people was often allocated by default.

> 'By the time I joined this case (young person) had already formed a good relationship with his keyworker and so I thought it would be better for them to do the direct work with him and for me to take on a much more secondary role. To be quite honest I wasn't clear what my role was. It was my first experience of using the Service. I was a bit out of my depth really.' (Social worker – Referred assessment)

There were some exceptions to this. For example, one social worker had within a short time of a young woman's referral to social services established a very good relationship with her and her family and was keen to continue working closely with them both. When this young woman was referred to the AAS for a placement, it was agreed at the APM that most of the direct work with her should be undertaken by her social worker.

Examples of such joint work were quite rare. Overall, only 14 per cent of social workers who were involved in a Referred assessment commented that they had undertaken any direct work with the young person, either alone or in association with another worker from the AAS. Although twice as many social workers in the Routine group stated that they had been involved in direct work with the young person, the majority of them, nevertheless, still regarded this as a task which should be undertaken by others, be it a carer, or other agency professional.

> 'Basically our role was to assess Mum's capacity to care for the children and to see what sort of support was needed to help them at home. It was the official solicitor's role to engage with the children to see what they wanted.' (Social worker – Routine assessment)

> 'My role was to act as link person between all the different agencies and individuals involved. We deliberately decided to keep the number of people involved with them to a minimum, with all the direct work being done by the residential staff and the educational psychologist.' (Social worker – Routine assessment)

As Table 8.2 shows, the Routinely assessed group had even less face-to-face contact with their allocated social workers than those who underwent a Referred assessment. Much of this difference is accounted for by the preponderance of emergency admissions amongst the Referred group, who, in the initial stages at least, seemed to be accorded a much higher priority on social work caseloads than young people in the other two main 'event' groups.

However, in spite of this, most of the young people we spoke to felt that the amount of contact that they had with their social

Table 8.2 Amount of face-to-face contact social workers had alone, with young people, during the assessment period

	Referred %	Routine %
None	14	14
At least weekly	27	19
At least fortnightly	18	25
At least monthly	27	19
Less than monthly	14	23
	100	100

workers was probably about right. Indeed, it was not the regularity or frequency of social work contact that was most important to them, but rather their ability to see or speak to their social work-ers if and when the need arose. However, some young people preferred not to have too much contact with their social workers because they felt uncomfortable; others had concerns over confidentiality.

'If I had any worries I think I'd talk to my Mum first. Then I'd talk to my foster parents. Then I'd ask them to get in touch with my social worker. But actually, I don't really like talking to my social worker. I'm just not used to talking to social workers and that, about what I'm feeling.' (Young person)

'You know sometimes they're really good to talk to but then you find out that they've been telling your parents what you've said. All my social workers have written things down and talked to my parents so it's just not worth it any more. So I just keep quiet and talk to my friends. That's the easiest.' (Young person)

'My Mum had a social worker and I had a social worker. My social worker would tell my Mum things and my Mum's social worker would tell me things. And then they'd try and get me and my Mum to talk. And like my social worker would tell my Mum things that I wanted her to keep to herself, and then my Mum would start shouting. And in the meetings it would be the same. They'd just be sitting there assessing what each of us had been saying to them.' (Young person)

In spite of this, they still recognised the importance of continuing social worker involvement, albeit in the role of a 'fixer', or mediator of resources, rather than as a 'confidante' or friend.

Given that many social workers saw direct work with young

people as the responsibility of others, how did the young people's carers or other professionals approach the task of engaging young people in the assessment? One of the ways in which the AAS tried to encourage young people to participate in the assessment process was by inviting them, with the assistance of their carers or key-workers, to prepare a report for their Final Assessment Conference. However, only six young people in our study were either able, or willing, to contribute to their assessments in this way, in spite of the efforts made by some of their keyworkers or assessment foster carer.

> 'At the beginning of our work in the Assessment Fostering Scheme we found this aspect of the work quite difficult. You know 'cos sometimes you'd get this young person that you know very little about, and they can't express themselves properly. What we try and do is to give them the confidence to write a report for themselves, or they can make a tape about themselves if they want. Sometimes I'll put it onto the word processor so that their style of presentation isn't any different from that of all of the other typed reports, but it is daunting for them.' (Assessment foster carer)

Getting young people to talk about their feelings can also take time and it was felt by some to require significantly longer than the six- to eight-week period within which the AAS hoped to achieve a plan for the young person. As one Assessment foster carer explained,

> 'For some young people the time-scale involved is OK, but others definitely need longer. The first three or four weeks that they are here can be quite awful. Everything's new and we're just getting used to each other. Then after a while things start settling down – they start opening up a bit more, start to trust you and talk to you.' (Assessment foster carer)

Attendance at decision making meetings

It has been established good practice for many years, reinforced by the Children Act, to invite children and young people to come to meetings where their welfare is to be discussed and decisions made about them. While attendance at meetings is not in itself an indicator of participation, as Hodgson points out, being invited to attend meetings can have 'tremendous symbolic significance' for children and young people. Moreover, he argues that even young children should be encouraged to attend meetings:

> Children may not fully comprehend all the details of discussion. But attending the event itself accustoms children to the reality that people other than their family are involved in decisions and can be used later

in conversations and explanations about important changes in the child's life. (Hodgson, 1991)

Marsh and Fisher would add that enabling young people to attend meetings helps to bring home to them the realities of their options and what can be achieved within current resource constraints (Marsh and Fisher, 1992).

Overall, more than two-thirds of the young people in our study, 70 per cent, were said to have been invited to attend their final decision making meeting. There was a marked difference between the Routine and Referred forms of assessment in this respect; all of the young people in the Referred group were invited to attend their meetings, compared with only 39 per cent of young people who were Routinely assessed.

In the Routine group social workers gave various reasons for not inviting young people to attend. The most common reason was that it was not departmental policy to invite them. However, as noted earlier, it seems that social workers' understanding of policy in this respect is limited and indeed flawed.

Another reason social workers gave for not inviting young people to attend meetings was that they were considered to be too young or 'immature' to be able to understand or participate in the meeting in any meaningful way. Others felt that young people would find the meetings too painful and wanted to protect them from any possible distress. Too often, however, there was confusion amongst social workers and others as to whose responsibility it was to make the invitation, with the consequence that some young people missed the opportunity to participate. This was highlighted by the responses of one mother when asked why her son had not attended the meeting with her:

> 'Nobody told me that he could come. I know he wanted to, but I told him I wasn't sure if he could. I'd have brought him with me if I'd known. I think he should have heard all of this. I'm sick of doing all the talking for him.' (Parent)

This illustrates the gap that can exist between the standards of practice articulated by senior managers and those operating at case level and perhaps supports the need for the clear statutory frameworks for practice that have been established by the plan and review Regulations and Guidance of the Children Act.

Of those young people who were invited, all but two were asked to attend the whole of their meetings. On both occasions this was because there was a professional disagreement which the participants did not wish the young person to witness. For instance, in the case of a young black man who was being considered for a long-term foster placement, the professionals felt there were still issues to resolve about the best way to meet his racial and cultural needs.

> 'Community fostering indicated that a white family was available right away and it had to be decided whether the professionals felt it was important for him to be placed in a black family or not, particularly as he could be waiting some time for this. We needed to discuss how suitable this white family were for him. We didn't think it was appropriate for him to be involved in this discussion. I'd already discussed this with him beforehand and he said he would happily move into a white foster home. But he's so desperate to please he would have gone for any family that was put in front of him. We wanted to avoid that. However we did agree to inform him of what had been discussed in his absence. We felt that it was an issue which needed to be discussed between the professionals.' (Social worker)

In the event only 34 young people (less than half of the total) actually attended their final assessment conference or other decision making meeting – a disappointingly low level of participation by attendance at key planning meetings.

Again, there were significant differences between the Routine and the Referred groups. First we look at the attendance of young people where the final assessment meeting took place as planned. As Table 8.3 shows, significantly more young people attended those meetings which were held within the AAS, compared with those which were organised by district social workers or other professionals.

Table 8.3   Young people's attendance at final decision making meeting

	Yes	No
Final Assessment Conference	16	10
Other final meeting	18	31
	34	41

However, this table considers only those cases where the assessment process was *completed*. There were a number of cases in the study where, for a variety of reasons, the assessment did not complete its course. If we include these cases, and consider the attendance of all young people at their meeting (which could be an assessment review, assessment planning meeting or placement review), then the figures are even less encouraging, dropping to 53 per cent for Referred cases and only 38 per cent for Routine cases. Given the AAS's declared policy of inviting young people to attend *all* of their assessment meetings, an attendance level of just over half in the Referred group seems discouragingly low.

Of course not every young person will wish to attend their planning meetings, and it would be wrong of social workers to insist that they do. Nevertheless, if we look at some of the comments made by young people about their meetings it is clear that more efforts could have been made to make their attendance easier.

'I used to get angry sometimes and I'd burst into tears; I couldn't talk to anyone because I felt it was all my fault, I was causing everything. Because when you see a whole load of people talking about you, just one person, it doesn't feel right; it felt strange – I didn't like it ... I couldn't tell them how I felt because my Mum was there and if I did say something we would start arguing and then they would cancel the meeting.' (Young person)

'You know I'm supposed to be studying so I just haven't got time to sit around talking in meetings all day. There are too many of them. Assessment meetings, planning meetings, review meetings, meetings with my social worker and my keyworker. It's the final assessment meeting that's the most important. That's where the decisions are made – the real ones.' (Young person)

'It's not that I'm scared of meetings or anything. It's just that they don't have any interest in what I have to say. Even if I didn't agree they wouldn't listen. And if they did listen they wouldn't take any notice.' (Young person)

'I won't go if I had to come out of school to go, because they know that I don't like missing school.' (Young person)

Here we see that there is still much to be done to ensure that the rhetoric of involving young people is, in practice, a meaningful and satisfactory experience for them. Moreover it seems likely that the difficulties with meetings which these young people articulated will be related to the lack of direct contact between the young people and their social worker which was noted earlier. However, the examples from this Authority, whose managers felt they had tried hard to involve young people, represent a more universal concern. The responses that young people gave to a questionnaire in the Who Cares? magazine, like the above quotes, illustrate the real pain that can be caused to young people through poor practice in managing meetings, however well-intentioned. Those views were summarised thus:

The strongest conclusion to be drawn from the answers on decision-making is that, even where young people feel they are listened to, they do not feel involved in the decisions which so crucially affect them and their futures. They feel ignored and patronised and that their opinions are of little value. (The Who Cares? Trust and National Consumer Council, 1993)

Working in partnership with parents

The idea that assessment should be undertaken in an open and participatory way with families has long been identified as an essential element of good social work practice (see Mind Working Party, 1975; Hoghughi, 1980; British Association for Social Workers, 1983; DHSS, 1981; Maluccio, 1981; Adcock and White, 1985). However the reviews of research undertaken by the Department of Health pointed to significant failures in translating this into practice (DHSS, 1985; Department of Health, 1991a). Several findings are of particular relevance to involving parents in the assessment process: evidence that social workers often had only a limited knowledge of the family history and did not share an understanding with parents of the problems to be faced (Packman with Randall and Jacques, 1986; Fisher and others, 1986; SSI, 1989); parents of children in care reported feeling 'frozen out' by the care process (Millham and others, 1986); parents were rarely invited to attend or contribute to key decision making meetings (Sinclair, 1984; McDonnell and Aldgate, 1984; Vernon and Fruin, 1986; Farmer and Parker, 1991; Thoburn, Lewis and Shemmings, 1993); parents' feelings of powerlessness in the face of the social services bureaucracy (Millham and others, 1989; Parton, 1991; Marsh and Fisher, 1992). Despite the strong moral arguments and increasing awareness of the benefits to children from involvement by parents, prior to the Children Act this was the exception rather than the rule.

'Research shows that partnership with parents has not been integral to past or current social work practice. Some fundamental changes in attitude will be required if the spirit of the new Act is to be fully implemented. (Department of Health, 1991a)

The concept of partnership with parents is one of the key principles which underpin the Children Act. More specifically, under the Act local authorities and other agencies are required:

- to consult with and inform parents before taking any decisions regarding their children (including anyone with parental responsibility, and 'other significant family members');

- to ascertain the wishes and feelings of parents about placement plans for their children;
- to enter into written agreements with parents;
- to avoid compulsory measures as far as this is consistent with meeting the child's needs.

Although the research study reported here commenced prior to the Children Act, it seemed important to examine the extent to which parents were involved in the assessment process – first to explore further what the concept of partnership with parents may mean in practice, and second to examine how working with parents may enhance or impede the assessment process itself.

We illustrate this using research findings from three aspects of the assessment process, namely:

- the information which parents were given about the assessment process, and the service and resource options;
- the use of written agreements with parents;
- working directly with families.

Information about assessment

Most of the social workers interviewed confirmed that they had explained the purpose and content of their own interventions to parents (or at least to the main caring parent, for as we reported in Chapter 6, a large proportion of young people in our study (44 per cent) came from lone parent families). However, as with young people, social workers assumed that the input of others would be explained by each of the relevant professionals and agencies concerned. As a result, social workers were, again, often unsure whether parents had been fully informed about the assessment process:

> 'I explained what my role was. I also discussed the Statementing process with the parents, as did the school head. Presumably the other professionals who had contact with them and (young person) did the same. I don't know what was said though.' (Social worker – Routine community assessment)

As we saw earlier, within the AAS the plans for an assessment would normally be discussed and agreed with parents and young people at the Assessment Planning Meeting. Encouragingly, most of the parents of youngsters who were assessed by the Service were able to attend these meetings. Where this was not possible, for example, in the case of unaccompanied refugee children, an older brother or sister was often in attendance.

For the Routine assessments there were no specific procedures for informing parents about the process and content of assessments. Although some of these assessments were preceded by planning meetings, parents and young people were commonly excluded from such meetings. Furthermore, as many of these young people's admissions and placement changes were organised at short notice, there was often little opportunity for parents to visit placements before young people were placed there.

Even when parents were informed about the assessment, it was important to ascertain what they understood by the term 'assessment' and whether they had any concerns. Most of the parents we interviewed whose youngsters had undergone an assessment with the AAS said that the process had been explained to them; this was less likely to be the case with Routine assessments. Even where parents did know an assessment was taking place, aspects of the process were often still unclear to them.

'I'm clear about what they're doing at the DAU. I took him down there and they told me what they were doing. It's to assess him, to see whether he's ready to go into secondary school or not. I mean they can watch him from a distance can't they? They told me there was an Art Therapist there too. You can tell a lot about someone from what art they do and that.' (Parent – Referred community assessment)

'My social worker has been doing this thing with me and (young person). They (social services) want to know how I live and what sort of routine we have at home. So she (social worker) comes here a couple of evenings a week and watches us then writes it all down on a piece of paper. She told me why she's doing it but I can't remember what she said.' (Parent – Routine community assessment)

'I don't know why my daughter went there. I know she didn't want to come home. But no-one ever told me what they would be doing whilst she was in the children's home.' (Parent – Referred residential assessment)

'I was told at the first meeting that this outreach worker would be coming round to do an assessment, write a report about us and then we'd discuss it all at a meeting. I didn't feel as though I had any choice about it though. I didn't ask them to come. It was social services who said that they needed to come into my home. I didn't know whether I had a legal right to refuse them entry or not.' (Parent – Referred assessment)

Not surprisingly for those parents of young people who were in care, such issues as whether their youngster was safe, being looked after properly, and how long they were likely to be there were what concerned them most. Indeed, some parents said that they had become so worn down by the experience of trying to deal with their son's or daughter's difficult behaviour, on top of their other problems, that they had not given much thought to what an assessment might entail.

'I know my social worker told me what everyone would be doing with my son, but I can't remember what they said. To be honest, I just don't think about it. Not really. I just live from day-to-day and go along with what they tell me. All I know is I can't go on like this. He's been like this for three years now. Something's got to change. I thought I'd go along with this as I'd tried everything else.' (Parent)

'I'm clear about what they are doing at the Assessment Service place. I just don't know how long it's going to last.' (Parent)

Written agreements with parents

As these comments from parents show, even if social workers believe they have properly informed parents about what is going on there is still much uncertainty among parents. This further reduces the capability of parents to be active partners in helping their sons and daughters. One way to help reduce this uncertainty is through written agreements between parents and social services (Tunstill, 1989). As we saw in Chapter 1, efforts to improve the standards of child care practice in the past decade have included an increasing use of written agreements – although evidence again suggests that the intentions outlined in policies and procedures did not always translate into practice (Reeves, 1986; Aldgate, 1989; Farmer and Parker, 1991). It is hoped that the clarification of social services interventions with children and families will be enhanced with the requirement of the Children Act for written Care Plans and Placement Agreements.

Social workers in this study were asked whether any agreements about the assessment process had been made between the parents, the social workers and other carers. The majority of social workers remarked that this had been done, but that these were usually verbal, rather than written agreements. In total, from our scrutiny of files we could find evidence of only 17 cases where written agreements had been made with parents.

Direct work with parents

In a previous section, when discussing the limited amount of direct work with young people undertaken by social workers, we reported that social workers felt that their main responsibility was to work with the young person's parents. Indeed, some social workers re-

ported that one of the main advantages of referring to the AAS was
that it enabled them to spend more time dealing directly with the
parents.

So what were the plans for direct work with families and how
much contact did social workers in our study have with the parents
of the young people? In only nine cases was direct work planned
with the parents, plus an additional 13 cases where such work
with parents and the young person was planned. There were no
notable differences in this between cases assessed Routinely and
those Referred for assessment. This does seem surprisingly little,
given the preponderance of relationship problems in precipitating
the 'event' and the fact that the single most cited reason for undertaking the assessment was to judge the parents' capacity to provide care.

Social workers had even less contact with parents than they did
with young people (see Table 8.4). If we exclude the 13 cases (17
per cent of the total) where young people had no family carer (unaccompanied refugee children, parents deceased, or where contact
with parents had lapsed during the time that young people had
been in care), less than one in four parents, 21 per cent, saw social
workers at least weekly, and only an additional 18 per cent on a
fortnightly basis. Nearly half, 47 per cent, saw their social workers
between one and four times during this 12-week period, whilst 18
per cent (11 parents) did not see their social worker at all. Perhaps
not surprisingly, there was significantly more contact with parents of young people who were being considered for care and admitted to care than with parents of young people who were
experiencing a placement breakdown.

Table 8.4   Social work contact with parent(s) during 12-week assessment period

	Referred	Routine
None (parents deceased/resident abroad)	7	6
None (other)	3	6
At least weekly	7	6
Fortnightly	6	5
Monthly	10	8
Less than monthly	6	5

Most of this contact was with mothers (and where applicable their partners). Less than one in four (21 per cent) of fathers were seen by social workers, and in only eight cases were other relevant family members consulted. This limited contact with extended family is in marked contrast to the emphasis given to involving the wider family and community within the Children Act. Social workers explained the difficulties they encountered in consulting other family members when parents had little contact with their own family or where there was enmity between them. Similarly they found it problematic to involve birth fathers in situations where the young person had not had any contact with their father for some time and had no desire to see him again. In addition, some felt that contact with the father might create problems in working with the mother (see case studies contained in Chapter 11).

Our findings also show that social workers have less contact with parents than had been planned. A range of reasons were offered for this: parents found it difficult to keep to appointments, especially when they had work and/or child care commitments; social workers found it difficult to make time to see parents, when they were still having to deal with all of the problems posed by the young person; once the immediate crisis was over, parents saw less reason to work with the social worker; and of course the standards of individual workers varied.

'As a fieldworker with case-load and duty responsibilities I don't have much time. I really want to keep up the goodwill with Mum, but she's only available after 5.30. Plus I've got one really heavy child protection case on my hands at the moment, which is eating into all of my time.' (Social worker)

'I did try and engage them (parents) in discussions about his background, but I never really found time to take this very far, as I've spent all my time just dealing with his (young person's) behavioural problems and placement changes since then. I think it might have been easier to engage the family if another worker had been working with me. Even though he was supposed to be being 'assessed' by the Assessment Service, I seemed to spend virtually all of my time dealing with him, and none with the family.' (Social worker – Referred assessment)

'She isn't like a social worker really. She's for me and (young person). I can see her when I want and I know that she sees my daughter weekly. And if I leave messages I know that she'll return them. It was completely different with my other social worker. I could never get hold of her. In fact before (young person's) placement with the (foster carers) broke down I only saw my social worker twice during the eight months that she was there.' (Parent – Routine assessment)

Racial and cultural needs

An important dimension to working with parents and young people is understanding racial and cultural needs. In spite of long-standing concerns about the disproportionate number of black, and particularly mixed parentage, children and young people in the care system, relatively little attention has been paid, in the research literature at least, to how social workers and other relevant professionals assess the needs of young people from different ethnic groups.

While awareness of racial and cultural issues in social work has increased in recent years, what research evidence there is suggests that for many white professionals this is an area of their work where they feel less confident and competent. Often the outcome is either a failure to acknowledge race and culture at all in the assessments of black young people and their families, or, alternatively to place so much emphasis on cultural explanations (often based on crude and/or racist stereotypes of minority ethnic groups) that important economic, emotional and psychological factors are overlooked (Ahmed, 1986, 1989; Barn, 1993; MacDonald, 1991; Pinder, 1983; SSI, 1985, 1993a; Brummer, 1988; Clifford, 1994).

Although the requirements of Section 22(5)(c) of the Children Act – to give due consideration to 'a child's religious persuasion, racial origin and cultural and linguistic background' – were not in force at the time this research was undertaken, the ethnic diversity of the authority's population (see Chapter 4) should make this a highly significant component of any assessment process. This raises a number of research questions: what consideration did social workers and other relevant professionals give to these factors in their assessments of young people's needs? Were assessments sensitive to any attempts made to help young people maintain links with their heritage and promote a positive black identity? How was their race, culture, religion and language portrayed in assessment reports and social work records? Was there any acknowledgement by social workers and others of how racism may have impacted on the situation of these black young people and their families?

Additional questions are raised when we look in more detail at differences between the white and black groups of young people in our sample. However, in breaking down this data for further analysis, caution must be exercised in interpreting the results because of the small numbers of cases in any one category. The ethnic composition of our sample was fully described in Chapter 6 and indicated that the majority of young people in our study, 63 per cent, were black or from a range of different minority cultural, religious and linguistic backgrounds.

It has already been reported in Chapter 7 that there was no difference between the Routine and the Referred groups in terms of ethnicity, but some other important differences were noted. For instance, less than a third of black young people (32 per cent) were at home or in some other community location at the time of their assessment, compared to almost half (47 per cent) of the white young people.

There were differences also in both the source of, and reasons for, the referral. Referrals of black and Asian young people were far less likely to come from parents than was the case with young white people. Young black people (50 per cent) were more likely to be referred by other agencies than young white people (35 per cent) – these figures exclude refugees who, with the exception of one sibling group, were all referred by a voluntary agency working on behalf of young asylum seekers. Also, amongst the black group, requests for care were twice (57 per cent) as likely to come from the young person themselves as with the white group (23 per cent) – moreover such requests were more likely to be agreed if the young person was black or Asian. Only one in five requests for admission to care made by white children resulted in an admission compared with more than two out of three requests made by black youngsters.

Analysis of the reasons for referral show that the black group were less likely to be referred for short-term respite but more likely to be referred following allegations of abuse (26 per cent compared to only 9 per cent for white young people). Moreover, as we saw in Chapter 7, black young people were both more likely to be admitted to care following referral than white youngsters, and more likely to be admitted faster.

While the numbers in our sample are small this does resonate with the findings from Barn. In her analysis of the care careers of black children in an inner city local authority, Barn found that whilst black parents (with the exception of Asian parents, whose children were vastly under represented in that Authority's care system) were as likely as white parents to refer themselves to social services for assistance, their children were much more likely to be admitted to care, and at a much faster rate than their white peers. This signified to Barn an inability on the part of white social workers to engage in any effective preventive work with black families.

While great efforts were made not to admit white children into care, the same was not true for black children. Social workers' negative perceptions of black families led them to develop a 'rescue mentality' which came into force very quickly when dealing with these families. Social workers' image of black parents as 'hostile and uncooperative' prevented them from working effectively with black families. (Barn, 1993)

To what extent are these differences between the two groups in our sample the result of the assessment process? Although the majority of social workers in our study said that they had given these factors some consideration during their assessments, the degree of attention which was given to these important dimensions varied considerably, and was very often limited to recognising the importance of 'same-race' placements. For example, when asked whether there had been any plans to look at young people's racial or cultural identity as part of their assessment, the majority of social workers either did not regard this as a priority issue, or felt that it would be more appropriate for a black worker to undertake this task.

'There weren't any plans to look at his racial or cultural identity. The main problem was neglect by his Mum, which has nothing to do with his race or culture. We did feel it was important for him to be placed in a black family, as it didn't seem helpful to assess his needs in an environment which was strange to him.' (Social worker)

'No one ever discussed his racial identity with him. I left this to his foster Mum. She's black and I thought she'd be much better at this than me.' (Social worker)

'She seemed to have a positive sense of identity, but it's not something I've raised with her. Her keyworker's black although that wasn't a deliberate thing and, as far as I know, she has black friends in the community. We didn't make any specific plans regarding her race or culture during the assessment. It just wasn't an issue.' (Social worker)

Where issues of identity were mentioned, this was almost exclusively with reference to cultural issues and generally related to young Asian men and women. Indeed, social workers seemed to find working with Asian young people and their families to be a particularly difficult and challenging experience. As we saw earlier, Ahmed has demonstrated how an overdependence by white social workers on simplistic cultural explanations can lead to inappropriate assessments of the needs and problems of families from minority ethnic groups. This was most apparent in work with Asian youngsters, whose difficulties were frequently explained by reference to 'cultural conflict' (Ahmed, 1986). Social workers in this study recognised the difficulty in finding the right balance of respecting cultures without making generalised assumptions.

'Although we tried to give a lot of thought to her cultural and religious upbringing when she came into care, we were very conscious that she has very few links with the Muslim community. We've tried to get her to join a girls' group at one of the community resources. We've also sought advice from them about how we should approach issues of identity with her. But she's just not prepared to discuss it with anyone at the moment. She's just so anti-Moroccan because of her anger at what her father had done to her. She's also ostracised by other Muslim girls at her school because of the behaviour and the fact that her father has disowned her.' (Social worker)

'The contract that we drew up with the foster carers was much stricter than it would be normally for a 16 year-old in care. But we were very keen to respect her family's wishes. The AAS are used to dealing much more flexibly with 16 year-olds, but it just had to be different in this case because of religious and cultural factors. It was a totally new experience for us, them and the assessment foster carers.' (AAS staff member).

As we discuss elsewhere the lack of appropriate resources, in the form of ethnically matched placements, was a major difficulty. One social worker recorded how she had dealt with this in relation to a young Asian woman admitted into care following allegations of sexual abuse:

'We discussed with her and her parents about her routine at home, and her cultural traditions. We were also very aware of her mixed religion. Her father was Hindu and her mother Christian. We knew it would be difficult to match this, so we encouraged as much family contact as possible.'

While our study does provide some evidence of cultural stereotyping, we also found examples of social workers trying hard to think through the issues while recognising their own lack of experience.

'The decision to use two workers was very much influenced by his Muslim family background. When you're working with a family with a very strong Muslim cultural base it's important to have someone other than a female working on the case. I needed a male to reinforce my views.' (White female social worker)

'We gave a lot of thought to their cultural traditions. For example, like being very conscious of undermining Dad's position in the family. There are other little things that you need to consider when working with Muslim families. For instance I wouldn't dream of going round to their house wearing a mini-skirt as I know I'd just have no credibility.' (White female social worker)

'The fact that there were two workers on the case, one male and one female, was in response to the fact that the father did not have a particularly high regard for women. But that's just the way he is. It's difficult to know whether another Muslim male would have responded the same way as I haven't any other experience of working with Muslim families.' (White female social worker)

At present there is very limited knowledge about the number of Muslim children who are being looked after by local authorities and workers still exhibit a lack of confidence in working with Muslim families (The Islamic Foundation, 1993; Marchant, 1993). Another group of young people who presented relatively new experiences for this department were unaccompanied refugee children mainly from the Horn of Africa. The Authority had few resources to support workers, with only one Section 11 post (specially funded post to support minority ethnic populations) in the department. Staff were encouraged to use their initiative to seek advice from other agencies; and in the example of the refugee children, in most cases social workers approached local community resources for advice on cultural and religious issues. However seeking outside help is not without its problems as in the case below where both parents and social workers were concerned about confidentiality.

'As a white Christian I felt very ill-equipped on how to work with (young person) and her family. Her school also needed a lot of guidance and support. The family felt very victimised and so I was keen to get a Muslim worker involved. However we don't have any in this department so I contacted a Muslim advice centre to see whether they could suggest where I might get the right sort of help. Although they didn't have a qualified social worker they did offer to get involved anyway. However, I was very concerned about confidentiality. Her parents were also very reluctant to have anyone from their own community involved as they were very embarrassed and ashamed about what had happened. They were useful though. I got a lot of advice and guidance from them about how to deal with her religious and cultural needs.' (White social worker)

These issues are not only important for social workers; school staff were also major contributors to the assessment process. In interview, social workers reported that some schools were not particularly sympathetic to different cultural and religious traditions and the schools' lack of understanding was often felt to contribute to the poor reports on young people that were prepared as part of the young person's assessment. For instance, there were examples of reports containing complaints that parents kept children away from school on certain religious festivals, and that parents were unsupportive of their daughters' education, which the school interpreted as linked with cultural traditions.

One school report, which was presented as part of a young person's assessment, illustrated the problems of racial stereotyping while failing to recognise the importance of racism in the lives of young black people. This report consisted of four lines on the young person's attendance record, four lines on his 'bizarre and unpredictable behaviour' and a full page on one particular incident involving a fight with another pupil. Although it was reported that the fight had broken out because a boy had called A's parents 'bad names', the focus of the report was on A's response to being punished for attacking the boy. He was said to have gone into 'a wild and frenzied dance; thrusting his pelvis and grinning'. The recommendation of this particular schoolteacher was that he should be removed from school and placed in a psychiatric unit.

In assessing the needs of young black people we found very little recognition of racism within our society and the needs of young black people to learn to confront this constructively.

> ... in their assessment reports social workers could and should incorporate the racial dimension in social work .... The fact that an individual's sense of identity depends not only on how the child's parents value him or her, but also on how the parents were valued by society, is not acknowledged. Invariably, the demoralising effects of rejection by society remain unwritten. (Ahmed, 1989)

While there is now greater awareness of many of the issues in appropriately assessing the needs of black young people, this is not always reflected adequately in the models or tools of assessment that are available to assist social workers (see Clifford, 1994, for a suggested anti-oppressive assessment method).

Inevitably the standard of practice in the research Authority varied; we found examples of both very good and very poor practice. However, in general we felt that social workers recognised both the importance and the complexity of addressing issues of race, culture, religion and language and the need to further enhance their skills in this area. For a largely white staff group dealing with a care population that has a majority of black young people, this is a formidable task.

> Prescription is easy; practice is hard. One point being made here is that in cross-cultural work with children, white workers need to maintain the balance between addressing the subjective experiences of the child,

without forcing the issue of ethnicity, and acknowledging the importance of addressing, rather than politely ignoring, issues of ethnicity
and colour when they emerge in the work as *central* to the experience
of the child. (Brummer, 1988)

Summary points

- Social workers' definitions of assessment varied widely; Adolescent Assessment Service (AAS) staff were more precise. But
  in general most agreed that it was a dynamic process concerned with identifying needs and problems, and finding appropriate responses.
- Few social workers were aware of any departmental principles
  regarding child care assessments – many said they would welcome this. Helpful guidelines existed to the conduct of AAS
  assessments but had not been produced for the department
  more widely.
- There was a proliferation of forums in which child care plans
  and decisions were made. Apart from the AAS procedures, we
  were aware of seven separate arrangements. Social workers,
  clients and researchers alike found this confusing.
- AAS and the Community Fostering section had produced some
  useful tools to facilitate assessments. However most social
  workers seemed not to use them.
- Social workers found young people's and families' previous records insufficiently detailed and, consequently, of limited use.
  In many cases Statements of educational need had not been
  copied for social work files.
- Social workers were usually unaware of how other professionals, such as psychiatrists or educational psychologists, approached their assessments.
- Encouragingly, most young people interviewed said that they
  were aware that an assessment was taking place and what this
  entailed. Despite having insufficient say in the process, they
  were nonetheless mostly satisfied with the arrangements that
  had been made for them. Young people were confused by the
  roles of different professionals.
- About one young person in eight was without a social worker
  for a significant period. Yet for those with social workers, direct contact was surprisingly infrequent, although most young
  people were satisfied with the level of contact. There was some
  confusion amongst social work professionals about who was
  responsible for face-to-face work.

- More than a third of young people experienced breakdowns in their assessment placements.
- Seventy per cent of our sample were invited to their final decision making meeting. This applied to all the Referred group but a minority of the Routine. Significantly more of the Referred group also actually attended but overall this must still be seen as disappointing. Furthermore the experience of many of those who attended was unsatisfactory.
- Not all social workers had explained the objectives and process of the assessment to parents. Parents who were interviewed mostly stated that they understood what was happening, although this was less clear in Routine assessments. There were few examples of written agreements with parents.
- Planned direct work with parents was infrequent: 13 cases with parents and young people, and nine with parents alone. Figures for Referred and Routine assessments were similar. Contact with parents was even more sparse than with their offspring, with only half being seen at least fortnightly. Most planned contact was with mothers and very little with fathers or extended families.
- Despite social workers being aware of the significance of this area, issues associated with racial and cultural identity were neglected during the assessments. Social workers felt particularly ill-prepared to work with Muslim families. Unaccompanied refugees also posed new challenges.

9. The results of assessment

In this chapter we examine what the assessment process achieved. We begin by looking at how many of the assessments that were planned were actually completed within the proposed time-scales; which aspects of the assessment were considered to have gone well; which were problematic and why. In particular we consider which parts of the assessment were still outstanding at the time when the final planning meetings took place, and what action, if any, was taken to remedy this situation. We then go on to examine the outputs of the assessment process, in terms of the recommendations and decisions that were made.

Were assessments completed on time?

We asked social workers whether they felt all of the various assessment tasks had been completed by the time the young person's Final Assessment Conference or other decision making meeting took place. Although all of the young people in our study had, according to our definition, undergone some form of assessment, it was difficult for social workers to respond to this where they did not consider that what they had been doing constituted assessment activity. Tables 9.1 to 9.3 therefore give the results only for those 60 cases where an assessment was said by the social worker to have been planned.

As Table 9.1 shows, fewer than one in five of these assessments (17 per cent) were reported to have been fully completed by the time the Final Assessment Conference or other social work decision making meeting was held. In fact, fewer than half (45 per cent) were said to have been completed in at least most respects, whilst in 11 cases (18 per cent) none of the assessment tasks were considered to have been completed. This latter group includes four young people who were either reported to be 'missing' during the course of their assessments, or who were absent from their care

Table 9.1   Extent to which assessment tasks were completed on time

	Number	%
Fully	10	17
In most respects	17	28
Only partially	20	33
Not at all	11	18
Don't know	2	3
	60	100

placements for virtually the whole of the assessment period. In a further two cases, social workers felt unable to comment on the degree to which these assessments were completed, as they were only allocated to the young person towards the end of the assessment process. These cases had to be recorded as 'don't know'.

In Chapter 8 we considered the time-scales that were set for these assessments and noted that, overall, the deadlines for completion were slightly shorter within the Referred system than those which were undertaken Routinely; the objective in the former being to arrive at a plan of action within 6 to 8 weeks, compared with an average time-scale amongst the Routinely assessed cases of three months. However, this appeared to make little difference to the outcomes from these two assessment systems. As Table 9.2 shows, the percentage of assessments which were completed in at least most respects was remarkably similar whether the assessment was undertaken Routinely (44 per cent) or with reference to a specialist assessment service (42 per cent).

Table 9.2   Type of assessment and the extent to which tasks were completed

	Referred %	Routine %
Fully	17	12
In most respects	25	32
Only partially	40	25
Not at all	14	24
Don't know	4	7
	100	100

The time needed to complete an assessment may of course vary: according to the range and depth of issues to be covered; the complexity of the case; the availability of resources; and the skills and knowledge of the professionals involved. Our analysis explored possible differences in the types of cases and the completion of assessments.

Interestingly, seven of the ten assessments which were reported to have been fully completed involved young people who were already well known to social services and who were assessed following a breakdown, or threatened breakdown, in their care placements. Indeed, by the time these young people's assessments took place all seven had been in the local authority's care for a minimum of six months. A considerable amount of information had, therefore, already been gathered on this group. The other three assessments involved a sibling group (of three). These brothers were admitted to care shortly after their arrival in this country as unaccompanied refugee children and were assessed together in a short-stay residential unit.

The ten fully completed assessments were also more likely to be undertaken by social workers who were familiar with the young person. For example, in seven cases the social worker had been allocated to the young person for at least 12 months prior to this 'event' taking place. In contrast, only four (13 per cent) of the 31 young people whose assessments were either partially or not at all completed, were reported to have been allocated to a social worker for this long. The majority of these cases were either not active prior to the 'event' taking place or were not allocated a social worker until some time after this had occurred.

Not surprisingly, the cases where assessments were completed were also regarded by their social workers as being some of the most straightforward on their case-loads. Not only did the young people involved present fewer behavioural problems – for example, only two of the ten were reported to have any behavioural problems at all, compared with 63 per cent of the study group as a whole – they were also less likely to be referred to other agency professionals. In fact, in only one of these ten cases was an educational or health professional said to be directly involved in the assessment process. This compares with more than half of all assessment cases. Fully completed assessments were therefore less dependent on the availability, time and skills of other agency professionals.

The young person's age also appeared to affect the extent to which assessments were completed. As Table 9.3 shows, assessments of younger teenage children (11 to 13 year-olds) were more than twice as likely to be completed in at least most respects than those which involved older adolescents. And, of the 11 assessments which were not completed at all, all but one involved an adolescent of 14 years or over.

Table 9.3   Young person's age by the extent to which assessment completed

	Fully / in most respects %	*Partially / not at all* %
Under 14	73	27
14 and over	31	69

This finding – that increasing age is associated with less successful outcomes – is neither new nor surprising. For example, research studies of foster care outcomes have long shown a higher breakdown rate amongst placements of older teenage children (Parker, 1966; George, 1970; Berridge and Cleaver, 1987; Rowe, Hundleby and Garnett, 1989). Similar findings were also reported by Farmer and Parker in their study of 'home on trial' placements (Farmer and Parker, 1991). More significantly, Rowe, in her analysis of all types of child care placements, found that where the primary aim was 'assessment', placements of teenagers were less likely than those of younger children to meet this aim.

Of course older adolescents do tend to present carers with more difficult and challenging problems; often they have come to the attention of social services because of their troublesome behaviour. They are also highly mobile compared to younger children, and are more likely to initiate placement endings themselves, either by running away or by requesting a move (Packman with Randall and Jacques, 1986; Millham and others, 1986; Farmer and Parker, 1991). Indeed, of the 15 youngsters in our study whose assessment placements broke down, all but two were initiated by the young people themselves.

More interesting, perhaps, is our finding that the venue for assessment appeared to make little difference in the rate of completion of assessments. Although slightly more residential assessments were reported to have been completed in at least most respects than those undertaken at home or in foster care, this difference was not statistically significant. Whether the assessment took place at home, in residential or in foster care, the older the young person, the less likely it was to be completed.

Which parts of the assessment were still outstanding?

As we saw in Chapter 7, many of the assessments which had been planned for these young people involved significant contributions from health and education professionals. For example, nine young people (15 per cent) had either been referred for a Statement of educational needs, or were already undergoing the Statementing process at the time when their social services assessment began. In addition, six young people (10 per cent) had either been referred for a psychiatric assessment or were already engaged in one at the time when social services became involved. A further eight young people (13 per cent) had been referred with their parents to other agencies for the purposes of a 'family assessment'. Four young people (7 per cent) had been referred to clinical psychologists, whilst three (5 per cent) had been referred to other health professionals for the purposes of a full development assessment. (For the purposes of this section these are referred to as 'specialist' assessments.)

Overall, fewer than a third of these 'specialist' assessments (30 per cent) were said to have been completed in time for the young person's Final Assessment Conference, or other decision making meeting. In fact, some of them had not even begun by the time that these meetings were held, whilst others had been abandoned, either because of difficulties in securing the young person's and/or their families' cooperation, or because of a change in the young person's circumstances.

As Table 9.4 shows, only one of the nine Statements of educational need that were planned for the young people in our study was actually completed in time for the young person's FAC, or decision making meeting, and this one was already well underway at the time when the social worker became involved in the case. In contrast, six out of the ten cases involving other educational assessments were said to have been completed by the time the young person's final assessment meeting took place.

The identification and assessment of special educational needs, under the 1981 Education Act, is of course a far more detailed and comprehensive process than most other educational assessments. It involves contributions from education, health and social services agencies as well as representations from the parents of the children concerned. In our study cases, the length of time taken to complete this Statementing process ranged from six to 16 months – the average length of time taken being just over ten months. This compares with a completion time of between three to six months for the other education assessments in our study.

Table 9.4   Number of 'specialist' assessments that were completed

	Planned	Completed
Statement under 1981 Education Act	9	1
Other education assessment *	10	6
Family assessment (i.e. with family		3
therapists)	8	
Psychiatric assessment	6	1
Psychological assessment	4	–
Specialist health assessment	3	1
Total	40	12

(* Educational assessments undertaken by the DAU, or other specialist off-site unit.)

Although the time taken to complete young people's Statements was somewhat longer than the six months recommended by the Department for Education and Welsh Office, this is by no means unusual, and in fact is rather quicker than some other Local Education Authorities (LEAs). In a recent Audit Commission report on the Statementing process, all 12 of the LEAs studied took longer than the recommended period to complete their assessments – the median length being 12 months. Indeed, in one of these 12 authorities studied the average time taken to complete the Statementing process was reported to be just under three years! (Audit Commission, 1992).

The number of assessments which were successfully completed by family therapists, psychiatrists and other 'specialist' health service professionals was also disappointingly low. Overall, only five such assessments were completed out of the 21 that were planned in time for the young person's final decision making meeting, whilst ten of them were never completed at all. So why were assessments not fully completed? We look first at 'specialist' assessment and then at social work assessments.

'Specialist' assessment

Interviews with social workers suggested a number of explanations why the 'specialist' assessments were not completed: difficulties in gaining access to other professionals; their different time-scales; coordinating the assessment task; gaining the cooperation of families and young people.

Difficulties in getting access to other agency professionals

Not only were some social workers unsure about how to make

contact with health and education agencies, when they did make referrals they often found that these other professionals were unable to respond as promptly as they would have liked, because of the many other demands that were being placed on their time. This was particularly evident in the case of family therapists and psychiatrists, whose client waiting lists were often several weeks longer than the time-scales which social workers had set for assessment completion.

'Soon after he was admitted into the assessment foster home he started to present quite disturbed and bizarre behaviour. We felt a psychiatric assessment was needed and felt it would be useful to involve his family in this .... Unfortunately, the family psychiatrist was not able to offer us an appointment for at least another three months. We had hoped to get all of the assessment work done within nine weeks as his assessment foster placement was only supposed to be short-term.' (Social worker)

Social workers also complained about the length of time they had to wait for an educational assessment. Although lack of resources coupled with an increasing demand for Statements in recent years may have been responsible for some of these delays, some social workers felt that the LEA had at times been deliberately slow in responding to their referrals because of the potential financial implications involved.

'It's been really difficult to get the Education department moving on this case. Even when they get the work done there'll still be the question of who would pay for any special education. Maybe that's why they're stalling us, as in another few months he'll be 15 and he'll slip through the net.' (Social worker)

Similar findings were reported by the Audit Commission study, which concluded that the main cause of delay in the completion of educational assessments, in their study authorities, was the lack of priority which LEAs gave to the Statementing process.

In many cases LEAs had taken no action to reduce delays and one LEA introduced an additional administrative process with the expectation that it would increase the time taken. It is unusual for LEAs to act in this manner. That they do so is symptomatic of the difficulty in managing demand consistently when the group eligible for additional resources is so open-ended. The situation is exacerbated by the in-built financial incentive to delay the completion of statements. (Audit Commission, 1992)

It may be recalled that one of the reasons social workers gave for referring young people to the AAS and other assessment services was because they assumed that specialist health and education professionals would be more readily accessible. However, whilst this may have been the case some years ago in residential observation and assessment centres, many of which routinely undertook educational and psychiatric assessments, this was not so in the AAS. Although the Assessment Service did have good links with some health and education professionals, apart from a small number of teaching staff in the DAU there were no other agency professionals attached to the Service. Nor were there any formal arrangements for getting access to specialist health or education resources. Indeed, given the changes in purchasing arrangements between the NHS and the local authority, some AAS staff were unclear about what use they were allowed to make of these services. Recent structural reorganisations within the health and education services also resulted in changes in personnel which made joint planning difficult.

> 'We have at various times built up good relationships with some people in the health service but it's getting much more difficult now. We've got two health regions here and they're quite competitive, very anxious about resources ...'

> 'Although we've had quite a bit of negotiation with the family therapy service in the past, we've never signed anything. We still run our services in parallel without much overlap and discussion about how people end up in one system or the other or how they're connected.' (AAS staff member)

Social workers were therefore often disappointed to find that once they had made a referral to the AAS, they were then required to mobilise all of the other relevant professionals themselves.

> 'I found it all very confusing and frustrating. I just couldn't understand why I felt like I was the only person who was working on this case when this was one of the reasons why I'd contacted the AAS in the first place.' (Social worker – Referred assessment)

Another commented that she had only become aware of this fact some weeks after she had referred a young person to the AAS, thus leading to further delays in the assessment process.

> 'Linking in and liaising with all of these other professionals took up so much time. Every time we approached a resource we'd have to repeat the details of the case. This made it very difficult to move on when the wheels turned so slowly. When we referred to the Assessment Service we assumed that they would have all of these resources at their fingertips. It was only later that we found out that they didn't.' (Social worker)

Although the arrangements for involving other agency professionals in assessment often differed between the Regional Resources, they too experienced problems. One young man in our study was still waiting for a psychiatric assessment several months after his admission to a Regional Resource centre. Rather than delay plans for him further, it was decided to make a recommendation for his future placement – a CHE – and to move him on, hoping that provision for a psychiatric assessment could be made for him there.

Differing time-scales

A further difficulty that social workers reported was the different time-scales to which some of these other agency professionals worked. For example, a 'family assessment' undertaken in the context of an NHS clinic might take a family therapist several months to complete; that is, assuming that all of the relevant family members were willing to participate in this assessment process and were able to attend all of the necessary appointments. Not surprisingly, some families found it difficult to sustain this level of commitment, and their attendance often tailed off after the first couple of sessions.

> 'The families that we deal with often require a lot more support and encouragement than the sorts of people that these other agencies are used to dealing with. Family therapy services can be very restrictive. If for some reason Mum or Dad can't make one of the sessions, they cancel them until everyone turns up. Some families find this approach very unhelpful. It also means it can take forever to get anything done.' (Social worker)

Overall only three such assessments were completed by family therapists during the course of our study out of the eight that were originally planned. In the remaining five cases, the process had to be abandoned as the families concerned were either unwilling or unable to continue.

Coordinating the assessment tasks

Social workers also experienced difficulty in sequencing all of the various assessment activities on time. As the following worker explained, this often had a 'knock-on' effect on their own assessment work.

> 'I think the main issue is one of coordination, particularly when lots of different people are involved. Getting professionals to meet together and moving on to a final plan can be quite difficult. Constraints on time also means that you can't actually get your own work done. Cases can

then drag on and events often overtake them so there often isn't an end product, that is, a plan.' (Social worker)

In addition to problems in organising and coordinating all of the necessary appointments on time, there were also issues around which part of the assessment should be completed first. Often this was because agencies were, understandably, reluctant to accept social workers' referrals without more detailed background information on the young person and/or their families. For example, we were told that educational psychologists were often unwilling to complete the Statementing process until social services had undertaken a full assessment of the young person's family and home situation. This was because they felt that non-attendance and underachievement at school could be a result of problems at home, rather than any special educational needs.

Similar problems have been shown to arise between social work and health agencies in the investigation of child abuse cases (see, for example, Hallett and Birchall, 1992) as 'each agency wants the other's input first: the former wants urgent therapeutic investigation to confirm whether abuse has occurred while the latter wants confirmation before referral for therapy' (p299).

Gaining the cooperation of young people and families

Finally, even when social workers were successful in getting a prompt response from other agency professionals, there was still the problem of securing the cooperation and commitment of young people and families involved. Indeed, when asked why assessment aims were not fully achieved, the most common reason given by social workers was because of a failure, either on their part or on the part of other professionals, to engage fully the young person and/or their parents in the assessment process (see Table 9.5).

Understandably, some young people were reluctant to undergo a health assessment and refused to keep any appointments that were made for them. The number of young people who underwent routine medical examinations was also low. Of the 26 young people in our study who were admitted to care, less than a quarter completed a statutory medical. In the majority of cases, this was because social workers were unable to secure the young person's cooperation.

We have already commented on clients' low attendance at family therapy sessions. Similar problems arose with the completion of young people's psychiatric assessments. Although most of the young people who were referred did attend at least one session with the psychiatrist, half of these assessments were subsequently abandoned as the young people concerned refused to attend any further appointments. Some young people complained that they simply did not 'get on' with the individual professional concerned (an opinion shared by teenagers from other studies (Triseliotis and others, 1994)). Others did not understand the purpose of such an assessment and therefore did not see any point in attending.

> 'She (young person) wasn't happy about going to see the psychiatrist. She was supposed to meet with him regularly but failed to keep to the planned appointments. But I told her this was the only way that she was going to get the placement that she wanted. After that she agreed to go.' (Social worker)

Similar difficulties arose with some of these young people's educational assessments; another reason why these assessments were delayed or not completed was the young person's poor attendance at school or other educational unit.

Given their chaotic lifestyles, turbulent relationships and histories of abuse and disrupted placements, it is perhaps not surprising that the take-up of appointments was so low. Moreover, as we saw in Chapter 6, this was often not the first time that young people had been referred to other agencies. Indeed, the majority of young people in our study had already been subject to some other formal assessment procedure in the ten years prior to this 'event'. Not surprisingly, some parents and young people were sceptical about the ability of these other professionals to effect any positive change, particularly when they had seen them before.

> 'I wasn't convinced that it would do any good talking to that lot at the (family therapy clinic). It doesn't hold very good memories for (son) or myself. That was about four years ago when I first asked for help. He was starting to get into trouble at school and he was really getting naughty. They said to me, you need help, so we started going to the (family therapy clinic). After that he went into care, so it all sort of ties in, you know.
> Anyway this time I thought, what have I got to lose? I'd tried everything else. So we went along again a couple of times. But it didn't help. He didn't like going there and I thought some of the things that they said were just plain stupid. So I told (social worker) I wasn't going anymore. I'd tried it and it hadn't worked. It was me that said no.' (Parent)

It should also be borne in mind that the majority of young people in this study, 72 per cent, were either accommodated under voluntary arrangements or were living at home under no legal jurisdiction. Social workers were therefore not in a position to enforce assessments upon young people and/or their families. Indeed, beyond encouraging their cooperation, there was little that social workers could do.

Social work assessments

Health and education professionals were not the only people to experience difficulties in completing their assessments. Less than half of the social workers in our study (46 per cent) regarded their own assessment tasks or those undertaken by carers or other social work professionals, such as *guardians ad litem*, as having been completed in at least most respects by the time the young person's FAC or other decision making meeting took place. One in five did not regard any of their assessment tasks as having been completed.

As with 'specialist' assessments, the most common reasons social workers gave for this was the difficulties they and/or carers had in engaging the young person and/or their parents in the assessment process. For example, two young people were removed from care by their parents before their assessment could be completed, whilst another two returned home at their own initiative. Although attempts were made to continue working with these young people and their families, this proved difficult once the young person had returned home.

> 'After a few weeks in care the physical distance between him and his Mum made it easier for them to get on. As their relationship improved they started saying that they didn't need me anymore. Then Mum discharged him home. I felt that this was too soon and that they still had a lot of things to sort out. I tried to set up some outreach work with them but I couldn't persuade either of them to get involved. They said they could sort out their own problems. I'm very pessimistic about this, though. I don't think it'll be long before Mum's back in the office asking for him to come into care again. In fact every time the phone rings I think it's going to be about him.' (Social worker)

A further 11 placements were terminated either at the request of the young person or as a result of them persistently running away. In some cases another placement was found and the plan was to continue the assessment there. In the remaining four cases the assessment process had to be temporarily abandoned as the young people concerned were either 'missing' or absent from their care placements for virtually the whole of the assessment period. Two of these young people refused any further contact with social services and were subsequently discharged from care. The other two resurfaced some weeks later. One was placed in a Regional Resource and the other in bed and breakfast accommodation.

Although it is possible that some of these breakdowns would have occurred whatever the assessment venue, most of these young people's social workers felt that, in retrospect, a different type of placement might have been more appropriate. The problem was, however, having the right resource available at the right time.

'Our main difficulty was getting him to sit still for long enough for any assessment work to be done. He ran away five times and so we just seemed to spend our time responding to crises. He never really engaged with anyone and so it was difficult to get any sense of what his problems were or about what he wanted. It simply confirmed what I'd thought from the beginning – that he needed a very structured and secure regime which could stabilise him before his needs could be identified. Unfortunately we don't have that sort of resource in this department and getting access to one proved very slow.' (Social worker – Residential assessment)

'Although I felt it was right that we should try for a foster placement, in retrospect it probably wasn't suitable, particularly the location. It was just too far away from home which made it difficult for his parents to visit. His IT officer was also very disappointed about the distance as the placement was so far away from the IT project. This made it difficult for them to organise any constructive out-of-school activities for him, although it didn't prevent him from going into the West End and continuing with his previous lifestyle. Because of his criminal activities we decided that should he come into care again, we'd go for an assessment in a regional resource. It's the only option left as we just don't have any local resources which can contain his behaviour.' (Social worker – Foster assessment)

'Initially she was placed in bed and breakfast accommodation with a view to moving her into one of the assessment units. However it was another six weeks before a place became available. She only stayed in the unit for three days and then she was off. Since then no-one has been able to hang on to her. I think the main problem was that she was left to drift in B and B for too long. The whole system seemed to work too slowly to meet her needs. She's living in a squat now and the only time I see her is when she comes in to the office to pick up her weekly allowance, or if she's had a brush with the law. I've told her it's her decision if she wants to accept help from us or not. She's 17 soon, so if she decides she doesn't want to cooperate we'll discharge her.' (Social worker – Residential assessment)

'I felt at several points during his assessment that he should move out of his home, at least for a short time, just to give him and his Mum a break and allow him a bit of space to let go. Relationships at home were so fraught this simply aggravated his problems and made it difficult for anyone to communicate with him .... Maybe if he'd been a year younger he'd have been admitted to care – but at 16 I got the impression that he was regarded as being too old. Even if he'd agreed to it, there was still the problem of finding somewhere suitable for him.' (Social worker – Community assessment)

'(Residential unit) was originally proposed as a short-term emergency measure until an assessment foster family became available. However, this took some time to find. (Residential unit) didn't prove to be the best place for him. He's easily led and although the staff managed to keep them out of trouble, he has found it difficult, particularly with his education. It's not the best environment to be in for someone as highly motivated as he is.' (Social worker)

Others felt that the time-scale for assessment was too short for some young people and that they needed more time to settle before any direct work could begin. However, allowing young people to set their own pace for assessment also had its problems, not least because of the pressure on short-term assessment beds.

'There was no problem with the placement as such, it was more to do with the slow pace with which we had to work with (young person). We were just going along with her feelings the whole time, which in retrospect was probably a mistake. For example, in the beginning she wouldn't allow any contact with her parents and at the end of six weeks we were still no further on in terms of assessing the viability of a return home. Although the foster carers were willing to keep her for longer this wasn't possible because of their assessment status. We decided then that we would have to go for a longer-term placement. Once we'd made that decision she decided to start communicating with her family again. Things then started to turn around very quickly and she decided to go home.' (Social worker)

As we saw in Chapter 8 involving parents in the assessment process also proved to be a difficult task for some social workers, especially in the primary assessment task of compiling family histories.

'Although we managed to establish what his needs were, getting background information on the family history and particularly on the parents' marital history was really difficult. It requires real skill and time to get at this sort of information and in this case neither parents were very forthcoming. In fact there was so much conflict it was impossible to work with them together. When meetings took place we had to see them separately in order to accommodate their wish not to attend together.' (Social worker)

'I felt that the key to his behavioural problems must lay in his past.

But we were unable to find out any more from his parents. Both of them were very resistant to talking to us about this. They were much more concerned about the here and now and couldn't see any point in going over the past in any detail.' (Social worker)

This comment, and that which follows, highlight the different perspectives that social workers and parents have of the purpose of social services intervention, and in this instance of social work assessment. So perhaps it is not surprising that the most common reason given for not completing an assessment within the expected time-scale was what social workers perceived as problems in gaining the cooperation of the parents – see Table 9.5.

'You know I've been very good the last three years. I've done everything they've (social services) asked me to do. Try this, try that, try something else. But they just don't know what it's like. You've got to live here to know what he's like. You really have got to live here. When, (son), is not here I'm really carefree. I'm like another person. But the minute he comes through that door I get moody and that. They just don't know what it's like to live here.' (Parent)

Table 9.5   The main reason given by social workers for assessments not being fully completed

	%
Difficulties in getting parents to participate in assessment	26
Difficulties in getting young person to participate in assessment	13
Difficulties in getting parents and young person to participate in assessment	11
Breakdown in assessment placement	15
Lack of time	13
Problems between client/assessor	9
Lack of resources	9
Lack of other professional input	4
	100

Having focused on explanations of why not all assessments were completed within three months of the precipitating 'event', we look briefly at which particular aspects of the process the social workers felt to be most influential in helping or hindering the assessment.

Key factors influencing the assessment

When asked which aspects of the assessment had gone well and which proved to be more problematic, the responses of the social workers reinforce the findings from the previous section – namely, that assessments went well where the worker was able to gain cooperation from the parents or the young person, and of course vice versa.

In thinking about aspects that were positive, social workers identified two important factors: first the assessment process was useful in helping to settle the young person – 'she has settled in the foster home well'; 'he has calmed down a lot'; 'for the first time in a year he is attending school' – achievements which have great value in themselves as well as assisting the assessment. Second, assessments were more successful when someone found time to engage in direct work with the young person – 'the foster carers' work with him was very successful and he has begun to trust them'; 'he really benefited from the one-to-one relationship with the psychologist'; 'the DAU worked hard on building his self-esteem'.

However while some workers were able to use the assessment process to get to know and work well with the young person, a recurrent theme from many was an inability to get below the surface – 'although she talked to me I never got to the root of her unhappiness and depression at home'; 'I got closer to him, but emotionally he was completely frozen'; 'although he has moved on, he's not divulging much'. So for some young people the assessment process had a stabilising influence, but for others a period of stability may be necessary before a deeper assessment can be successfully completed – but achieving that stability was not always easy.

Overall, when social workers were asked how useful they found the assessment, two-thirds of those responding said they found it very useful or useful, in contrast to only 15 per cent who felt it was not useful. There were no differences in these responses between the Referred and Routine assessments. The explanations the social workers gave reflect not only the role of assessment as a focus for information gathering but also the concurrent intervention, especially in terms of the placement provided.

'Yes, it was useful because it gave us a clear and honest picture of her care for the baby, and it gave her a good idea of how she was doing with the baby.' (Social worker)

'Yes, there was a pretty intensive piece of work done by (foster officer) on the foster placement and on A's needs. This highlighted how inappropriate the foster placement was and that A needed to move on. The assessment enabled us to do that in a planned way.' (Social worker)

'It gave us an opportunity to get to know her and her overall needs; it clarified where S was at with her education and an appropriate education place found for her; it has given a positive experience of social services which had not always been the case.' (Social worker – DAU assessment)

'It was useful to work with the AAS, particularly the regular meetings, as it helped us to keep informed and gave her a forum to express what she wanted.' (Social worker)

'It seems to have ended up with a really suitable foster carer; I'm not clear what the assessment consisted off except to set him up in a foster home.' (Social worker)

Here we see clearly the link between a positive intervention and a successful assessment; but perhaps most crucially this section highlights again the importance of social workers getting to know the young people they are working with through undertaking direct work with them – and how often that was missing from these assessments.

The recommendations and decisions reached

Finally we look at the recommendations or decisions that were made at the end of the three-month assessment period. Although not all assessments were completed, in all but five cases a formal plan was made and recorded. Obviously the content of these decisions will vary to meet the particular needs of each of the 75 young people. However there are key areas which one could expect to be covered by every assessment – where the young person is to live; their legal status; education, training or employment; health; contact with parents and family; racial, cultural and religious needs; contact with social worker. The extent to which these topics were covered in the plans made for each of the young people in the study will be taken up in the next chapter, when we examine the outcomes for the young people from the assessment process. Here we report the overall objective which was determined for each young person, together with the broad range of topics addressed by the care plans.

The record of each Final Assessment Conference or other decision making meeting was scrutinised. However in 12 instances no minutes were recorded and here we depended upon the social workers' notes or interview responses. Table 9.6 records the overall plan for the young people.

Table 9.6   Overall Plan for each young person

Plan	Referred	Routine
To remain at home/relatives	9	11
To return home/relatives	7	1
To remain/move to semi-independence/independence	4	9
To remain in care		
– residential care	6	3
– foster care	10	7
To remain/move to boarding school	0	3
No plan/plan pending	3	2
Total	39	36

These overall plans represent the broad objective of social work service to these young people. A range of other decisions are likely to be needed if the objective is to be met and if all the needs of the young person are to be addressed. We chose 20 topics where decisions are likely to be needed and noted whether these were included in the recommendations made for each of the 75 young people. Table 9.7 lists these subjects and records the number of cases in which they were included in the decisions made at the Final Assessment Meeting.

This table demonstrates the limited range of issues which were the focus of decisions at these meetings – a topic we shall return to in subsequent chapters.

The specificity of decisions

There is now a considerable body of research literature which indicates that, to be effective, decision makers must do more than be comprehensive in their coverage of the key issues – they must also record those decisions in ways that identify clearly the tasks to be performed, who is to perform them and the time-scale in which implementation can be expected (see, in particular, the research reviews published by the DHSS, 1985, and the Department of Health, 1991a). The limited specificity of decisions which many of these research studies noted influenced the new regulations and guidance on Plans and Reviews in the Children Act. However the report of a major social services inspection undertaken since the Children Act, while pointing to a reassuringly high level of planning, did note a continuing lack of specificity.

Table 9.7   Content of decisions from the Final Assessment Meetings

Subject matter	Number of cases
Education/employment	59
Contact with parents	39
Parents' capacity to care	33
Contingency plans	33
Emotional needs	23
Leaving care	14
Cultural needs	13
Links with professionals	13
Links with other networks	12
Behaviour/control	11
Health needs	11
Linguistic needs	7
Religious needs	6
Parents' finances	6
Contact with carer	3
Parents' health	3
Racial needs	3
Parental networks	2
Young person/family history	2
Parents' relationship	2

Many of those (plans) viewed by the Inspectors lacked clear aims, objectives, allocation of responsibilities and time-scales, although there were some notable exceptions. (SSI, 1993a)

With this in mind we examined the characteristics of the decisions taken, noting the extent to which social workers considered and recorded the 'who, how, when and why' of the decisions relating to each young person. In the great majority of cases (83 per cent) the tasks to be performed where clearly identified either fully or in most respects, with a greater tendency for this to be so in Referred assessments (see Table 9.8).

Table 9.8   Were tasks clearly specified?

	Referred	Routine
Fully specified	11	11
Specified in most respects	25	14
Specified little/not at all	1	1
No record	2	10
Total	39	36

However when it came to recording time-scales, workers were much less certain – in less than half of the cases (47 per cent) was a time-scale recorded for all or some of the decisions made (see Table 9.9). However here there were no significant differences between the two types of assessment.

Table 9.9 The recording of time-scales

Time-scales recorded	Referred	Routine
In all decisions	11	9
In some decisions	8	7
Not at all	18	10
No record	2	10
Total	39	36

Before leaving the decision making process it is interesting to note the extent to which these final meetings took account of the views of the young people and their parents. Information on this was gathered from accounts of meetings together with questions to social workers. In the previous chapter we discussed the inclusion of parents and young people in the assessment process and noted a surprisingly low level of attendance of young people at their planning meetings. It is therefore reassuring to note that in over two-thirds of our sample cases (68 per cent) the views of the young people were reported and discussed at the meeting. As expected, the corresponding figure for the presentation of the views of parents was much lower at 47 per cent. There was no significant differences between the Referred and Routine assessments in this respect.

The last three chapters have described, in some detail, many aspects of the assessment process and the outputs from that, in particular comparing the two types of assessment, the Routine and the Referred. It is time now to look at the outcomes from the assessments, and that is the subject of the next two chapters.

Summary points

- Fewer than one in five assessments were said to have been fully completed by the time of the Final Assessment Conference or within the three-month assessment period. Another 28 per cent were concluded in most respects. There were no noticeable differences between Referred and Routine assessments in this regard, nor with the venue of assessment – at home, in foster or residential care.

- The older the young person, the less likely the assessment was to be completed.
- Fewer than a third of other professional 'specialist' assessments were completed before the Final Assessment Conference; some had not even begun by that date. Only three of the eight family therapy assessments were ever finished. The average duration of assessments of special educational needs under the 1981 Education Act was ten months. This incongruence in time-scales and the efforts required to coordinate led to difficulties for social workers in their planning.
- Fewer than a quarter of the 26 young people who were admitted to care had a statutory medical examination. Adolescents were often unwilling for this to occur. Young people frequently withdrew from psychiatric assessments. Gaining parents' compliance was also difficult for professionals.
- Nonetheless, a clear majority of social workers had found the assessments useful and worthwhile; this opinion was influenced by the quality of the relationship between the young person and their social worker.
- A range of plans were produced by the assessments. However, these often covered a limited range of issues.
- Tasks identified in plans were usually quite specific, particularly resulting from Referred assessments. But time-scales tended to be more vague.
- In over two-thirds of cases, the views of young people were reported to, and discussed at, the final meeting. The representation of parents' views was lower, only half. Referred and Routine assessments were alike in these respects.

10. The young people one year on

Thus far the information from the empirical study has related to the young person's circumstances at the time of the 'event', the assessment process and the services offered in the three months following the event. A key question which the research addresses is whether there are any discernible differences in the outcomes for these young people depending on the nature of the initial assessment. To answer this, a further round of information was gathered approximately one year after the end of assessment, or 15 months after the original 'event'.

In this chapter we report on what actually happened to the young people in the intervening period and how far this was in accordance with the social worker's plans. In the next chapter we examine outcomes more specifically and relate these to the original form of the assessment.

Data collection for follow-up

Data collection for this research was designed around three points – the occurrence of a transitional event; the completion of an assessment; and one year later. As the previous discussions have indicated, the assumption of a three-month period in which to complete the assessment was exceeded in some cases and was unnecessary long for others. This in turn has led to some variation in the length of the follow-up period. Approximately one year after the assessment was completed, contact was made with the social worker or the social work office of the 75 young people. Data were gathered from each of the files, from interviews with social workers, and, where possible, from interviews with young people.

From the sample group of 75 young people included in the first round of data collection, a quarter of these were no longer open cases to the social services. In addition, a further eight cases were officially open, but they were not active – no work was being done with the young people, nor were they receiving services.

Where cases had closed, the interval between the end of the assessment and case closure varied, with a few cases closing immediately or soon after the assessment was complete and some remaining open for almost another year. Correspondingly, the information which was gathered from the files also covered variable periods. Where a case had been closed and the social worker was still available, interviews were held. But in some instances this was not possible – for example, if the case had been closed for some time and the previous worker was no longer in post, it may be that no one had information on the young person's current circumstances. Similarly, for active cases where there has been a change of social worker, the new worker may have current information on the young person, but may find it difficult to relate this to the assessment process.

Despite this variable picture, it was decided that all available data should be gathered and analysed. As a consequence the number of responses to questions in this follow-up varies, as does the time-period for some aspects of the data. This will be made clear in the reporting of findings.

Case closures

The case status of the 75 young people at follow-up is shown in Table 10.1.

Table 10.1   Case status at follow-up

	Number	%
Case open	48	64
Case open, not active	8	11
Case closed	19	25
	75	100

So one year on, almost two-thirds of the original group were still receiving a social work service. Of the 19 cases that had closed, 10 had done so within 9 months of the original 'event'; a further 7 within 12 months, with 2 cases remaining open for over one year after the event. One young person had died in the intervening period – despite some mental and physical health problems, she had been supported by social workers in her wish to return to her mother in Pakistan, but had died unexpectedly a few weeks after arrival there.

Looking at the reason for closure of the other 18 cases, only one of these could be said to have closed positively and in accordance with the original plan. The closure of the cases of three unaccompanied refugee brothers was not in accordance with the plan but was for positive reasons – an uncle arrived to take them home following a political coup in their home country and the release of their father from prison. In the majority of the remaining cases the young person, sometimes on their own, sometimes in conjunction with their families, decided to withdraw from social services, most often it seemed because the social services department was unable to provide a service that was perceived by the young person and the family as helpful in meeting their needs. About two-thirds of these young people went or remained at home, the rest moved to live independently, some more securely than others.

Following a residential assessment it was recommended that L remain in care and a foster place be found for him. Seven months later he was still in the residential unit, his mother was unhappy about that and decided to have him home, so he was discharged to her from care. (Derived from case record)

S was received into care at 16 following a physical assault by her father. She was placed in an assessment foster home for six weeks with an agreed plan to find a long-term foster home. After ten months in the assessment foster home, with no indication when a long-term place would be available, S simply moved in with her boyfriend and leaving the social services with little option but to discharge her from care. (Derived from case record)

In many ways this proactive role by families and young people is reminiscent of the findings of Vernon and Fruin (1986):

In many instances there was no social work involvement in the child's discharge, parents and children being the direct initiators of change. (p69)

Similarly in their study of disaffected adolescents who were returned 'home on trial', Farmer and Parker (1991) found the pressure for change often lay elsewhere than through the social worker:

… the way in which decisions were made (or at least the way in which they were recorded) suggested a rather laissez-faire approach in which outside influences of various kinds, rather than social work initiation, were the key factors. (p142)

It is perhaps unsurprising that a substantial proportion of these young people had returned home, as we know from statistical information and research studies that the great majority of children who come into care do eventually go home (Rowe, Hundleby and Garnett, 1989; Bullock, Little and Millham, 1993). The Dartington study also highlights the stresses involved in going home and the need for continuing support, so the early closure of the cases in our sample may give some cause for concern. However we must remember, unlike the other studies mentioned, our sample of young people were generally older and mostly in voluntary care. We must also recognise the value in young people and their families making decisions and choosing options for themselves.

What is more concerning is the element of 'drift', rather than a purposeful planned return, as advocated in *The Children Act Guidance* – 'The aim should be to achieve a planned ending to a placement with careful preparation and transition' (Department of Health, 1991e). Rather we find that often the choice to return home is made for negative rather than positive reasons. This supports the findings of others, that young people may be able or willing to return to their families even when there appears to be little or no change in either behaviour patterns or in the quality of their relationship with their parents (Bullock, Little and Millham, 1993). The period apart can allow for a reassessment, perhaps of increased tolerance of each other, and a more accurate view of the alterations that social services can offer (Farmer and Parker, 1991).

The type of assessment, whether Referred or Routine, was not an important factor in whether cases were likely to be closed by follow-up. However, six out of the eight cases that were open but not active had been assessed routinely within the district team.

The age of the young people at follow-up

The focus of this research is social work with adolescents. In fact, two-thirds of the sample group were between 14 and 16 years at the time of the 'event'. At follow-up, on average they will be 15 months older, giving a modal age of 16, with 19 of the young people in the sample being 17 years or older. It can be seen from Table 10.2 that, as expected, a higher proportion of the cases that were closed or inactive were of the older age groups.

Social work input

In an earlier chapter, we noted the relatively low priority that is often now given to social work with adolescents and the conse-

Table 10.2 Age and case status at follow-up

Age	Open	Open but not active	Closed	Total
10–11	3	0	1	4
12–14	14	0	5	19
15–16	24	3	5	32
17–18	7	5	7	19
Total	48	8	19	74

(The child who died is not included.)

quent difficulties in undertaking assessment when awaiting allocation of a social worker. This would appear to be a continuing problem made worse by an industrial dispute in the research Authority. During the follow-up period 29 (almost 40 per cent) of cases were unallocated for a time – 24 of these for periods in excess of three months and 13 for periods in excess of seven months. Undoubtedly this had an impact on implementing assessment decisions.

> A had been sent by his mother in Nigeria to private foster carers in England, primarily to gain educational qualifications. He came to the attention of social services when he left this placement and was sleeping rough. The assessment decision was to place A with 'bridging' foster carers until a suitable long-term place was found and to support his education. When the social worker left, the case was unallocated for almost three months, during which time the young man dropped out of school, the foster placement broke down and he moved to a hostel. (Derived from case record)

In addition to periods with no allocated worker, in over 30 per cent of cases there was a change of social worker during the follow-up period. The impact on young people of changes in their social worker has often been noted; a situation which has been made worse with the constant reorganisations and restructurings which is now the norm in social services departments. An additional concern in this study is the impact of a change in social worker on the contribution of a social work assessment to continuing work to meet the needs of the young person. Ideally a well documented assessment should ensure that a new social worker has full and structured background information on the circumstances and needs of the young person and has a clear care plan to follow. Often this ideal was not reached. When asked at follow-up whether, in retrospect, the assessment was useful, 45 per cent of those responding said it was useful or very useful, but this falls to as low as 29 per cent in cases where there has been a change of social worker.

Many of the young people in the sample had long histories of social services provision and consequently had accumulated several volumes of files. New social workers felt that they rarely had the time to familiarise themselves with past family history by reading through extensive recordings in multiple files.

> 'These young people go back a long way – there are about five or six files on them. When I was given the case I had to get involved quickly in the current happenings – I didn't have time to read any of the old files.' (Social worker)

Social Services inspectors have noted that the vital link in the process of planning between information, judgement, or assessment and decision making is provided by the case record:

> Case records need to be accessible, accurate and intelligible; they are the basic tool of good social work practice. (SSI, 1989)

The standard of recording within the Authority was variable. While this was largely due to the style of individual workers and the standards set by the team leader, it was also true that the more formal or structured the assessment process the more accessible was the information in the file.

The circumstances of the young people at follow-up

In documenting the circumstances of the young people at follow-up, the researchers used a similar format in respect of each of the key aspects of legal status, accommodation, education or employment, contact with their family and people of the same ethnic origin and contact with the social worker. First a comparison was made by the researchers between the current circumstances and that which had been planned following assessment, and the reasons for any differences were noted. Then social workers were asked the extent to which they felt that plans had been implemented, together with any explanation for their response. This enabled us to offer two evaluations of the implementation of plans – that of the researchers and that of the social worker. In this section we shall record the changes over the year in the young people's circumstances in key areas and identify how far this was in accordance with plans. Later we shall consider more generally the quality and effectiveness of the plans which were made following the assessment.

Legal status

At follow-up fewer than half (44 per cent) of the sample group were being looked after, compared to 57 per cent at the end of the assessment period (see Table 10.3).

Table 10.3 Legal status at assessment and follow-up

	Looked after %	Not looked after %
At assessment	57.3	42.6
At follow-up	44.0	55.6

(*Including one child who had died.)

Direct comparisons of legal status at these two points is not easy, with the intervening implementation of the Children Act. As already noted, 19 cases were closed. In addition, 11 young people were admitted or readmitted to care or accommodation during the period. However, only four from the 'considered for care' group were subsequently looked after by the Authority. There were more care orders in force at follow-up (16 compared to 9), mainly due to transfer from wardships; no care orders were discharged. Fewer people were accommodated under Section 20 of the Children Act 1989 than had been in care under Section 2 of the 1980 Act. None of these was over 16 years of age, so at this very early stage of the implementation of the Children Act there was no evidence of older teenagers requesting accommodation.

Were these legal statuses as anticipated? This was so in about half of the cases, both in our estimation and that of the social workers. However, in about a quarter of cases no plan had been identified regarding legal status. At times it was possible to assume an implicit plan, for instance when the young person was receiving voluntary support or was on a time-limited supervision order and so no future action was required; at other times this could not be assumed, suggesting a real gap in the care plan. In the final quarter of cases, the current legal status was not that which had been planned, most often because of action initiated by the young person and/or their family – for instance, returning home and a subsequent discharge from care, committing offences or, as in three cases, requesting accommodation.

Accommodation

Table 10.4 summarises the accommodation plans that were recorded for the young people at the end of the three month assessment period. For 40 per cent of the young people the plan was that they should continue to live at home or that they should cease to be looked after and return to their family or friends. This figure is very similar whether the case was assessed by the AAS or routinely by the case worker.

Table 10.4   Plans made for accommodation following assessment

Planned accommodation	Referred	Routine	Number	%
Home	12	14	26	34.7
Relatives	2	2	4	5.3
Long-term foster	11	6	17	22.7
Authority's children home	1	2	3	4.0
Private/voluntary home	3	1	4	5.3
Semi-independent	5	9	14	18.7
No plan*	5	2	7	9.3
Total	39	36	75	100.0

(* Including assessments not completed.)

We can compare these plans with the actual situation of the young people at follow-up. Table 10.5 provides this information for both open and closed cases, although for eight of the closed cases it was not possible to ascertain where the young person was currently living.

Table 10.5   Actual accommodation at follow-up

	Number	%
Home	33	44.0
Relative/friends	5	6.7
Relative/fostering	4	5.3
Assessment/bridging foster care	3	4.0
Long-term foster care	5	6.7
Assessment – residential	1	1.3
Authority's children home	4	5.3
Regional resource	1	1.3
Private/voluntary	7	9.3
Semi-independent	3	4.0
Independent	1	1.3
Missing data	8	10.7
	75	100.0

When we compare Tables 10.4 and 10.5, the plans made for young people at assessment with their actual living situation one year later, then three differences are immediately apparent:

- there are more young people at home or with relatives;
- many fewer were in long-term foster care than was planned;
- few of the plans for semi-independent accommodation had materialised or been sustained.

We need to look at these results in more detail.

Young people at home

Looking at the group as a whole indicates that, overall, more young people were now living at home than had been planned. However when we break this down and look at individual cases we see an even greater level of discrepancy between the type of accommodation that was planned for the young person and that in which they were actually living.

In the earlier discussion on closed cases, we noted that a considerable number of young people had initiated actions that resulted in their discharge from care and that several of these had returned home, regardless of social services (earlier) intentions. This group accounts for the higher than planned number of young people at home. In contrast, if we compare the assessment plan against accommodation outcomes for those cases which were still open, then we find that only 24 young people were at home, when in 30 instances this was the planned outcome.

Some in this group will be the 'considered for care' cases, which were assessed while the young person was living at home or with friends and relatives. As we noted earlier only four out of this group of 27 were subsequently looked after; a considerable endorsement of preventive inputs. However, this does not necessarily mean that these young people had stable living situations. Only 11 out of the group of 27 had no change of care-giver. For the rest there was often a move to a different parent or relative and for some several changes of bed and breakfast or hostel accommodation. The regular shifting of living situations seems to have become an established characteristic for this adolescent group – whether prior to assessment, while being accommodated or after leaving care.

Long-term foster care

Undoubtedly the greatest failure in implementing accommodation plans was in securing appropriate foster homes. This was the plan for 17 young people but by follow-up this had been achieved for only five. Indeed a year later two people were still in assessment foster homes, which were now regarded as 'bridging'. Of the rest, seven had returned home, one was in residential care, one in a hostel and one in an independent bedsit.

The declared policy of this Authority, like that of most others, is to regard foster care as a preferred placement option for children who need to live away from their families. Yet this study, like so many over the years, is highlighting once again the problem that authorities can have in recruiting sufficient foster carers to offer appropriate placements, especially to older young people, many of whom are from minority ethnic groups (see Berridge, 1985; Department of Health, 1990; Cliffe with Berridge, 1991).

Although this is a comparatively wealthy Authority which offers generous fostering rates, it scores low on other factors which predict the supply of foster carers. In their study, Bebbington and Miles point to four characteristics of families which can be used to indicate the likely supply of foster families: households with five plus rooms; two parent families with males in full-time work and females not employed; families with children, but none under five; women aged 30-54 living in private households. Using this formula the predicted supply of foster carers in this Authority was actually the lowest for all authorities in the country (Bebbington and Miles, 1990).

Three problems which arise from this lack of long-term foster places, were identified to us by social workers and young people.

- those foster homes that were available were outside the borough, hence removing the young person from their family, school and friends and involving both them and staff in much travel;
- having no suitable placements to which young people could be moved resulted in the blocking of both residential and assessment foster places, thereby reducing the flexibility of the whole care system and the assessment service in particular;
- young people felt great insecurity when they had agreed to a plan to move to another place, yet over the months that was not happening.

'When I went there at first I was told it was going to be for six weeks ... they kept having meetings ... saying I would go to other foster parents but I just end up staying ... after I had been there for months I didn't know how long I was going to be there.' (Young person).

'It was protracted ... they wanted her to move into a community foster family ... that was left and left, with our link worker phoning, writing, me saying something, the young person saying something ... the young person was so disillusioned that in the end she said, I'm not going, just move me to a hostel …. She was so angry that she was still here….

We have got to know where we are working to … we've got to have a focus, even if the social worker is not clear about what's happening … we have got to have a plan to work with the young person.' (Foster carer)

Semi-independent living

Given the age of the sample, semi-independent living was likely to be an important option. This was the accommodation plan for nearly 19 per cent of the group; in fact only 4 per cent were so accommodated at follow-up. Of the rest, five were with parents, friends or relatives; three were in supported bedsits; two in private and voluntary hostels; and nothing was known about the other two young people. Again the problem was largely one of lack of immediate resources. The Authority had no semi-independent accommodation of its own and was reliant on placing outside the borough or in private or voluntary establishments. The opportunities to work with the young person in a structured way in these units was very variable, and often outside the influence of the social worker.

Number of moves

So far we have contrasted accommodation plans against the situation at one date about a year later. The *Child Care Now* study highlighted the need to view the care system in a dynamic way; presenting statistics as a snapshot at a certain point in time underestimates the substantial movement of young people within the care system (Rowe, Hundleby and Garnett, 1989). By noting the number of changes of placement throughout the follow-up period we were able to assess how much stability the young people experienced. This is particularly relevant to this study as inherent in the use of specialist assessment placements is the requirement for the young person to move on from the specialist short-term assessment facility, once the assessment is complete.

Table 10.6 sets out the number of changes of placements or caretaker that each of the 75 young people experienced between the time of the event and the follow-up or case closure, on average a period of 15 months. The majority of young people had experienced some change during this time; most had two or more changes of placement and a small number had multiple changes. Case studies of the young people with multiple moves are presented in the next chapter when we evaluate outcomes.

Table 10.6   Number of changes during 15-month period

	Number	%
No changes	14	18.7
1	19	25.3
2 or 3	30	40.0
4–8	10	13.3
8+	2	2.7
Total	75	100.0

Detailing all the movements of this sample group also highlights the role that residential care plays in the care system. The static picture of the type of placement in use at each of the three key points in this research period suggests that only a small number were in residential places at those times. But if we look at the total picture of all placements in use throughout the period, we find that well over half (57 per cent) of this sample have experienced at least one residential placement. This is very similar to the findings of the *Child Care Now* study of all placements in six local authorities, which found that 52 per cent of all placements for young people of 11 years or older were in the residential sector (Rowe, Hundleby and Garnett, 1989).

We should remember that not all of this sample are in the care system. As we noted earlier those receiving social work support at home were subject to similar moves – between relatives and friends or from one parent's home to another – often involving very makeshift arrangements. Again this highlights the findings from the Marsh and Fisher study that when relationships get difficult, whether in or on the edge of the care system, the solution is often for the family to effect the move of the young person or for the young person to make the choice to move somewhere else, all of which mitigates against any real effort to resolve underlying problems (Fisher and others, 1986).

Achievement of accommodation plans

Having looked at some of the detail, how can we summarise the extent to which accommodation plans were fulfilled? In our judgement accommodation plans were implemented fully or in most respects in 46 per cent of all cases, while social workers felt this to be so in 51 per cent of cases. This is not a marked difference, and is due to a tendency for social workers to discount delay in implementing plans. When the delay was substantial we regarded the objectives as being only partially achieved.

There was however a marked difference in the rate of successful implementation of accommodation plans according to the type of assessment: Referred assessments were less likely to result in accommodation plans which were fully or mostly implemented (43 per cent) compared with Routine assessments (58 per cent). We have noted already the particular problems associated with plans for long-term foster care and semi-independent living. These options were decided more often following referred assessments, which helps to explain the disparity in the rate at which accommodation plans were fulfilled.

Looking back, social workers rarely felt that the original decisions made following assessment were inappropriate; rather they felt the difficulties lay in turning plans into reality. Three factors seem important in the limited success of implementing these decisions – and we shall return to these later – the factors being a lack of appropriate resources, coupled with a lack of input in achieving these resources, and the degree to which young people and their families initiated decisions. The provision of social services is via a process of negotiation between social worker and young people and their families. As these young people get older it is both right and inevitable that the balance in the negotiation shifts towards the young person. But surely this must be an acknowledged process, rather than one which takes place as if by default – where the young persons' personal decisions are filling the vacuum left by a lack of planning or fulfilment of plans on the part of the social services department.

The assessment venue and the accommodation plan

In Chapter 2 we noted that one of the criticisms that had been made of the old O & As was a tendency for assessments by residential staff to lead to a further residential placement. Was that also apparent from these assessments? Table 10.7 shows the accommodation plans which were made at the end of the assessment period, by the venue for the assessment.

This table shows some major differences in accommodation plans, according to the assessment venue. However it will be remembered that the venue for the assessment was closely related to the nature of the case. For example, the majority of 'considered for care' cases were assessed at home and recommended that the young person remain at home. Similarly those assessed residentially were already in care, with 55 per cent being assessed follow-

Table 10.7 Social work plan by venue of assessment

Social Work Plan	Assessment Venue Residential Residential	Foster Home Foster Home	Community Community	Total Total
Remain or return home/relatives	4	5	19	28
Remain/move to semi-independent	7	2	3	12
Remain/move to independent	0	0	1	1
Remain in Authority children's home	3	0	0	3
Move to other residential care	4	2	0	6
Remain/move to boarding school	0	1	2	3
Move to long-term foster home	11	2	4	17
Plan still pending	2	1	2	5
Total	31	13	31	75

ing an admission to care and the rest following a placement breakdown.

Interestingly however, the above information shows no tendency for a residential assessment to produce a residential option. Indeed the residential assessments gave rise to the greatest number of recommendations for long-term foster care and semi-independent living. These were also the two plans least likely to succeed which, as we indicated, meant that Referred assessments were less likely to be successful in achieving their accommodation plan.

Education

In the intervening period, a further 27 young people had left school, leaving 34 of the original sample still under school leaving age; in addition, four young people over 16 were staying on in school. Of the rest for whom information was available, eight were in further education, mainly part time; one was on an employment training placement; one was employed full time as a nursing auxiliary and no fewer than 12 were unemployed.

Of those 38 young people of school age or on school registers, six were not in school at all; the rest attended the following educational establishments:

Mainstream day (14)
EBD day school (2)
Special day units (8)
Special boarding (6)
CHE (2)

When the characteristics of the sample were described in Chapter 6 it was clear that the majority of young people had significant educational problems. During the follow-up period the sample group still showed signs of unstable educational experiences. For instance, 40 per cent had changed school during the period and a similar proportion (41 per cent) had been excluded or been absent from school. Table 10.8 shows the total length of time the young people still in school at follow-up had spent out of school since the 'event'.

Table 10.8 Total period out of school in the follow-up period

Time	Number	%
None	1	2.6
Under 1 week	5	13.1
1 week–1 month	4	10.5
1–3 months	4	10.5
4–6 months	13	34.4
7–11 months	5	13.1
1 year +	6	15.8
Total	38	100.0

At the point of our follow-up, one person was temporarily excluded, three permanently excluded, seven were non-attenders and seven irregular attenders, leaving just over half the group (20) as regular attenders.

In Chapter 6 we saw the importance of problems associated with education in bringing these young people to the attention of social services. It is obvious from Table 10.8 that many were continuing to miss out on schooling, although it must be remembered that we are dealing with young people, many of whom are in their last years of compulsory education. The information on educational attainment that we were able to glean from files or from social workers makes equally gloomy reading. We were able to record that only four young people had sat any GCSEs and to find the results for two of these. Once again this repeats the findings from previous studies; first, that children are likely to leave care or social services support with poor educational records and, second, that social workers frequently do not take educational achievement sufficiently seriously to worry about GCSE results (Jackson, 1987; Fletcher-Campbell and Hall, 1990; Heath, Colton and Aldgate, 1989).

How do these educational outcomes accord with the social work plan? In assessing this there is very close agreement between our judgement and that of the social workers. First and most strikingly, we both agree that in over 27 per cent of cases no plans were made for the young person's education or employment. In just over a third of cases do we both agree that plans have been met fully or in most respects and in between 20 and 24 per cent of cases they have not been met at all. The young person's lack of cooperation was the most common cause for failure to meet plans; but also important, and recognised by social workers, was their lack of input, as well as that of other professionals, into securing education provision.

There can however be few excuses for such neglect of the educational well-being of these young people, a point forcefully made by Sir William Utting in his report *Children in the Public Care* (Utting, 1991). Perhaps this situation will improve with full implementation of the statutory requirement under the Children Act for all children looked after to have a Care Plan, which includes an education plan, and the implementation of Circular 13/94: *The Education of Children Looked After*, one of six circulars on Pupils with Problems issued jointly by the DFE and Department of Health in 1994.

Young people's contact with their families

In this section we shall examine the level of contact that the sample group had with their families during the follow-up period and the social workers' estimation of the quality of that relationship. First it is worth reminding ourselves of several factors when interpreting this data:

- not all of the group were in care placements; by follow-up about 44 per cent of the total sample were known to be living with parents or relatives;
- in almost one-third of cases it was known that there had been a change in the family or household composition during the period;
- the older age of the sample and the voluntary nature of most of the care meant that social workers very often left the young

person and family to make their own arrangements about contact. This in turn meant that social workers did not always have an accurate picture of how often the young people saw, or were in contact with, their family.

Social workers were asked about the pattern of contact that each young person was having with different family members and significant others at the time of follow-up and how that compared with contact levels at the time of the assessment; these are shown in Table 10.9. The particular pattern of contact varied greatly between the individuals in the sample, and between the young people and different family members. For instance, as other studies have shown, many more had regular contact with their mothers than with their fathers (Millham and others, 1986).

There were 13 young people who had no contact at all with any members of their family. Of these, eight were unaccompanied refugee children and four had no parents alive or whose whereabouts were known. Social workers, with some help of other agencies such as Asylum Aid, did make efforts to build contact between the refugee children and their families; but sometimes it had to be recognised that this was not possible, for instance where children showed reluctance to divulge information for fear of jeopardising their parents' safety.

Table 10.9 Contact at follow-up compared to a year earlier

	More	Less	Same	Total
Mother	17	4	31	52
Father	10	6	31	41
Other adults	2	4	8	14
Siblings at home	11	3	24	38
Siblings not at home	9	5	11	25
Grandparents	6	4	8	18
Significant others	5	1	6	12

In general one must view these figures as encouraging, as, overall, young people were having more contact with their parents and other family members now than previously. Some of this was due to social work effort, but case records and interviews with young people and foster carers suggest that often this could be viewed as *despite* rather than *because* of the social worker. Foster carers were also key in enabling the young person to remain in contact, sometimes taking greater initiative in this than either the young person or social worker anticipated or indeed may have wished.

Where significant input from the social worker was necessary in terms of arranging supervised visits this could have the effect of reducing both the amount and value of parental contact.

N and N, a brother and sister, were allowed supervised access to their father. Following complaints by the young man about his social worker, the siblings no longer had the same worker. There were marked differences in the attitudes of the two workers and the priority that they gave to arranging contact between parents and teenagers. This caused difficulty in facilitating contact. As a result, over the follow-up period few official contacts had been made, although one social worker felt certain there was informal contact with the father initiated by the young people themselves. (Derived from case records)

The social workers' estimation of the quality of the relationship between the young person and various family members is shown in Table 10.10. As before, these results can be seen as encouraging, in that the relationships with all family members were in general more likely to be better than worse, compared to a year earlier.

Table 10.10   The quality of the relationship at follow-up compared to a year earlier

	Better	*Worse*	*Same*	*Total*
Mother	19	6	21	46
Father	10	7	12	29
Siblings	14	6	28	48
Significant others	2	1	4	7

Implementation of social work plans for contact with families

Plans regarding contact with family were included in the final assessment in less the half of the cases in the sample. Social workers were most likely to record plans for contact with family where the young person was living away from home. There may of course be instances where contact arrangements need to be made for children living at home, for instance with a parent or grandparent who does not live in the family home. However in reviewing contact plans we have only included those cases, 46 in total, where the young person was not at home at the start of the follow-up period.

Table 10.11   Implementation of plans for contact between young people not living at home and family

	Referred	Routine	Total
Fully implemented	3	2	5
Partially implemented	10	4	14
Not implemented	4	4	8
No plan	7	12	19
Total	24	22	46

The implementation of these contact plans is shown in Table 10.11.

Even where the young person was living away from home, in over 40 per cent of cases there was no recorded plan for contact with the family. Such a situation would now be contrary to the *Arrangements for Placement of Children (General) Regulations 1991* (Department of Health, 1991e). However, where plans were made they tended to be implemented, at least in part. Those following Referred assessment were much more likely to be recorded and more likely to be implemented.

Race, culture, religion and language

Given the requirement of the Children Act to take due account of a young person's racial origin, religion, cultural and linguistic background, we would hope that the assessment of young people would include plans to promote positive racial and cultural identity by encouraging links between the young person and people from the same ethnic background. This is particularly important where the young person is living away from home and is from a minority ethnic group. It will be remembered that over two-thirds of this sample were from a very diverse range of minority ethnic groups.

First, we asked whether, at follow-up, the young people had links with people from the same ethnic community. In general, most young people did have such contact – some through school, some through their care placement, but mostly through their links with family, friends and the wider community. The allocation of a social worker of the same ethnic origin was not a significant source of contact for young people, and was only mentioned in one case. This arises in part because the social work staff group was predominately white, and in part because the department did not attempt any policy of 'ethnic matching' in allocating social workers to clients. Apart from equal opportunity dilemmas in such a policy, given the ethnic diversity of the client group, any attempt to allocate social workers according to race and culture and religion would be almost impossible to achieve.

The ethnic origin of carers was given consideration in placement decisions, although the overall shortage of foster carers meant that attempts at 'ethnic matching' were not always successful. Issues of ethnic background were fully covered in the training for foster carers, but some staff and foster carers did have concerns about whether any policy on ethnicity was given a sufficiently high priority by the Authority.

> 'When it comes to the real issues of racism and racial identity and culture, the Authority doesn't try hard enough .... Other boroughs can get black staff, so it's not a question of resources ... it is ideological commitment ... even if the Authority hasn't got a policy the young person's social worker should think ... they should try their level best to get the right family for the young person.' (Foster carer)

> 'As regards dealing with race and cultural issues I think we are working under difficult circumstances ... we have such a huge mixture of different cultures to deal with. We have a degree of expertise but I do sometimes wonder if we are good enough ... we have an authority that explicitly doesn't want to own a strong policy on equal opportunities as a council – this makes it a difficult context to work in – in many ways we are all struggling, but that should be a more open struggle.' (Team Leader)

There were however nine cases, over 12 per cent, where the social worker felt that the young person did not have any contact with people of their own race or culture.

It should also be noted that in more than one in five cases, the social workers felt that answering this question on the interview schedule was not relevant to the particular case. This was mostly where the young person was white and the social worker felt particular efforts in this area to be unnecessary. However in four instances social workers felt this to be the case where the young person was black.

The responses to these questions highlight the complex nature of the ethnic dimension to social work in such a culturally diverse area. As the following case example illustrates, one cannot make generalised assumptions about the way in which young people perceive their ethnic identity when their parents come from different ethnic groups (see Tizard and Phoenix, 1993).

One young woman in the sample was classified as White/Arab. When asked if she had contact with people from her own ethnic community, the social worker replied 'Yes, she goes to mass every Sunday with her grandmother and plays in an Irish pipe band'. This young woman's Egyptian father had left when she was a baby and she had been brought up by her white Irish mother in an Irish community. She was aware of her father's background, and proud of her stunning 'Cleopatra' looks but regarded herself as white. Both she and the social worker saw her ethnic group as Irish and no other consideration of ethnicity was made when her placement was considered.

Although we set out to ascertain whether plans were implemented to promote this racial identity, it proved to be a rather meaningless exercise – few care plans included any reference to ways of meeting young people's racial and cultural needs – for example, by ensuring that they had contact with people of their own community. Even fewer plans dealt with helping black youngsters develop strategies for dealing with racism. Overall, in only 16 instances was a plan related to race and culture recorded. Of these only nine were fully or mostly implemented. If we exclude those cases where the young person is white, the proportions do not improve markedly; rising only to 34 per cent of cases. For those for whom plans on promoting links are particularly important – young people who are black and who were living away from home – plans were recorded in only one in three cases.

Failure to take due account of ethnicity, religion, culture and language in the assessment process may have important consequences in the subsequent outcomes for the young people. However it should also be said that not all the young people whom we interviewed attached importance to race in quite this way. It may be that this is due to 'false consciousness' or because they have grown up in a multicultural society in a way that is still not true for many older professionals. Whatever the reason, this reflects the conclusions from a study of young people's views on choice and control within the care system (Gardner, 1987). Furthermore, where disagreements with family revolve around cultural issues, this adds to the complexity of the situation.

The nature of the assessment process had no influence on these results; almost identical proportions of Referred and Routine cases had no plan or had plans related to race and cultural needs that were not fully implemented.

Social work contact with young people

The final area of decision making that we consider is that of contact between the social worker and the young person and their family. We noted in Chapter 8 the surprisingly limited time which social workers spent with young people during the assessment. Similarly, during the follow-up period there was a substantial lack of social work input in many cases, due to changes of social worker and periods when cases remained unallocated. The priority given to planning the appropriate level of social work contact with young people is demonstrated by the fact that following assessment no plan for this was recorded for almost one in three cases, and that where plans were made only 58 per cent were implemented fully or in most respects.

Of course levels of social work contacts need to be flexible, with the worker responding to any changes in need as they arise; but the young person, and their carers, must be aware of the overall level of contact that they can expect from their social worker. Interestingly, in response to questions on the nature of social work contact, just over half (53 per cent) of social workers said they saw the young person on a routine basis, although a substantial minority, over a quarter, only had contact following a crisis for the young person.

The actual amount of contact which social workers had with young people was measured over the previous four-week period for the 56 cases still open. In 17 instances (30 per cent) the social worker had not seen the young person at all in the previous four weeks; in 25 instances (45 per cent) the young person had been seen once or twice and in 14 cases (25 per cent) the young person had seen the social worker more than three times. Young people's views about contact with their social worker was variable: some felt this was adequate or that they could see the worker more if they wished; others complained about the inaccessibility of workers and a difficulty in confiding in them.

'I don't often phone my social worker, but I see her often; yesterday she took me and my sister out to lunch.' (Young person)

'I don't know how often I see my social worker – she gets in touch with me sometimes and sometimes we talk on the phone. But actually I don't really like talking to my social worker – I'm just not used to talking to people like that.' (Young person)

This chapter has documented the circumstances of this group of approximately 75 young people, one year after their assessment. It has noted changes during the follow-up period and analysed the extent to which the plans made following assessment have in fact been implemented. The conclusions on this will be taken forward into the next chapter as one measure used to assess the outcomes from social services assessment for this sample of young people.

Summary points

- A quarter of cases were no longer open a year after assessment. A further eight were receiving no services.
- Of the 18 closed cases, only one of these had done so positively and in accordance with the social work plan. In most cases that closed, young people had initiated this themselves, feeling that the service being offered was not proving helpful.
- Forty per cent of cases were unallocated to a social worker during some stage of our follow-up, most of them in excess of three months. In addition, in almost a third there was a change of social worker.
- In retrospect, 45 per cent of social workers felt the assessment had been 'useful' or 'very useful'.
- Comparing assessment accommodation plans with the actual situation 12 months on, more young people were living at home or with relatives; many fewer were in foster care and more in residential care than planned; and few of the plans for semi-independent accommodation had materialised or succeeded. Overall, about half the accommodation plans had been fulfilled.
- Particular problems came in finding suitable long-term foster placements.
- Residential assessments did not recommend disproportionately subsequent residential placements. Nonetheless, residential care played a very significant role: well over half the sample had experienced a residential placement in the follow-up period.
- Most young people had at least two changes of placement or caretaker during the follow-up period. Two young people had more than eight changes.
- In only a third of cases were educational plans met 'fully' or 'in most respects'. Two young people in every five had changed school during the follow-up. A similar proportion had been excluded or absent from school at some stage, mostly for periods longer than three months. Of the 27 school leavers, its seems that only four sat any GCSEs.
- Encouragingly, levels of contact with parents and other family members had increased over the year. The quality of relation-

ships was also felt to have improved. However, this was not always attributable to professional input, as in two-fifths of cases of young people living away from home, contacts with family did not feature in social work plans.

- Young people's contacts with others of the same ethnic background was a complex area. Nonetheless, few care plans made reference to continuing links with the young person's own community: for those from minority ethnic groups it was only one in three.

- No plans for contact between the social worker and the young person were recorded in almost one in three cases, and that where plans were made, just over half were implemented fully or in most respects.

11. The outcomes of assessment

Introduction

In Chapter 3 we discussed the definitions that we would use to examine the outcomes from the assessment process. Using the terminology developed by Parker and colleagues, these are mainly service and professional outcomes, together with some indications of the outcome for the young person as perceived by the social worker (Parker and others, 1991). The examination of service outcomes is the first step in using research to identify lessons that can lead to practice development. If social services departments have intervened to help young people, it is important to know whether they are successful in following through their intended actions and what helps or hinders that process. Equally importantly, we must know what impact this has on the lives of the young people. So in this chapter we examine outcomes through the responses to a set of five questions. These are:

- to what extent were the plans which were agreed at the young person's final assessment meeting implemented; were there any components of these plans which were more likely to be implemented than others;
- what does the young person's current health, behaviour and well-being tell us about the impact of these plans;
- how do social workers view the young person's overall circumstances a year after assessment; compared to a year earlier, how do they regard the balance between the positive and negative features;
- what is the social worker's overall prognosis for the young person's well-being over the next five years;
- how far, in the view of the social worker, have the needs of the young person and the family been met in the past year; what contribution have social services made to meeting those needs?

Each of these measures of outcomes will be examined in turn.

Plans and their implementation

Scrutinising the extent to which the recommendations of an assessment are successfully implemented may seem an obvious way to monitor the effectiveness of social services intervention with a young person and their family (Buist and Mapstone, 1985). However such data must be interpreted with great care. In examining their implementation it is important to remember that these decisions will have been made in order to solve what is already, by definition, a problem situation. Social workers are aware that the plans that they make are often far from ideal but they may well be the best possible in the particular circumstances (Packman with Randall and Jacques, 1986). Planning for an individual child always involves a balancing of positives and negatives. In this sense the outcomes from these decisions will always have to be qualified. As Whittaker and colleagues say:

> Rather than think in terms of 'success', it is better and nearer to reality, to think in terms of a pattern of gains and losses or costs and benefits. (Whittaker, 1987)

Similarly, using the implementation of plans as a measure of 'success' needs to be treated with caution. Below we give just six ways in which a simple analysis could be misleading, together with brief case illustrations.

- non-implementation of a plan does not always mean that a child's welfare was not promoted and the outcome advantageous;

  Three brothers who had arrived in England from Ethiopia as unaccompanied refugees were assessed and a plan made for long-term care in a foster home. Unexpectedly, following a coup, their father was released from prison and an uncle arrived to take them home to Africa.

- in complex cases it is possible that the successful implementation of one decision can hinder or mitigate against the implementation of other decisions;

  In line with the plan agreed with two siblings, the social worker facilitated renewed contact between the young people and their father. However this resulted in their mother refusing to see them, thereby making the plan to maintain contact with mother impossible to achieve.

- despite the best intentions of the social worker, implementation may not necessarily improve the outcome for the young person;

A young person with no family in this country was placed, as planned, in a long-term foster home, carefully chosen for cultural appropriateness. Shortly afterwards the foster carers went on extended holiday. This necessitated several moves to other carers, which resulted in serious depression in the young person.

- where, due to the passage of time and the natural maturation of the young person, the original plan becomes irrelevant;

A 16 year-old young woman was placed in an assessment foster home, following an incident of physical abuse by her father. The agreed plan was to remain in care, in a community foster placement. When no placement was forthcoming, over the months the young person re-established contact with her family and developed a stable relationship with her boyfriend. Despite the agreed plan, the young person moved to live with her boyfriend and discharged herself from the care of the local authority.

- using the implementation of decisions as a measure of effectiveness may fail to highlight sufficiently those situations where no plan has been made and this is a significant factor in the adverse outcome for the young person;

J's mother is white and father black. The social worker reported that J regards himself as white and refuses to acknowledge his Jamaican background. When J was assessed the concern was around his neglect; no decisions were made regarding his racial identity. At follow-up the social worker reported that issues of racial identity were causing concern – this should have been addressed earlier but was on the agenda for the next review.

- where there is a change in circumstances which is genuinely outside the control of the social worker;

A young man was received into care as his mother was neglecting him, he was out of her control and he was not attending school. The plan to place in foster care had not been implemented when his father reappeared on the scene; the education department, unexpectedly, recommended a weekly residential boarding school placement, which was now acceptable as father could provide weekend care.

Noting these limitations on the use of implementation of decisions as an evaluative measure does not in any way diminish the importance of care planning (Social Services Inspectorate, 1989; Department of Health, 1991a). Indeed the highly dynamic lives of these young people which makes necessary a more sophisticated monitoring of implementation, is itself a cause for careful, if flexible, care planning.

Not only must there be clear procedures for making decisions, equally important is the need for effort to be directed at ensuring that decisions are implemented, or if necessary, new decisions agreed in a structured way (Sinclair, 1984). In this Authority the AAS had a clear mechanism for the review of assessment decisions during the period of its involvement. Outside of this, individual supervision and the six-monthly statutory review were the only mechanisms for monitoring decision implementation; these appeared to have much less impetus than the system for decision taking. This is an issue that is still likely to be relevant in the post-Children Act era, if the drawing up of Care Plans and periodic Reviews are not integrated into a continuous planning process.

Returning to the issue of decision implementation, bearing in mind the above caveats, what does this study tell us about the implementation of decisions as a measure of outcomes, from a professional perspective? In the previous chapter we examined decision implementation in six key areas: accommodation; legal status; education or employment; contact with family; links with people from the same ethnic group; and contact with social worker. The extent of decision implementation was assessed both by the researchers and the social worker and any notable differences in these judgements were reported. Here, in summarising those results, we shall use the researchers' judgement of the extent to which plans made after an assessment were successfully implemented. This summary is presented in Table 11.1.

Within these six key topics areas there was major variation in the extent to which decisions were actually made. For instance, in just 6 per cent of cases were no plans recorded in relation to accommodation, while this was true three times out of four in respect of decisions to maintain links between the young person and their ethnic community. This variation in the proportions in the 'no plan' category tends to distort the information on decision implementation. To gain a better understanding of the actual level of implementation of those decisions which were made, the 'no plan' and 'missing data' figures have been removed and the statistics have been presented in this revised format in Table 11.2. Here the columns will comprise differing numbers of cases, reflecting the number of cases which had recorded decisions in each topic area.

Table 11.1 Pattern of decision making and implementation (percentages) (n = 75)

	Legal Status	Accommodation	Education	Contact with Family	Racial Identity	Contact with Social Workers	Total
Fully implemented	45.4	25.3	24.0	10.7	2.7	25.3	22.2
Implemented in most respects	9.3	18.6	10.7	12.0	9.3	13.3	12.2
Partially implemented	4.0	22.7	17.3	10.7	4.0	22.7	13.6
Not implemented at all	16.0	22.7	20.0	14.6	5.3	8.0	14.4
No plan	25.3	6.7	26.7	52.0	76.0	28.0	35.8
Missing Data	0.0	4.0	1.3	0.0	2.7	2.7	1.8
Total	**100.0**	**100.0**	**100.0**	**100.0**	**100.0**	**100.0**	**100.0**

Table 11.2 Decision implementation in instances where decisions were made (percentages)

	Legal Status	Accommodation	Education	Contact with Family	Racial Identity	Contact with Social Workers	Total
Fully implemented	60.7	28.3	33.3	22.2	12.5	36.6	35.6
Implemented in most respects	12.5	20.9	14.8	25	43.7	19.2	19.6
Partially implemented	5.4	25.4	24.1	22.2	18.8	32.7	21.7
Not implemented at all	21.4	25.4	27.8	30.6	25	11.5	23.1
Total	**100.0**	**100.0**	**100.0**	**100.0**	**100.0**	**100.0**	**100.0**
n =	56	67	54	36	16	42	

Three main conclusions can be drawn from these tables:

- there are major gaps in decision making;
- there is a disappointing lack of decision implementation;
- the form of assessment has little impact on decision implementation.

There are major gaps in decision making in particular areas
More than a quarter of the assessments contained no legal status plan or plan for education; over a half had no plan recorded for contact with the family and over three-quarters of care plans made no mention of working to promote racial identity, for instance, through contact between the young person and others from the same ethnic community.

In the previous chapter we discussed possible explanations for this – for instance, legal status was often implicit and inferred from decisions about placement; decisions about contact with family and links with the community were seen as necessary only when the young person was living away from home. Nonetheless failure to make comprehensive plans was still a common feature of these assessment processes. Similar findings were found by the Social Services Inspectorate in a summary of inspections in 11 authorities. Although overall the inspections did find most children had written plans:

> they were often not very specific on the particular objectives of placement, nor did they identify the specific ways in which children's needs were to be met ... many lacked clear aims, objectives, allocation of responsibilities, and timescales. (Social Services Inspectorate, 1993a)

Where decisions were made, there is a disappointing level of implementation, particularly in relation to accommodation and education.

In less than half of those cases where decisions had been made relating to accommodation and education, was the decision implemented fully or in most respects. Fuller analysis of this was presented in the previous chapter. This finding raises three important considerations about decision implementation.

Firstly, the key question of the link between assessment of needs and the availability of resources. The whole concept of assessment of need, rightly in our view, assumes a 'needs-led' rather than 'resource-led' approach to decision taking (Department of Health, 1991h). However what this study shows is that this can lead to decisions – particularly those relating to long-term foster care and places in special schools – that may be unrealistic in their time-scale or in their assumptions about resource availability. Ideally, the making of individual care plans on the basis of assessed needs will, in the longer term, result in the creation of appropriate resources, especially if planning mechanisms enable individual needs to be aggregated into an estimate of overall demand for particular resources. (The report of a working party on the priorities for management information under the Children Act considers these issues more fully (Social Information Services, 1989).) In the interim, however, difficulty in finding resources to fulfil agreed plans can cause uncertainty and instability, which can be very detrimental for the young person. This difficulty in gaining access to resources is exacerbated where social services staff experience problems in working productively with other agencies (see Malek, 1993).

This leads to our second point. We have already mentioned that much less effort and fewer mechanisms are directed at ensuring that decisions are implemented in comparison to that given to assessment and decision taking. It is evident that this is particularly true where decision implementation is dependent on the actions of practitioners outside social services. Although the social worker carries overall responsibility for implementing plans, they often have limited knowledge and control over the progress being made towards implementation when this involves services from other agencies. Perhaps this is something that will be addressed in the new era of the contract culture when services will have to be demanded, supplied and monitored in a more formal way.

The third general point we would make is the importance of continuity of case management. Many of these young people were subject to changes in social worker and to considerable periods when their cases were unallocated. Inevitably this leads to a lack of impetus in getting decisions implemented.

The form of assessment had limited impact on the pattern of decision implementation.

A key variable in this research is the type of assessment – Referred or Routine. The information on decision making and implementation has been further analysed according to assessment type. This is summarised in Tables 11.3 and 11.4, which follow the same format as that used in Tables 11.1 and 11.2, but with the additional breakdown by Routine or Referred assessment. Table 11.3 summarises the pattern of decision making and implementation for each type of assessment and Table 11.4 shows the level of implementation for decisions that were made. As before, the

Table 11.3   Pattern of decision making and implementation, by type of assessment (percentage) (n = 75)

	Legal Status		Accommodation		Education		Contact with Family		Racial Identity		Contact with Social Workers		Total	
	A	B	A	B	A	B	A	B	A	B	A	B	A	B
Fully implemented	43.5	47.2	12.8	38.9	28.2	19.4	15.3	5.6	0.0	5.5	20.5	30.6	20.1	24.5
Implemented in most respects	15.4	2.8	25.6	11.1	7.7	13.9	18.0	5.6	7.7	11.1	12.8	13.9	14.5	9.7
Partially implemented	2.6	5.5	30.8	13.9	20.5	13.9	12.8	8.3	2.5	5.6	20.5	25.0	14.9	12.0
Not implemented at all	18.0	13.9	20.5	25.0	20.5	19.4	18.0	11.1	7.7	2.8	5.1	11.1	15.0	13.9
No plan	20.5	30.6	7.7	5.5	23.1	30.6	35.9	69.4	77.0	75.0	36.0	19.4	33.4	38.5
Missing Data	0.0	0.0	2.6	5.6	0.0	2.8	0.0	0.0	5.1	5.1	5.1	0.0	2.1	1.4
Total	**100.0**	*100.0*	**100.0**	*100.0*	**100.0**	*100.0*	**100.0**	*100.0*	**100.0**	*100.0*	**100.0**	*100.0*	**100.0**	*100.0*

Column 'A' – decision making following Referred assessments
Column 'B' – decision making following Routine assessments

Table 11.4   Pattern of implemention for recorded decision by type of assessment (percentages)

	Legal Status		Accommodation		Education		Contact with Family		Links Ethnic		Contact with Social Workers		Total	
	A	B	A	B	A	B	A	B	A	B	A	B	A	B
Fully implemented	54.8	68.0	14.3	43.8	36.6	29.2	24.0	18.2	0.0	22.2	34.8	38.0	31.1	40.7
Implemented in most respects	19.4	4.0	28.6	12.5	10.0	20.8	28.0	18.2	42.9	44.5	21.7	17.2	22.5	16.2
Partially implemented	3.2	8.0	34.3	15.6	26.7	20.0	20.0	27.2	14.2	22.2	34.8	31.0	23.2	20.0
Not implemented at all	22.6	20.0	22.8	28.1	26.7	29.2	28.0	36.4	42.9	11.1	8.7	13.8	23.2	23.1
Total	100.0	100.0	100.0	100.0	100.0	100.0	100.0	100.0	100.0	100.0	100.0	100.0	100.0	100.0

Column 'A' – implementation of decisions recorded following Referred assessment
Column 'B' (italics) – implementation of decisions recorded following Routine assessment

number of cases in each of the columns in this later table will be variable. Decisions following a Referred assessment are labelled 'A' and those following a Routine assessment are labelled 'B' and shown in italics.

While these tables do show some differences, overall the pattern of decision implementation is very similar for the two types of assessment. Because of the small numbers in some cells, often due to the lack of plans in certain areas, it is not possible to carry out tests of statistical significance on all the decision making areas. However where this is possible, for instance, in the key areas of accommodation and education, there is *no statistically significant difference between Referred and Routinely assessed cases in the pattern of decision implementation.*

In following these cases for one year after assessment, it is evident that as time passes the quality of case work and case management by the social worker becomes a more important determining factor in the outcome for the young person than any differences in the assessment process. This is not to say that the assessment process is not important in the making of clear and appropriate plans, but its direct influence on outcomes is considerably weaker as time passes.

Factors associated with decision implementation

So far we have concentrated on the reasons why decisions have not been implemented, but of course almost half of all decisions taken were implemented. Previous chapters have pointed to positive aspects of the assessment process which have contributed to this. In reviewing this at follow-up, using quantitative measures of service provision supported by qualitative responses, it is possible to identify four factors which were most commonly associated with decision implementation and positive outcomes for the young people. These are:

- continuing input from a social worker, ideally allocation of the same social worker;
- persistence by the social worker in pursuing the objectives of the plan on behalf of the young person;
- an ability by the social worker or other workers actively to engage with the young person and their family and to undertake direct work with them;
- a lack of dependence by social workers on input from professionals from other agencies.

The case study below provides an illustration of the application of these factors.

Case study 11.1

Eleven year-old P and his 12 year-old sister were Wards of Court. Their mother was very depressed, never leaving home, often not getting up. She was refusing access to all social workers, of whom she was very distrustful. (Essentially this was because her eldest daughter had been taken into care with what the social worker acknowledged was appalling case management by the department.) Neither child was attending school regularly and both were admitted to care for a short period when their mother couldn't cope. Consistent visiting and direct work by the social worker built trust with the mother, helped her with rehousing, enabled the children to return home, and encouraged her to get the children to school. When the mother moved house, she had great difficulty getting the children accepted into a new school. The social worker persisted in her advocacy on behalf of the children until school places were found. The children settled well and attended regularly. At the Court hearing the Wardship was replaced by a one year supervision order; the intention at follow-up was to allow the S.O. to lapse and to close the case.

Positive outcomes were not only more likely when the social worker acted positively as an advocate for the young person, but also when they enabled the young person to articulate their wishes and feelings.

Case study 11.2

The consultant psychiatrist regarded Y as 'terminally ill' because of her heroin use, suicide attempts and her high risk lifestyle. She would not remain at the specialist psychiatric assessment unit. The SSD was giving serious consideration to a secure accommodation placement. Y asked to attend the placement panel personally and to request a semi-independent placement. She was supported in this by her social worker. By presenting her case articulately and maturely she convinced the panel to accept her point of view. At follow-up, while she still had problems, she was no longer using heroin and had a much more settled lifestyle.

These findings raise important issues about the relationship between procedures, social work practice and outcomes. They indicate that positive outcomes from social service interventions depend to a significant extent upon the exercise of social work skills, and the development of a relationship between the social worker and young person.

However social work is delivered through an organisational context and, in this instance, as a public service. To provide such services equitably and effectively requires a system of accountability, with clearly stated policies and procedures. However it is also clear that procedures, in themselves, cannot compensate for a lack of basic social work inputs; that a balance must be achieved, both in the service as a whole and at an individual case level, in the emphasis given to planning and managing resources and that given to more traditional case work.

The welfare of the young people one year on

The second measure of outcome that we use is the social workers' assessment of the welfare of each of the young people at follow-up as indicated by their health, their behaviour and any pattern of offending.

Health

There is limited research knowledge about the mental and physical health of young people in care, but most suggests that the physical health needs of young people in particular have been long neglected and given low priority (Kahan, 1989; Bamford and Wolkind, 1988; Polnay, 1994), and that access to mental health services are an increasing problem (AMA, 1994; Kurtz, Thorne and Wolkind, 1994).

When interviewed immediately following assessment, social workers indicated that 33 (44 per cent) of the young people had health problems. There were, however, definite signs that health was less problematic a year later. At this point only seven people were said to have problems related to health, 12 per cent of those for whom information was available. This positive result is supported by the opinion that, of those whose health was thought to have changed during the year, 11 were showing improvement, whereas only two young people were thought to have greater health problems. Some of the improvements in health were due to more stable lifestyles than was apparent at assessment, others to better control over a particular condition.

> 'HH's physical health is much better now he is at the Home. He likes their food arrangements where he can help himself when he likes and now eats like a pig.'

'Now that DM is less likely to run away and live on the streets his general health has improved.'

'AA has her epilepsy under control now, she sees the doctor every three months to monitor her condition.'

The two young people whose health had worsened give cause for concern. (Their case histories are summarised below). In both cases there were delays in finding an appropriate placement and in one this was greatly compounded by a lack of response by the young man and his family to the help that was offered.

Case study 11.3

BB is a refugee from Ethiopia and the plan following assessment was for a long-term foster home. However in the past year that has not become available and BB has had several very unsatisfactory placements. Although she has older siblings in this country, she blocks any attempt to contact her family at home. During the year BB also heard that her father had died in prison. BB's social worker says she is very unhappy and this is manifesting itself in poor sleeping patterns, with many stress-related symptoms, which have resulted in her visiting hospital on several occasions.

Case study 11.4

MB is a highly disturbed young man with a very difficult relationship with his mother. He has been attending the Day Assessment Unit and living at home. Attempts to engage the family in family therapy or therapeutic counselling were not successful. As his behaviour worsened, with more incidents of heavy drinking, depression and self-harm, it was agreed to refer to Child and Adolescent Psychiatry and try and find a placement in a therapeutic community. Neither of these plans had been successfully implemented by follow-up and MB's condition was worsening, including several incidents of firelighting.

In Chapter 9 we discussed the problems of ensuring that psychiatric assessments were completed. In looking at those instances where psychiatric or psychological counselling help was included in the plan, it was apparent that there were considerable problems in persuading young people and their families to take advantage of these services. This negative view of psychiatric and psychological services which is apparent in other studies, is an issue which must be addressed urgently if the real needs of the young people are to be appropriately addressed (see Triseliotis and others, 1994). Neither did there seem to be any consistent monitoring of whether such help was being received and an alternative service offered if necessary. A similar feeling of lost opportunity comes from the report by Farmer and Parker (1991):

> social workers often faced an uphill task in securing the assistance of other agencies, but the records also suggested that in many instances steps were not taken to explore these possibilities ... some in our group are very difficult and disturbed. Yet there was little evidence that attempts had been made to provide or to encourage them to accept therapeutic help.

Even if such encouragements were given, there is no certainty that services would be available. There is now extreme worry in many quarters about the disarray in mental health services for young people (AMA, 1994; Kurtz, Thornes and Wolkind, 1994).

> There is widespread anecdotal evidence that services for the prevention, assessment and management of mental health problems in children and young people may be diminishing or even disintegrating. (Department of Health, 1993c)

Offending

It is apparent from the previous chapter that the data collected on the sample group at follow-up was variable in its completeness. However this was not true of the offending record, even in those instances where cases were closed to social services. Case files appeared to have complete and accurate accounts of recorded offences, much of this originating from the Police or the Courts.

During this follow-up period 21 (28 per cent) of the group of 75 had committed at least one offence. Overall this is marginally higher than at round one where 20 young people had committed offences in the previous year. Obviously some young people will have offended in both time periods, however taking the two years together, 44 (59 per cent) of the group of 75 young people had committed no offences at all. Eleven of those who had not committed any offences at the point of assessment had offended by follow-up. However, on the plus side, exactly half of those who had offended previously did not offend again in the second year.

How do we assess these findings? The first point to make is that the sample were of an age when offending activities is likely to be high. The modal age of our sample was 15 at assessment and 16 at follow-up; the modal age of female offending and for all car related crime is 15 years; the modal age of all offending is 18 and for juvenile offending it is 17 years (House of Commons Home Affairs Committee, 1993). Statistics produced by the Home Office show that, in 1991, 8.7 per cent of all 14 to 16 year-old young men were known to have offended and 12.3 per cent of all 17 year-old youths had offended. The equivalent figures for young women were 2.3 per cent and 2.2 per cent (ibid).

The offending rate of the sample is therefore higher than the overall population. However, young people looked after by the local authority are more likely to have committed offences than other young people; for many, offending behaviour is a significant factor in bringing them to the attention of social services, whether as contributing to unstable home relationships or because they have been remanded to care. Surprisingly, given the level of concern, there are no official statistics on the offending behaviour of young people in the care system. However, statistics prepared by Birmingham Social Services Department for a recent enquiry showed that 13 per cent of those young people aged 10 to 17 who had resided in residential care in the current year had appeared in court charged with an offence (Birmingham SSD, 1993). These figures differ from those for our sample in two ways – the age range is wider and it takes into account only appearances in Court when charged with offences – both these factors would suggest that our research group could be expected to have a higher proportion of offenders than that reported for Birmingham. A study of adolescents placed 'home on trial' showed a rate of offending of 55 per cent, which was higher than that for this group of adolescents (Farmer and Parker, 1991).

While the pattern of offending during the follow-up period can be regarded as relatively positive overall, for a small number of the sample group offending was a serious problem. Table 11.5 shows the number of recorded offences committed by the young people in the year prior to the follow-up point.

Table 11.5 Offences committed in the previous year

Number of offences	Number
0	54
1 or 2	8
3–6	7
7–9	4
10+	2
Total	75

For most of the young people their offences were relatively minor, generally theft or car related offences. However, one young man in the group had committed several minor infringements, followed by the serious offence of rape and was now serving a Section 53 Order in a Secure Unit. He was among the small group who had committed multiple offences and, for two of these, the number of offences recorded in the year had reached double figures. These are very much the group of 'persistent offenders' that are causing the Home Secretary such concern (see *Hansard*, 11 January 1994) although when one reads their case details it is the complexity and longstanding nature of their problems which stands out.

Case study 11.5

LM, a 14 year-old African-Caribbean young man, was received into care for assessment as his father was no longer able to cope with his disruptive and offending behaviour. (There had been two referrals in previous years but these had never been followed-up.) The plan following assessment was for a weekday placement in an adolescent psychiatric unit for a full psychiatric assessment. However this placement was a long time coming and in the meantime LM had four placements, two in residential units in the Authority, two in regional resources, none of which was able to respond to his behaviour problems and mental health concerns. When at last LM did get a place in the psychiatric unit he was unable to settle and was moved to a P & V therapeutic unit which also failed. Another temporary placement in a children's home followed. At follow-up he was placed in a specialist private resource for black young people where it was hoped he would get appropriate psychiatric help.

LM had once been attending a special EBD day school, but the request for a review of his education Statement was never enacted, nor were any steps taken by the education department when he failed to attend the special educational unit as planned. During this period LM had continued to offend, always with others, when he is stressed or under pressure from his peers. To date these had been relatively minor offences, but he was awaiting a Court hearing for a further burglary and for carrying an offensive weapon.

When asked about the prognosis for this young man his social worker, perhaps not surprisingly, was cautious: 'He is now in a very appropriate placement to which he is committed, and for the moment is settled. If he remains there long enough and can accept the help on offer, then the potential for saving him from a very destructive road is still there'. Looking back the social worker has no doubt that the weekday placement was wrong and that a therapeutic community should have been planned and found sooner.

Case study 11.6

GM, a white young man, had been known to social services for most of his life. He had had an educational Statement at the age of eight and had been at a residential EBD school. He was admitted to care at 15 years having been excluded from his school some months earlier; was alleging his father was physically abusing him, and he was at risk of self-harm. He was an extremely anxious young man with very poor self-esteem; his relationship with his parents was not good; he was described as a laughing-stock among his peers and was prone to making intense, inappropriate relationships.

He was placed in a specialist P & V assessment unit. This unit could not manage him so, according to the social worker 'they drove him to London and dumped him on the doorstep'. In his first year in care he had four placements, including a regional resource. None of these were able to deal with his self-destructive behaviour and he was absent frequently. He was also receiving some help from the IT section of the Authority and from Child Psychiatry. The assessment plan at this point was for him to remain in care and to move into bed and breakfast with preparation for independence. GM had made it clear he did not want another residential establishment, nor could any be found that would accept him.

One year on the outlook was bleak: his behaviour had deteriorated; his offending had increased; he has had two spells in secure units and one in youth custody. Although GM was on a full care order, his case remained unallocated for almost six months after his social worker left. He has moved around from various 'B and Bs', and returned to his father's home for several short stays. SSD found him a place in a Probation and Bail Hostel, but he would not stay. Shortly after this follow-up interview he was sent to a Young Offender Institution.

Behaviour problems

Social workers were asked whether the young people had exhibited any of a given list of behaviour problems during the previous year. These particular problems were chosen because of their use in other studies and in widely used assessment schedules (Hoghughi, 1980). Their responses are shown in Table 11.6.

Before commenting on this table it is worth reflecting on the way in which social workers responded to this question. First, many felt that they would not necessarily be aware if the young person had any of these problems.

> 'I've seen her "high" (on drugs) once, but I don't know how much of a feature this is of her life. I wouldn't rule it out as a problem, but she denies it.'

Second, these responses inevitably contain a large element of subjective assessment and so social workers varied in their judgement of when certain behaviours could be regarded as a problem. For instance, how much or how often does a young person have to be drinking alcohol for this to be regarded as a problem. Similarly most did record a positive response to drug abuse if they thought that the young person was smoking cannabis, but not all would have regarded this as a behaviour problem.

Overall this represents fewer behaviour problems than reported at round 1, but of more interest to assessing outcomes is the extent to which these problems have lessened or grown worse for individual children. Looking, for example, at those young people who were known to have attempted suicide or caused injury to themselves either at round 1 or round 2, then there is some overlap between those identified in the two time-periods: half the young people noted to have problems at round 1 continued to have these problems during the follow-up year, while others had found a way out of this pattern of behaviour.

Table 11.6 Behaviour problems identified by social workers

Behaviour problems	Number
Suicide attempts	3
Self-injury	6
Prescribed drug abuse	1
Drug misuse	10
Solvent or alcohol abuse	9
General behaviour problems	20

Case study 11.7

Q was known to social services virtually from birth and had a history of very inconsistent care from her mother. She had several earlier periods in care before being admitted on a full Care Order at the age of 11. In the intervening years she had over ten placements. According to the social worker 'She has never had a planned placement in her life'. She was admitted several times to hospital because of overdosing; the psychiatric prognosis was very gloomy and there was some talk about whether she was 'sectionable'. Q's behaviour was very aggressive and abusive, and she frequently went missing. It became almost impossible to complete the assessment because of responding to constant crisis. At this time it was felt that the only two options left were 'B and B' or to try another regional resource. It was decided that 'B and B' was too risky, largely because of her perceived vulnerability, as a girl, so she went to the regional resource. At this time the only positive factor seems to be that Q still attended her educational unit regularly. At follow-up, she was reported to have settled down; to have matured and learned to articulate her anger rather than to 'lash out'. She was still in the same placement and was maintaining her educational progress.

What helped to break the previous very destructive pattern? The residential placement did not have any extra or specific resources compared to others that had failed. While she did have some relationship problems within the unit, there were enough positive aspects to enable them to hold on to her for long enough to assist her to settle down. Her commitment to education was very important and something that could be built upon. Finding a residential resource where staff had the skills necessary to engage with the young person long enough for them to work with her, helped to break the previous destructive pattern.

The behaviours we have listed here, characterised by a self-destructiveness, are often the hardest for social workers to deal with. For some of those who have attempted suicide or who have injured themselves, this is a longstanding pattern of behaviour (Bullock, Little and Millham, 1991). Indeed of the six young people who had inflicted self-injury in the follow-up period, five had had a period of residence at a regional resource and the sixth was currently awaiting a place in a therapeutic community. All had been referred for psychiatric assessment but, as explained earlier, these were rarely completed.

As we shall see in Chapter 12, when we consider the relationship between the costs of assessment and outcomes, this study does indicate that young people with the greatest needs were being offered appropriate resources, often expensive specialist residential care, although this did not always result in improved outcomes.

Some research has argued that the services offered to young people with challenging behaviours by the different agencies – health, education, social services, justice – can be somewhat arbitrary (Malek, 1993; Grimshaw with Berridge, 1994). One service manager in the research Authority saw it thus:

> 'With a young person with very challenging behaviours, what tends to happen is we will either be very passive and we will run away from the child, and the child will make the running by their own behaviours. Or we will get anxious and we'll play it by the book and probably take over-severe action; so you get where the kids are in bed and breakfast or they're in secure units and actually they're completely interchangeable – and that's a nonsense.' (Service Manager)

We have already had a glimpse at the events in the life of GM (see page 234), leading eventually to his imprisonment. Two further case summaries are presented here. In many ways these three cases illustrate the range of options that are available to meet the needs of disturbed adolescents – a therapeutic community; minimal support in the community, having tried everything else; and the input of specialist help while the young person remains at home.

Case study 11.8

MA had been in care, as a Ward of Court, since she was ten years old. Although originally placed with a relative, this placement ended as did the next two, due to MA's behaviour; she was using drugs and was violent to herself and others. She was placed in a regional resource unit, with continued input from a psychiatric assessment unit. The assessment decision was to seek a placement in a therapeutic community, which was achieved with minimum delay. MA has settled and will remain at the therapeutic community until she is 18.

Case study 11.9

MB, a small white youth, was 11 years old when referred for assessment following a request by his mother that he should be received into care. He had had two previous periods in care and some family therapy after which the case had closed. As before, his mother was requesting care because she felt she had no control over him; he was not attending school and was consistently running away to stay at his father's or sister's home.

Following assessment, the decision was that MB should remain at home, which was what he wanted, with help from the DAU and family therapy. However over the summer MB did not attend any of the DAU activities, he was very depressed and began to self-harm. A referral was made to a psychiatrist for a full assessment, but this was not followed-up. As his situation deteriorated, a planning meeting in September agreed that he should be placed in a therapeutic community. At follow-up more than six months later, MB was still at home awaiting a long-term placement. His situation had deteriorated with further incidence of drinking and self-harm.

Of these three cases only MA could be said to have a positive outcome from the plan agreed. Again we note our earlier proposition that there are four factors which appear to be related to successful implementation of plans: consistent input and persistent advocacy on behalf of the social worker; ability of staff to engage with the young person; and limited dependence on professionals from other disciplines and agencies – and of course the corollary applies, cases which lack these factors are more likely to lead to poor outcomes.

Broad-based outcome measures

Having identified particular problem areas, social workers were also asked, as a broad-based assessment of outcome, whether they felt in respect of behaviour, health, and emotional problems, that the young person was better, worse or much the same as a year earlier (see Table 11.7).

Table 11.7 Broad-based assessment of outcome

	Behaviour	Health	Emotional development
Better	20	11	26
Worse	10	2	4
Much the same	24	42	20
Number of responses	54	55	50

In addition, social workers were asked to look at the young people in the round and to say, in general, whether they felt their situation had more positive features or more negative ones, or whether these were equally balanced compared to a year earlier. The responses are shown in Table 11.8.

Table 11.8 The balance in positive and negative features

Judgement of current situation	Number
More positives	34
More negatives	9
Equally balanced	8
Child since died	1
Cannot judge	16
Number of responses	68

Taken together these are encouraging responses. In these key areas of welfare, compared to a year previously, significantly more young people were judged to be faring better now and, in general, social workers were able to say they had more going for them than going against them. In general the group of unaccompanied refugee children coped well in the follow-up period, as illustrated below.

Case study 11.10

Two teenage sisters, T and A, arrived in Britain from Ethiopia as unaccompanied refugees. They stayed at first at a refugee centre where the other young people were Eritrean. This was clearly inappropriate. The social worker allocated to the case throughout fought hard to have the sisters received into care and supported by the Authority and was successful in finding a suitable long-term foster placement. At follow-up the sisters were very settled in the foster home and doing well at school – A was sitting GCSEs and was intending to stay on at school. Although T and A had no contact with their family and didn't wish any to be made, the social worker maintained contact with the Refugee Relief Society and their worker brought news from the girls' home country. Both sisters made friends with other Ethiopian young people in the community.

However in nine instances the outcomes were seen to be more negative. We examined these cases closely to see if there was any discernible pattern to them. All were living away from home in a variety of situations; the majority were boys (seven males, two females) but the causes of their more negative situation were very varied. Three were due to a breakdown in the relationship with home, and father in particular; three related to the consequences of continued offending; and another was a refugee child who had no family and who had a very unhappy experience in foster care. One young person was now completely out of school; and for another his mental health had deteriorated. In most of these cases, although not all, with hindsight the social worker thought things could have been done differently. *In none of these cases did the social worker see the poor outcomes related to the actual decision that was taken at assessment; rather it was to do with the failure or delay in mobilising resources to implement agreed decisions.* Additionally, in two instances social workers recognised a failure to deal with the young person's emotional problems and questioned whether a fuller assessment at an earlier point in time would have helped.

Without diminishing the less than successful outcomes in these cases, they do represent only a small proportion of the total group, and must not overshadow the gains that have been achieved for the majority of the sample. Given this fairly optimistic assessment of the current position, what prognosis did the social workers have for the future of these young people? Many found it almost impossible to predict the outcome for the young person five years ahead; the pattern indicated by summaries of the responses is provided in Table 11.9.

Table 11.9   Looking ahead five years

Prognosis	Number
Very good	3
Good	14
Alright	8
Not good/bad	15
Uncertain	11
Missing data	24
Total	75

In analysing the reasons for these prognoses, it becomes clear that the key variable in predicting a favourable outcome on the part of the social worker was stability; not only *stability* in placement, but more important in emotional state.

'DD is now in a permanent, caring foster home, with black foster carers who are helping him deal with uncertainties over his family. He is doing well at school. It is hard to see what can go wrong; the only little concern is a flirtation on the fringes of the law, but hopefully this is the normal teenage thing.' (Social worker)

In contrast it is apparent from the case files and talking to social workers, that the factor which most often lay behind a poor outlook was unresolved relationship and emotional problems leading to continuing patterns of destructive behaviour.

'I don't think he will develop emotionally at all; how much anger and resentment will come out in the future is uncertain. I don't think the outlook is good; I think he will get depressed and wouldn't fulfil his potential.' (Social worker)

Many social workers recognised the very limited help they felt that they could offer to older adolescents in this situation.

'I felt that there wasn't much that we could do to help him. We have endeavoured to provide options for him and keep him in the community, but he has not followed-up on this. We have provided accommodation and IT; he has had money from us and he continues to see me regularly. So we can provide the basics but cannot deal with the personality. And it is too late to undo the damage that was done to him in the early years. I'm not confident that we can do anything now beyond meeting his basic needs. It's sad but I feel he is a lost cause.' (Social worker)

Again this raises the question of whether more help could have been offered earlier and the role of assessment in identifying what help, if any, could have been more effective. This leads to the final measure of outcome used in this study, namely the role of social services in these outcomes for this group of young people.

The social services contribution

Having examined the situation of the sample group one year after their assessment, the final important question is how much of this can be regarded, legitimately, as a result of social work support, or indeed a lack of input from social workers or other professionals; how much occurred despite social workers; and how much was due to changing circumstances and natural maturation. Social workers were asked, for each case, what contribution they thought social services had made to the young person's current situation. On its own, of course, this will not give us objective assessment, but it is an additional perspective which can be added to those already employed. Moreover the social workers did appear to be fairly frank in their responses – which was perhaps easier as many were referring to the contribution of the department as a whole or to previous workers.

First, a summary of social workers' responses. Perhaps the most important point to make is that no-one felt that social services intervention had actually made the young person's situation worse. One-third felt that the contribution of social services had made little or no difference to the young person's current situation; 'not a lot'; 'bugger all'; 'a roof over her head, nothing else'. For several others the main contribution of social services was to provide income maintenance or some sort of placement, but with little other support.

'She viewed the social services positively, although she only came to us in a crisis when she was out on the streets or in trouble with the police. We supported her financially, but she didn't want any other sort of contact and wouldn't attend any meetings, or accept the offer of counselling.'

But it is important not to underestimate this contribution, when the alternatives may be worse. It may be as much as the young person wants or can handle and it gives some support while the young person is still maturing.

'We have prevented him from deteriorating – he would be homeless and penniless without us – so we have met his material needs. We have also kept his family alive for him, but otherwise we have not met his emotional needs as he hasn't been able to make use of the support we offered.'

Given the situation with which they are presented, staff in social services have to be realistic about what they can hope to achieve – what may seem to some to be small victories can have a significant impact for the young person. The social worker for the young man found guilty of rape felt that social services had made a positive contribution to his present situation, as shown in the following quotation.

'F would be in a Young Offender Institution if we hadn't intervened – now he is in Secure Accommodation and he shall still receive support from us. He has got a lot of support from his family, especially his mother and brother – that may not have been there if we had not intervened to encourage it.'

Two-thirds of respondents felt that social services had made some or a lot of difference to the young person.

'We have provided her with a stable family life with foster carers that she enjoys; we are holding the situation together for her; we manage it and the foster parents do all the work; the social worker is another person that she can talk to about her family and foster family.'

'We prevented a Care Order being made on all four children and enabled the family to stay together and to get rehoused.'

Overall the considered comments from social workers on each of
these cases suggest that the Social Services Department did make
a significant contribution to the relatively positive outcomes for
young people that have been reported in this study.

In summary, the outcomes for this group of 75 young people
inevitably show a high degree of variation; some are more settled
and secure than a year previously, while for a few there are significant needs which have not been met. However, overall the picture
must be regarded as relatively positive.

What is more difficult to disentangle is the particular contribution to this of the original assessment. Certainly this chapter has
pointed to significant gaps in the plans made following assessment
and only limited success in implementing these plans. However,
despite difference in the procedures for undertaking Referred and
Routine assessment, there were no marked differences in the outcomes between these two groups.

Our sample group were of an age, late adolescence, when we can
expect frequent movement and changes in circumstances and
where young people can be very influential in the decisions that
were made and taken. While this calls for a flexibility in social
work input and service provision, this needs to take place against
a knowledge of the young person, and here assessment has a crucial role to play.

When cases are analysed in more detail, the findings demonstrate that assessment and planning, of themselves, are of limited
value if they are not supported by sufficient good quality social
work, including working directly with the young person to address
their needs.

Summary points

- Caution should be exercised in using the implementation of
  plans as a means of evaluating assessments. Nonetheless,
  major gaps were identified in assessment plans, including regarding legal status, family relationships and contacts with
  others from the same ethnic group.
- There was often a disappointing level of implementation of
  assessment plans, especially in relation to accommodation and
  education. Three issues were seen as important here: the availability of resources; dependence on other professional groups;
  and changes in social workers and/or the unallocation of cases.
- Significantly for this research study, the form of assessment –

whether Referred or Routine – had limited impact on the implementation of decisions.

- Instead, the implementation of decisions seemed to depend more on the quality of social work input than organisational features. Four factors were identified which were related to positive outcomes for young people: continuity of input from a social worker; persistence in pursuing objectives on behalf of young people; in-depth involvement with the young person and their family; and a lack of dependence on contributions from professionals from other agencies.

- This suggests there may be a need to rethink the emphasis given, at both service and case level, to planning and resource management, compared to more traditional casework.

- Social workers were asked to assess the welfare of young people one year after their assessments in three specific areas. First, significant improvements were noted in their general health; however delivering psychiatric and psychological support was problematic. Secondly, there was a slight increase in offending a year later but half of those who had offended previously did not reoffend in the follow-up period. But it should be borne in mind that many in our sample were reaching the peak age for offending and that most infractions were relatively minor. Thirdly, an amelioration in general behaviour problems was reported over the 12 months.

- There were four times as many young people whose general situation was felt to have improved rather than diminished. However the future prognosis was more uncertain.

- Encouragingly, two-thirds of social workers felt that social services involvement had made a positive contribution to the welfare of young people. *No-one* felt that young people had deteriorated as a result of this involvement.

12. The costs of child care assessment

Jennifer Beecham and Martin Knapp[1]

Background

In this penultimate chapter we outline the work and findings relating to the costs of assessment activities. The research in this specialist field has been undertaken by the Personal Social Services Research Unit (PSSRU), University of Kent. From the outset of the research it was felt to be important to incorporate a costs dimension to the study. We live and work increasingly in a costs conscious age and recommendations from research that fail to acknowledge the economic context in which services are provided may be of limited relevance. This aspect of the study builds on many years of costs research by PSSRU, much of it relating to child care and associated activities.

This costs evaluation is designed to address three groups of questions:

- What is the cost of assessment? How is it spread between different agencies and services? These descriptive cost questions will be examined for two time-periods: three months after the event which precipitated assessment for the young person, and 12 months later (that is, 15 months after the event).
- How does the cost of assessment vary between different types of assessment? What, indeed, are the service components which comprise these different assessment types?
- What factors appear to account for the differences in assess-

---

1   This chapter draws on research undertaken by Ruth Sinclair, Louise Garnett and David Berridge at the National Children's Bureau. The authors alone bear responsibility for the results but thanks are extended to Amanda Dansie for her assistance in calculating costs, Andrew Fenyo and Ann Netten for their comments and advice and to David Peters for his early work on the analyses.

ment costs? Also, is there a relationship between costs and outcomes, for example in terms of care careers, and changes therein? Does a high initial investment in assessment pay dividends in terms of lower subsequent costs and better outcomes?

The broad design of the costs study closely followed that of the Bureau approach, allowing description and analysis of the data for 75 young people along similar dimensions of assessment (Referred or Routine), venue (residential, foster care and in the community) and the event which precipitated assessment (considered for care, admitted to care and placement breakdown). Based on information collected by the Bureau researchers, the costs study examines the services received by sample members and their associated costs for the two study periods. A comprehensive approach to costing is taken, which ensures all elements of service packages are included. Whilst broadening the scope of the costs data beyond the assessment process itself and beyond the confines of what are normally regarded as child care services, this approach recognises the interrelationship between service elements which comprise a 'package' of care.

The conceptual framework within which these research questions are addressed is the *production of welfare*. This has informed PSSRU research over the last 18 years and has been fully described with reference to child care services in Knapp (1987). The basic assumption of this approach is that final and intermediate outcomes are influenced or determined by the level and modes of combination of the many and various resource and non-resource inputs. *Final outcomes* are changes in the users' welfare, ends in themselves; whereas *intermediate outcomes* are couched in terms of the means to those ends, such as provision of services or offering a supportive, high quality residential environment. *Resource inputs* (summarised by costs) are defined as tangible items such as staff, buildings, provisions and other consumable items which go to create service packages. Resources are scarce, and therefore society must make choices: economics examines choice under scarcity. *Non-resource inputs*, by contrast, are those determinants of final outcomes which are neither physical or tangible: they are embodied in the personalities, activities, attitudes and experiences of the main actors in the care system or process, and may be influenced by factors outside the system or process (see also Knapp, 1984; 1993a).

Methods

The current work builds on previous child care research under-taken at the PSSRU. Over the last 12 years the Costs of Child Welfare programme has examined the costs of care for foster and residential placements, the mixed economy of child care services, foster placement terminations, child care outcomes, and the cost-effectiveness of intermediate treatment. For better or worse, the PSSRU remains one of the few suppliers of cost information on child welfare services.

In earlier work, and as outlined in Chapter 3, we suggested four principles to be followed in cost evaluations (Knapp, 1984; 1993b). First, costs should be measured comprehensively, and include all components of service packages, regardless of the agency to which they fall. Thus, the assessment of young people will include ser-vices provided by health and education authorities as well as those offered by the social services department (Fenyo and Knapp, 1988). All these elements should be included (although occa-sionally some elements are not costed due to data limitations or the complexity of the task). For example, earlier research identi-fied those 'hidden' costs of residential care, including social work support: Knapp and Baines (1987) suggest that the total costs may be 115 per cent of the direct cost of a placement in a community home.

The second rule suggests that differences in costs should not be ignored but examined and explained. We would expect these dif-ferences not only to be a result of the different service configura-tions for each young person but also to vary according to the characteristics of sample members. This leads us to the third rule: that comparisons drawn from such examinations should be made on a like-with-like basis. The fourth rule states that costs data are of greatest use when they are combined with data on final out-comes, or *changes* in client welfare. Although advances have been made in the measurement of outcomes (see, for example, Parker and others, 1991; Department of Health, 1991b) these data are hard to come by in child care research, and good intermediate outcome measures might provide a temporary, if inferior, sub-stitute. In this study, some measures of final outcomes have been included in the multivariate analyses; however, the small sample size means some caution should be used when interpreting these results.

The costs of services

To enable the total costs of care to be calculated, a unit cost must be estimated for each of the services used by sample members. This 'price' reflects local realities during the period of data collection and is calculated to approximate the *long-run marginal opportunity cost* of providing each service (Knapp, 1993b). *Marginal cost* is the addition to total cost attributable to the inclusion of one more user, and the *opportunity cost* reflects the resource implications of opportunities foregone rather than amounts spent. It is inappropriate to measure only the short-run cost implications of service provision for young people. Today's (short-run) average revenue cost, plus appropriate capital and overhead elements, is often close to the long-run marginal cost for most services and this is the convention adopted. This section is intended to give only a brief summary of the methodologies underlying the calculation of unit costs for services used by clients in this study. A more detailed discussion can be found in Allen and Beecham (1993) and Netten and Smart (1992). All costs data are expressed at 1990-91 prices.

For the purpose of calculating the unit costs of services a distinction is made between *facility-based services* and *peripatetic staff*. *Facility-based services* are those which tend to be based in a single building or on a single site and which provide a self-contained service to a fairly easily defined client group, for example, community homes or intermediate treatment centres.

The costs of these services are likely to vary by location, size, type of facility and user characteristics, and to apply one cost to these broad service types would disguise the enormous variation between individual units. Unit costs, therefore, are calculated using the adjusted revenue expenditure accounts, obtained from the managing agency, and include an estimation of the opportunity cost implications of the buildings. Thus, for the four Regional Resource Centres used by clients in this study, unit costs ranged from £1,673 to £2,561 per resident week. Places in community homes managed by the social services department in which the study was based were costed at between £526 and £925 per resident week.

For some independent sector residential services, revenue accounts were not available but convention suggests that the fee charged is representative of both revenue and capital costs, although care must be taken to ensure there is no hidden subsidy from another service within the same organisation. Earlier work has suggested that fees set by the independent sector are lower than their costs and that the managing organisations, therefore, subsidise the cost of local authority placements from their own resources (Knapp, 1986a; Knapp and Fenyo, 1985). We could not examine if this was so for the voluntary sector residential services used in this study. The mean cost of these facilities per resident week was £628.

A similar methodology was used to cost foster care placements, and included the 'set-up' costs of the placement. The social services department in the research Authority paid quite high fostering allowances (NFCA, 1991; Kind, 1992) at £221 per week (11-14 years) with higher costs allocated for placements in which specialist assessment duties were undertaken. The costs of social work support for these placements was also higher, adding another £47 per week. Kavanagh (1988a and 1988b) highlights the issue of foster carers subsidising placements, suggesting they should receive proper compensation for their extra expenses, the work undertaken and stress endured. Calculation of these costs requires a far more in-depth study than possible in this current work and they have not been estimated for this evaluation. The costs of a young person living at home were calculated using data from the Family Expenditure Survey (CSO, 1991), following the methodology used in earlier studies (Knapp, Brysan and Lewis, 1984).

Social work services play a major role in the assessment process and for this reason have been costed using the 'facility-based' methodology. The social services department identified each team as a cost centre allowing social worker costs to be calculated for each area, thus reflecting local variation. Including provision of support, supervision and use of the building the unit cost was between £14 and £17 per 'team hour'. Some cost variation can be accounted for by the composition of each team; however, a greater source of variation can be found in the working practices (such as the amount of time spent travelling) and the needs of clients on their case-load.

The second category for calculating unit costs of services is *peripatetic staff*. For most professionals involved in the study, national pay scales apply and to these were added regional weighting, national insurance and superannuation contributions, travel and subsistence expenses, overheads (such as for support staff or heating and lighting) and the cost implications of office space. A cost per hour was calculated using information on working hours per year, taking into account holidays and other leave. These peripatetic services accounted for only a small part of the total costs of assessment packages, but they should not be overlooked in a comprehensive costing exercise as they often represent costs that fall to agencies other than the main provider. Examples of services used by young people in this study and costed using this methodology were probation officers at £17 per hour and police officers, £28 per hour.

. To calculate the costs of service packages during the assessment period (time 1) or at follow-up (time 2), the unit cost for each service was combined with data on the amount of services received by each young person in the study. Ideally, for the assessment period, we would focus on the period between entry-to-study and the completion of the assessment for each child, time periods which may vary around the three months covered by the first round of data collection. This was not possible, and so an alternative approach was required for the costing work. Service use and the associated costs for all clients were examined for *the assessment period*, taken to be the 13-week period following the event which precipitated assessment and during which the greater part of the assessment activities would be completed. Costs data are expressed as an average cost per week. Although this 'flattens out' the service picture over time (clients actually receive service in 'lumps': maybe seeing an educational welfare officer four times in three months, or perhaps moving to different accommodation facilities twice within that period), this approach facilitates comparison with costs data for the follow-up period.

The service packages of the sample group

As with the overall study, the research sample comprises 75 young people who were categorised by assessment type (Referred or Routine), venue of assessment (residential, foster care or community) and event which precipitated assessment (considered for care, admitted to care or placement breakdown). Earlier chapters in this report provide more detailed information. Table 12.1 shows the number of young people comprising the costs sample in each of these categories at time 1 (the assessment period) and time 2 (the follow-up). As we saw in Chapter 10, at the follow-up interview 19 cases were found to be closed and a further eight cases were 'not active'. It was not possible to calculate a cost for the closed cases or for three of the inactive cases, as service use and other data were not recorded in sufficient detail. The sample for the follow-up study, therefore, is 53 young people. Noticeably, it is from the two larger categories, *routine / community* and *referred / residential*, that sample attrition has been greatest.

Table 12.1 Numbers of young people in the costs study by study category

Assessment type and venue	Considered for care		Received into care		Placement breakdown		Total	
	Time 1	Time 2	Time 1	Time 2	Time 1	Time 2	Time 1	Time 2
Routine/residential	–	–	1	1	8	8	9	9
Routine/foster care	–	–	1	1	3	3	4	4
Routine/community	18	9	1	1	4	3	23	13
Referred/residential	–	–	16	9	6	6	22	15
Referred/foster care	2	2	7	5	–	–	9	7
Referred/community	7	4	–	–	1	1	8	5
Total	27	15	26	17	22	21	75	53

Services used

Detailed information on service use is required to calculate the costs of care. This information also provides a valuable description of the young people's service packages during the study periods, quantifying the breadth of service involvement in child care. Information on frequency and duration of accommodation placements, education and social work input (the three main components of the packages in terms of their contribution to assessment and the associated costs) was recorded in some detail on the main interview schedules. However, for other services (which have a more peripheral influence on total cost) only information on whether the young person received that service was recorded. For these services one of three approaches was used to quantify service use: contact was made with the providing agency to ascertain probable or typical levels of receipt; data from other clients in the study were used where standard levels of care were provided; or assumptions were made on the basis of previous work in the area.

Receipt of services was calculated for each young person for both study periods. For the period between entry-to-study and first data collection (the assessment period) the total amount of any service received over the three months was examined. For the follow-up period, service use data were collected with reference to the four-week period preceding interview, and adjusted to account for changes in residence or education over the previous 12 months (for example, where a boarding special school was closed for the holidays and the young person returned to their own home or to another residential establishment). For illustrative purposes, service use and the associated costs for four young people are detailed later in this chapter to show variation in receipt at the individual level.

In this section service use for the whole sample is described. Following our rule of comprehensiveness, all services recorded on the interview schedule have been included. Tables 12.2 and 12.3 list accommodation and service use (and costs-related data) for both time periods but care should be taken when making comparisons as the data cover different time periods. Young people may use more than one service in any group compiled for Table 12.3 so the total adds to more than the component figures.

Table 12.2 shows the range of *accommodation* placements used during the two study periods. At follow-up the use of specialist assessment placements is, not surprisingly, considerably reduced, but several young people remained in assessment/bridging foster care. We saw in the last chapter the dearth in long-term fostering

arrangements in the Borough. Out-of-borough residential placements appear to be used quite frequently and there is a slight
reduction in the number of placements at Regional Resource
Centres between time 1 and follow-up. In addition, boarding special schools (returning home or to another residential facility during holidays), residential units provided by the voluntary sector or
other social service departments, bed and breakfast establishments, and several community foster places were used. The
young person's *main* place of residence formed the basis for categorising the venue for assessment, but many changed their accommodation within the study periods so the total number of
placements adds up to more than the number of clients. Furthermore, addresses are counted only once for each young person, so
multiple changes between the same addresses are not included in
the figures.

Table 12.2 Young people's accommodation

	Number of placements	
Setting	*Time 1* n = 75	*Time 2*[1] n = 53
Community home (SSD)	10	31
Community home (assessment)	25	–
Community home (out-of-area)	10	20
Regional Resource Centre	8	6
Community fostering	11	12
Assessment/Bridging fostering	10	12
Family	29	23
Friends/relatives	8	5
Special boarding school	4	4
Hospital	4	–
Bed and Breakfast	6	7[2]
Missing/Homeless/Squat	4	3
Remand/YOI/Police cell	1	3
Homeless persons' hostel/Jesus Army	–	1
Mother and Baby Unit	–	1
Family Centre	–	2
Total number of placements	130	125

Notes:
1. During the year prior to follow-up interview.
2. Includes one young person who stayed in six different bed and breakfast
   facilities over 28 weeks.

Social workers held direct case responsibility for nearly all
sample members during the assessment period (Table 12.3). Two

cases were held by student social workers (who would have been supervised by a qualified social worker), one by a member of staff from the Day Assessment Unit, and a team leader had responsibility for a further two young people. Social workers spent between 17 and 875 minutes on each case per week, around a mean of 182 minutes, with little variation between assessment types. This figure includes both direct care (face-to-face contacts usually occurring in the young person's place of residence) and indirect care activities (travel, administration tasks and supervision). Time spent preparing for and attending client-specific meetings is included with the costs of meetings (see below). Many young people in foster care tended to receive high levels of input per week although, interestingly, the amount of time spent travelling to placements accounted for much of this (see also Knapp, 1986b). Across the whole sample, team leaders spent an average of 12 minutes per week in supervision activities with the case-holding social worker.

At time 2 only 66 per cent of the cases for whom we have costs data were continuously open and allocated for the full year, although social workers held direct case responsibility for all 53 sample members at some time during the year prior to data collection. Just under half the sample had seen the case-holding social worker once or twice within the four weeks prior to interview and no contact was recorded for 11 sample members.

In the follow-up interview only frequency of contact with the social worker was recorded whereas, for cost purposes, information is also required on duration of input. To estimate these values, the time 1 data were examined to discover if there was a statistical relationship between frequency of contact and duration of visit. About half the variation in duration of contact could be explained and the equation was then used to predict duration of social work visits for each young person at follow-up. The mean (predicted) length of face-to-face contact per week was 10.1 minutes (range 0 to 49.6 minutes). Although one might hypothesise that social work input during the assessment period would be higher, this approach is more accurate than using a simple arithmetic mean. The time implications of indirect care activities were added to this figure. It is interesting to note that for those people in the time 2 costs sample there was no significant difference in the number of social work visits at time 1 (0.78 per week) and at time 2 (0.73).

As Table 12.3 shows, the *social services department* provided a range of other services to more than four-fifths of the sample during the assessment period. Of particular note is the number of

Table 12.3: Services used by the young people

Service Groups	Time 1		Time 2	
	% using service	% total cost	% using service	% total cost
Accommodation	100	**66**	100	**79**
Social worker	**96**	**13**	**100**	**9**
Social Services[1]	**88**	**6**	**59**	**1**
Assessment Service	28		9	
RSW/outreach	11		2	
Fostering officer	29		32	
Other social worker[2]	44		0	
Intermediate Treatment	19		15	
Payments	36		28	
Miscellaneous[3]	5		6	
Meetings		**2**		**1**
Education	**79**	**9**	**62**	**9**
School/College[4]	32		53	
School psychology service	12		2	
Education welfare officer	25		4	
Teaching staff/school nurse	6		0	
Careers/YTS	4		15	
Health Care	**48**	**3**	**28**	**1**
General practitioner	28		19	
Hospital inpatient	8		9	
Outpatient/A & E	13		11	
Other medical specialists	20		9	
Law and Order	**28**	**1**	**42**	**1**
Child Protection Team	11		0	
Court appearance	17		28	
Legal service/solicitor	8		9	
Police officers	11		34	
Probation service	1		4	
Other services	**39**	**1**	**23**	**1**
Interpreter/translator	9		0	
Advice Centres	7		0	
Counselling/therapy[5]	18		11	
Playscheme/Youth Club	4		4	
Charitable grants	3		4	
Miscellaneous	9		8	

Notes:
1. Excludes case-holding social worker.
2. Includes social worker of another family member, Duty Team leader, Assistant Divisional Director and Divisional Director.
3. Includes home help service, escort service, after care team and respite care.
4. Includes education provided through intermediate treatment centres, literacy classes, tuition courses and home tutors.
5. Includes art therapy provided at the day assessment unit.

young people who saw the Assessment Service personnel and the fostering officer, each mentioned at least once for nearly a quarter of the sample. Social work input (over and above that of the case-holder) was recorded for nearly half the young people. Section 1 and other payments were made to more than a third of the sample, usually related to accommodation and subsistence (these are included in the accommodation costs).

From the follow-up data we found that social services departments provided support to just over a half of the sample. Notably, and not surprisingly, the major difference in service receipt at time 1 and at follow-up was the reduced level of involvement of the Assessment Service and residential social workers or outreach services. The fostering officer was still used by more than a third of cases, and Section 1 or other payments from the social services department were received by nearly a third although full details were not always recorded.

The main service provided by the *education authority* was, as one might expect, schooling. In order to ensure comparability of costs, all education services (including mainstream schooling) which the young people used have been costed. This approach ensures comparability for those in boarding schools and also allows the inclusion of the financial cost of not attending school (for example, due to exclusion or age) as zero. During the assessment period 11 young people of school age received no education at all and 12 young people were attending secondary school only occasionally but a wide range of alternatives to mainstream schooling was used. Thirteen clients were over school leaving age at the time of data collection, eight of whom were either unemployed or for whom no daytime activity was recorded. Other services provided by the education authority came from individual professionals such as the educational welfare officer (including educational social worker), the education psychology service, and the careers service.

At the follow-up interview, about a third of the sample attended school, a slightly higher percentage than at time 1. Fifteen of the costed sample were over school leaving age, most of whom were not employed and many would not have been eligible for social security benefits unless registered on an Employment Training Scheme. Mainstream schooling remained the most commonly received form of education and other education services were used by only a few sample members. The data, for example, show a reduction in the numbers of young people using the psychology and welfare officer services.

At both time periods the most commonly used *health care service* was the general practitioner, many of these contacts relating to statutory requirements. During the assessment period, nearly half the sample members received some health services, including three young people who were seen by psychiatrists or the police surgeon. At follow-up just over a quarter of the sample members had received medical care in the previous four weeks.

Use of *law and order services* at time 2 shows a different picture to that during the assessment period. Table 12.3 shows that just under a quarter of the sample members had some contact with law and order services during the three-month assessment period, often in connection with court appearances (more detail on offending is provided in Chapter 11). For two children there was contact with the Home Office concerning their immigration status but these costs have not been included due to the complexity of obtaining and disaggregating data.

Even given the shorter time-scale, police officers appear to be involved with more of the young people at time 2 and there was a slightly higher number of young people with court appearances. The legal status of some of the young people had changed with the implementation of the Children Act 1989. Although this involved the social services department legal section it was not possible to estimate the cost implications of these activities.

Accounting for only a small proportion of the total costs of assessment, the *other services* category included people providing specialist advice and support, for example, translation or interpretation services. During the follow-up period only eight young people were referred to services which they did not appear to attend, compared to 15 during the assessment period.

Meetings provide a format in which professional and other interested parties express opinions and provide advice, and in which decisions can be taken concerning the young person. Preparation for and attendance at such meetings absorbs a considerable amount of professionals' time and the number and mix of people attending any meeting varies considerably. Table 12.4 lists the types of meetings and the percentage of meetings attended by different professionals for each time period. One hundred meetings where decisions were made were recorded for the young people during the assessment period, attended by a wide range of different interest groups. For the year following, 137 meetings were recorded (note that these refer to a sub-sample, 48 young people, as data were not available for eight young people). The costs of meetings include those associated with social workers (case-holding, residential and other), who attended a high proportion of these meetings. The young person and family members attended slightly over a third at either time period, not a high proportion. For the follow-up period there was a drop in participation from the Assessment Service personnel, medical staff and Child Protection Officer although attendance from court officers and solicitors was slightly higher.

Table 12.4   Percentage of meetings attended by different participants

Participant	% of meetings attended	
	Time 1	Time 2
Social worker of young person	86	84
Other social worker[1]	75	76
Residential unit staff	60	70
Relative(s)/informal carer(s)	36	35
Foster carer	22	26
Young person	38	42
Assessment Service staff[2]	61	19
Assistant Divisional Director	7	3
Community fostering officer/Linkworker	21	23
Intermediate Treatment staff	21	28
Child Protection Officers	13	9
School representative/EWO	35	29
Medical staff[3]	24	11
Court officer/Solicitor	9	21
Miscellaneous[4]	4	12
Total number of meetings	100	137

Notes:
1. Includes, for example, mental health and Family Services Unit social workers and area team leaders.
2. Includes staff from the Day Assessment Unit.
3. Includes school nurse, child and family psychiatrists, educational psychologist, registrar and paediatrician.
4. Includes art therapist, interpreter, National Society for the Prevention of Cruelty to Children (NSPCC) officer, National Association of Young People in Care (NAYPIC) representative, after-care team member and case conference organiser.

The costs of assessment and follow-up care

The costs of assessment packages

To calculate the total costs of assessment for each young person in the study, unit costs of services were attached to the component parts of each young person's assessment package. The costs of assessment, therefore, include all accommodation placements and service elements used by the young people.

Total costs for the assessment period vary by a factor of 18. Costing £1,809 per week, the most expensive assessment package was in the Referred/residential category. This young person had spent a considerable proportion of the 13 weeks in Regional Resource Centres. The least expensive assessment package (£79 per week) was for a young person Routinely assessed by a social worker in her family home. Table 12.3 shows how the total costs of assessment are distributed between the service providing agencies.

Accommodation represented the largest cost element, accounting for 66 per cent of the total, and includes the costs for each place of residence. A higher percentage of total costs is absorbed by accommodation where staffed residential facilities were commonly used. The mean cost of accommodation for young people referred to the specialist Assessment Service was approximately £250 per week more expensive than for those undergoing routine social work assessments, reflecting the higher use of residential venues over the period. We relate this later to the characteristics and needs of the young people involved.

Table 12.3 highlights the resource consequences of social work inputs to assessment, accounting for the largest proportion of total costs after accommodation. This is an unusually high percentage for a peripatetic service, emphasising the important role social work plays in the young people's lives and in the assessment process. Significantly, two-thirds of the social work costs were for indirect care activities (travel, administration and supervision).

Generally, it would appear from this table that costs accruing to any service type other than accommodation, social work or education pale into insignificance when they are considered as a percentage of the total costs of assessment. Moreover, when this is considered in the light of the evidence on funding of accommodation services, there can be no doubt that the social services department bears the major costs burden. However, setting these costs data in the context of the service receipt information clearly shows that services provided outside the department have an important, albeit small, part to play in assessment. Often these are specialist services which the social services department does not provide, but providing organisations, particularly smaller independent sector organisations, are not always directly recompensed for the service. Although a small part of the costs of assessment, the costs of setting up and maintaining such services may be substantial.

The costs of care packages at follow-up

The mean total cost of care per week for the follow-up period was £593. Again, the range is wide, from £105 to £1,437 per week.

Two-thirds of the cases had costs between £301 and £899 per week. The costs of care at follow-up are not presented by assessment categories as this might encourage invalid comparisons.

As Table 12.3 shows, across all cases the largest share of total costs (79 per cent) was absorbed by accommodation-related services. (The information on accommodation over the year prior to interview date has been used to calculate costs.) Social work still played a major role in the care of these young people, one year after the assessment period. For example, there was no reduction in the average number of visits per week at follow-up. The costs of social work inputs absorb nine per cent of the total costs and other support provided by the social services department accounts for two per cent. Use of education services for the year prior to interview accounted for 13 per cent of total costs across all sample members. Health, law and order and miscellaneous services together absorbed three per cent of the total cost and attendance at and preparation for meetings contributes just under one per cent.

Case studies

In order to provide some illustration of the sorts of young people and circumstances we are discussing, four case studies are described below providing data on the care packages recorded at both data collection points. This may help balance to some degree the essentially statistical analysis contained in this chapter. As will be seen, these four cases represent both Referred and Routine assessments, and placements in foster and residential care as well as in the community. We are not suggesting that these four are in any way representative of our wider sample. Table 12.5 lists the costs per week of the services which comprise each of the care packages.

Case study 12.1

A 15-year-old female, who was referred to the specialist Assessment Service when she was admitted into care. During the three-month period between the event which precipitated assessment and data collection, she spent nearly eight weeks at home and four weeks at a social services community home and also spent eight days in hospital. The case-holding social worker spent, on average, 30 minutes per week in face-to-face contact with the young person and client-related indirect care activities absorbed about the same. During the period, her attendance at mainstream secondary school was described as sporadic, with the educational welfare officer monitoring attendance. Home tuition was being considered. She was seen by the general practitioner twice while resident at the community home and also by a child psychiatrist. The young person also attended an Intermediate Treatment (IT) Centre two evenings a week and appeared at court once although the case was dismissed. One payment from social services, was recorded, £10 for a Christmas present. Three decision making meetings were held during the assessment period, one of which was the Final Assessment Conference. Professionals recorded as attending these meetings were: case-holding social worker; the psychiatric registrar; head of assessment; and other residential staff, one of who made two home visits. The mean total cost of the package is £690 per week, of which 53 per cent is absorbed by accommodation costs. The social services department funded 55 per cent of the total costs. The case was closed at follow-up.

Case study 12.2

Aged 16, this young woman was assessed by a social worker in the course of their normal activities after a placement break-down. She was briefly placed at a regional resource centre from a social services community home and spent the remainder of the three-month period prior to data collection at an independent community home in Surrey. She also spent two nights in hospital. Excluded from mainstream school three years earlier, this young person received individual tuition three half-days a week at an out-of-borough centre (a taxi transported her to and fro) and attended a college on work experience one day a week. She saw the case-holding social worker seven times during that period, the social worker also spent a considerable time on administrative tasks. She was referred to an IT group. A psychotherapist and the head of assessment were consulted about alternative placements. Social services made a payment of approximately £330 for clothing and travel. No decision making meetings were recorded for this young woman although it is known that three-monthly reviews were held. The total costs of assessment over the three-month period were £1,329, 74 per cent of which were absorbed by accommodation services. The social services department funded 84 per cent of the total costs. At follow-up the case was still active and had been continuously active for the whole year. The young person had been living at the same accommodation unit for the year prior to data collection, with the exception of two weeks spent at a private community home in

London. She attended a further education college full time. Over the four weeks prior to data collection she had seen her social worker twice and received four telephone calls. Her only other service receipt was a short hospital inpatient stay and outpatient appointments. During the year three decision making meetings were recorded, attended by the social worker, team leader and residential staff from both her and her siblings' community homes. The costs of care for this young person were £1,056 per week.

Case study 12.3

A 14 year-old female who entered the study when she was homeless and was considered for admission to local authority care. She was referred to the specialist Assessment Service and spent nine weeks in an assessment foster home followed by placement in an SSD community home. She was pregnant and had not attended school for the last year. Over the three-month period covered by the interview, she had two social workers and there was an average of 40 minutes face-to-face contact per week. She had some contact with the general practitioner, Intermediate Treatment staff, and the hospital. Only one meeting was recorded over the period, a planning meeting attended by the social worker, team leader, link officer for the assessment foster placement and residential staff. A report was prepared by the foster carers. The total costs of care over the assessment period were £696 per week, 57 per cent of which was absorbed by the accommodation costs. Seventy-five per cent of the total cost was funded by the social services department.

The follow-up data showed that the young person was resident at the community unit and foster carers before moving to a Mother and Baby Unit. During this period she continued to receive tuition. She returned to her family home and received £30 per week from social services (Section 17 payment) in addition to social security benefits. The case remained active over the year since the assessment data was recorded and the young person had weekly contact with her social worker. No other service receipt was recorded for the four weeks prior to data collection and no meetings were recorded. The costs of care for this young person were £515 per week.

Case study 12.4

This young woman was referred to the specialist Assessment

Service by the duty team and spent nine weeks with foster carers in Kent and four weeks living with her parents. She attended a special tuition unit but then returned to mainstream school. The case was allocated to a social worker two months after she was admitted to the care of the local authority and then was visited every fortnight. A medical and school report were completed as well as a social worker's report. A planning meeting and a review were held, attended by the social worker, team leader, assessment service representative, foster carer and linkworker and a police officer from the child protection team. The total costs of care over the assessment period were £342 per week, 53 per cent of which was absorbed by the accommodation costs. The social services department funded 56 per cent of the total costs of care.

By the follow-up data collection point, the young person was over school leaving age and had attended a youth training scheme and further education college for nine months. She had used the careers service in the four weeks prior to data collection. The case was considered active over the year but had not been allocated to a social worker for four of the 12 months. During the four weeks prior to data collection the social worker had visited the young person once and telephoned twice. The schedule suggests that the young person had briefly used some services (counselling, child guidance and youth clubs were recorded) and had been formally cautioned once by the police. A placement panel report had been completed. Over the period covered by the schedule the second part of the Final Assessment Conference was held (five months after the event which precipitated assessment) and a statutory review. The costs of care for this young person were £403 per week.

The relationship between costs and young people's characteristics

In this section the associations between the costs of assessment and care received during the follow-up period, and the characteristics and needs of the young people and their outcomes, are considered. Data on all 75 young people are included in the analyses of the assessment costs; however, as we have seen, costs data were not available for 22 members of this sample at the follow-up period. These 'closed' cases came from categories which contained both the most costly and the least costly packages of care. The spread of total costs of both groups was similar but the closed cases were found to have a lower mean assessment cost ($p < 0.1$) and a lower median. Although accommodation costs were also lower, this

Table 12.5 Component costs of care packages for four illustrative case studies, £ per week

Services[1]	Case study 1 Time 1 £	Case study 2 Time 1 £	Case study 2 Time 2 £	Case study 3 Time 1 £	Case study 3 Time 2 £	Case study 4 Time 1 £	Case study 4 Time 2 £
Residential care	343.35	981.04	913.37	234.92	367.02	0	0
Foster care	0	0	0	140.88	28.85	165.64	339.72
Living at home	25.65	0	0	0	11.20	15.81	0
Other accommodation	0	0	0	0	8.52[2]	0	0
Total accommodation costs	369.00	981.04	913.37	375.80	415.59	181.45	339.72
GP/nurse	2.67	0	0	0.17	0.34	0	22.13
Hospital services	214.80	23.55	5.99	159.85	0	0	0
Education	48.92	192.08	70.43	0	0	123.29	0
Court/police	5.95	0	0	0	0	0	2.11
Social worker[3]	19.06	41.30	64.26	47.18	81.23	21.92	32.39
Intermediate treatment	15.04	7.52	0	11.19	0	0	0
Other assessment staff	2.15	1.26	0	1.26	0	1.26	0
Fostering officer	0	0	0	37.16	0	3.48	5.66
Payments	0.77	79.59	0	60.15	4.60	0	0
Meetings	10.90	0	1.54	3.41	0	10.27	0.96
Miscellaneous	0.99	2.38[4]	0	0	12.85	0	0.47
Total cost, £ per week	690.25	1328.72	1055.59	696.17	514.61	341.67	403.44

Notes:
1. See Tables 12.2 and 12.3 and text for service receipt information.
2. Department of Social Security benefits.
3. Includes supervision from teamleader.
4. Includes psychology.

difference did not reach statistical significance. The number of visits from a social worker at time 1, on average 0.78 visits per week for the open cases and 0.84 visits per week for the cases closed at time 2, was not statistically different.

The analyses which include the follow-up data, therefore are based on information about 53 young people. Average weekly costs at time 2 for this sample (£593) are lower than at time 1 (£634) although the difference was not statistically significant. The distribution of costs changed only slightly: at assessment, 81 per cent of the cases cost between £100 and £999 per week; at follow-up 89 per cent of cases fell within this range.

It is important to examine the variation in the costs of assessment and the costs during the follow-up period. Central to this examination are the needs and other characteristics of the young people, as we would expect different mixes of services to be put together in response to individual needs. We would also expect that the assessments lead to the formulation of a service package that improves the welfare of young people. This exploration of cost variations might, therefore, provide insights for policy and practice. It certainly should ensure that comparisons are made on a like-with-like basis. We are thus now invoking the second and third rules of costs research.

The *cost function* approach estimates the relationship between the cost of providing a service and the characteristics of its users, employing multivariate analyses to explain the cost variations (Knapp and Smith, 1985). Taking total cost per week for each young person (a summary measure of the care received) as the dependent variable and the data collected on individual young people by National Children's Bureau researchers as the set of potential explanatory factors, a technique known as ordinary least squares multiple regression was used to tease out the relationship. Data were entered into the regression equation in an attempt to maximise the percentage of variance explained, though the statistical significance of individual regression coefficients and the interpretability of results were not ignored. Some of the potential explanatory variables are intercorrelated. This does not affect the power of the equation but it can make it difficult to disentangle the relative importance of the individual variables.

Costs and needs in the assessment period

Using this approach the first set of cost functions were run using the data collected three months after the event that precipitated assessment for the young person. These data include: biographical information; a description of the living situation and care history; educational, legal and Child Protection Register (CPR) status; and detailed information on the assessment and decision making process. These data are described in more detail in Chapter 6. For the costs analyses three conceptually different sets of variables were chosen. Most were entered as indicator or dummy variables (with the exception of age which is a continuous variable) where the value 1 indicates that the condition is satisfied and the value 0 indicates that it is not satisfied:

- *Background information* such as age, gender, first language spoken at home, security of their home base, ethnicity and religion. A selection of these variables explained nearly a quarter of the variation in the costs of assessment (as measured by the adjusted R^2 statistic).

- *Needs-related information* included: whether the young person had problems with their health, behaviour, relationships, social skills, or education; presence of any particular stresses in their lives; and whether they had committed any offence in the last 12 months. In addition, dummy variables were included to indicate the presence (or absence) of special needs, whether they had been 'statemented', and whether there was any likelihood of suicide, self-injury or substance abuse. Including some of these variables raised the explanatory power of the equation to 50 per cent.
- The final group of variables allowed in the equation against total costs per week during the assessment period were *service-related measures*, used as proxies for need. These included the young person's legal and CPR status immediately prior to event, previous contacts with services, whether the case was active at entry-to-study, and whether any siblings were in care.

When the service-related variables were added to the equation the adjusted R^2 – the proportion of cost variation 'explained' by the included variables – was raised to 60 per cent. This final equation, governed by conventional criteria of statistical significance (p value), parsimony and interpretability, is detailed in Table 12.6. Although introducing each of the blocks of variables changed the pattern of statistical significance, there was remarkable consistency in the variables which entered the equation each time. In fact, the 'next best' regression equations were little different from this one. One or two variables dropped out to be replaced by similar indicators, with the overall explanatory power of the equation slightly reduced. Table 12.6 gives a description of the variables, the proportion of the population who satisfied each condition, and the coefficient and significance values for each variable. (This format is also used for Tables 12.7, 12.8 and 12.9.) Overall, the equation reveals a strong association between the characteristics of individual young people and costs, suggesting that the assessment packages in themselves are tailored to the needs and circumstances of the young people.

Seven variables entering the equation have a positive coefficient, and are therefore cost-raising factors. The only *background characteristic* to enter the equation concerned ethnicity: young people from mixed or African/African-Caribbean families received more expensive assessment packages. Similarly, behaviour prob-

Table 12.6 Estimated cost function[1]: costs and needs in the assessment period

Variable Description	% satisfying this condition[2]	Coefficient value	p value
Constant term		272.16	.0094
Contact with education welfare in last 10 years	47	–204.21	.0033
Ethnicity: mixed parentage	20	249.76	.0028
Behaviour problems reported at event	63	195.95	.0060
Reported suicide attempt or self-injury	9	349.99	.0014
Legal status at time of event	67	278.85	.0003
Ethnicity: African or African-Caribbean	19	225.07	.0072
Religion: C of E or Roman Catholic	24	151.74	.0464
Charged with one or more offences	20	261.99	.0010
Stress factor in home base	61	–198.90	.0175

Notes:
1. Dependent variable: total costs per week for assessment period. $R^2 = 0.649$, adjusted $R^2 = 0.600$, F = 13.344 (significance .000).
2. Sample size: 75 young people.

lems and self-injury or suicide attempts reported at time of event tend to raise costs as services respond to *needs* measured along these dimensions. Two *service response* or proxy variables were significant: where young people were subjects of a statutory order (for example care, supervision or place of safety order); and where young people had been charged with one or more offences in the year prior to entry-to-study. However, young people who had offended were more likely to be on a care order.

Gender entered the equation when just the background and needs variables were considered (males costing more) but was dropped in the final equation where neither gender nor age reached significance at ten per cent. Although implying no discrimination in service provision by these factors, there was an inter-relationship between these and other variables entering the equation. For example, males were three times more likely to offend than females, and nearly twice as likely to have behaviour problems reported at the time of event which precipitated assessment. Older children were more likely to have offended and suicide attempts or self-injury were more commonly reported. The effects of these variables dominated over simple measures of age and gender.

Only two variables have a negative coefficient. Previous contact with educational welfare services tends to reduce costs, indicating that some elements of educational assessment may already have been undertaken during this earlier contact or some of the problems exhibited in this area have already been addressed. The presence of a third ranked stress factor in the young person's home base at the time of event which precipitated assessment (for example, disability or ill-health of a family member, relationship problems or history of abuse) also reduces the costs of assessment.

Costs, needs and outcomes in the assessment period

We would expect assessment to be related to the longer-term outcomes for young people in the study. That is, we would expect a good assessment to ensure appropriate packages of care are put in place which improve individual welfare. To test this assumption the following data were selected from the follow-up interviews: individual's changes in emotional and health status, social skills and behaviour in the previous year; the extent to which the social worker felt that the young person's needs had been met; and whether, overall, the social worker felt the young person's situation was more positive or more negative than a year ago. The outcomes for young people are described in the two preceding chapters.

These data were entered as dummy variables and the results of a stepwise regression can be seen in Table 12.7. The sample was reduced to 53 young people (that is, only those for whom follow-up data were available) but on the variables entering the previous equation they were similar to the full population: the adjusted R^2 was slightly lower (0.58) but each of the variables remained significant and the direction of influence of the coefficients remained the same. Adding the outcome variables into the equation raised the proportion of explained variation in assessment costs to 70 per cent. For those whose behaviour was reported as deteriorating since assessment, the costs of assessment were higher. However, higher assessment costs were also associated with meeting needs and an improvement in emotional state during the post-assessment period. An important finding, therefore, is that this association implies that a more costly assessment package engendered (a set of services which promoted) these welfare changes.

Table 12.7 Estimated cost function[1]: costs, needs and outcomes

Variable Description	% satisfying this condition[2]	Coefficient value	p value
Constant term		−106.11	.3362
Contact with education welfare in last 10 years	47	−222.93	.0044
Ethnicity: mixed parentage	25	250.37	.0082
Behaviour problems reported at event	66	255.15	.0028
Reported suicide attempt or self-injury	9	530.52	.0001
Legal status at time of event	77	201.69	.0395
Ethnicity: African or African-Caribbean	28	340.36	.0004
Charged with one or more offences	30	207.37	.0218
Needs reported as met in some respects	45	236.35	.0045
Deterioration in behaviour reported	17	238.25	.0307
Improved emotional status reported	49	209.23	.0133

Notes:
1. Dependent variable: total costs per week for assessment period
   $R^2 = 0.700$, adjusted $R^2 = 0.629$, $F = 9.806$ (significance .000).
2. Sample size: 53 young people.

Costs, needs and outcomes in follow-up period

The data collected by Bureau researchers were also examined to see if they could explain the variation in costs (the summary measure of care received) at time 2. Again, multivariate analysis was undertaken using the techniques described above. The relevant variables were entered in three distinct blocks:

- *Outcome data* which describe young people's changes in welfare.
- *Needs measures* from the time 1 data collection period, along the dimensions described above and including service response or 'proxy' measures.
- *Background data* comprising variables from the time 1 data set. These are characteristics which are essentially unchanging.

The first variables to be entered against costs at time 2 were the outcome variables. In fact, only seven per cent of the variation in cost could be explained by these variables alone. A greater proportion, however, could be explained once the other variables had been entered and examined for statistical significance. The final of these equations is shown in Table 12.8 which explains half of the variation in cost at time 2, and significantly it is the needs-related variables as measured at time 1 which dominate.

Table 12.8   Estimated cost function[1]: costs, needs and outcomes in the follow-up period

Variable Description	% satisfying this condition[2]	Coefficient value	p value
Constant term		439.53	.0000
Reported suicide attempt or self-injury	9	237.86	.0455
Ethnicity: White	30	−250.86	.0019
Legal status at time of event	77	197.76	.0412
Emotional problems reported at event	74	−253.81	.0149
Charged with one or more offences	30	276.01	.0011
Social skills problems reported at event	53	239.95	.0083
Overall situation reported as more negative	21	144.92	.0985

Notes:
1. Dependent variable: total cost per week at follow-up.
   $R^2 = 0.567$, adjusted $R^2 = 0.499$, $F = 8.393$ (significance .0000).
2. Sample size: 53 young people.

The only *background characteristic* which still features in the equation is ethnicity, suggesting that white children receive less costly packages of care at follow-up. Three *needs* variables which went towards explaining variation in the costs of assessment also entered the analyses of time 2 cost variation, again displaying their cost-raising potential. Self-injury or suicide attempts or threats reported at the time of event which precipitated assessment, and whether any offence had been reported both tended to raise costs for the post-assessment period, perhaps due to the extra supervision the young people required. Young people on some form of care order also receive more costly packages of care. This is a proxy for need, a *service response* variable indicating the legal relationship between the child and the local authority which we have assumed reflects a higher level of needs. The increased costs may well reflect the implementation of the local authority's statutory duties towards these young people.

The effect of the two problem-related variables is interesting. Social skills problems reported at the time of event raised the costs of care at follow-up. Where personality or emotional problems were reported, however, these young people tended to receive less costly packages of care. Although these two variables were positively correlated, it is possible that the latter problems were of a less enduring nature or that the main manifestations had passed by the time follow-up costs data were recorded. There was no correlation between these measures at time 2 and costs at the time of the follow-up.

The final variable listed in Table 12.8 is an *outcome measure*. In the follow-up interview, social workers were asked whether, overall, the young person's situation was 'more negative' or 'more positive' than a year ago (see Chapter 11 for more information). Where the young person's situation is reported as more negative than a year ago, costs at time 2 are higher. This is a global measurement but it does not mask any effects on costs from other, more specific outcome variables. We would expect to find the opposite, that increased resources expended on the young person's care promote positive, rather than negative outcomes.

The final task in these analyses was to test whether any activities undertaken during the assessment period had an effect on costs at follow-up. The regression equation is the ideal vehicle for testing these ideas as the resulting equation can be used to standardise for different needs or outcomes that are associated with costs. For example, Parker (1988) suggests that the foster care population is likely to be 'less difficult' on average than the residential care population. So a direct comparison of the average costs of foster and residential care may exaggerate any differences between the two options, whereas by basing comparisons on multivariate analyses such differences in characteristics can be taken into account (Knapp and Fenyo, 1989).

The residual cost, that is the costs per week *not* explained by the equation reported in Table 12.8, was calculated for each young person in the study and used as the dependent variable in a further multiple regression analysis. The independent variables indicated whether the following professionals were directly involved in the assessment process: health worker, Intermediate Treatment worker, psychiatrist, teaching staff, educational welfare officer or psychologist, or social worker. In addition, indicator variables were computed for the type of assessment and venue of assessment according to the categories defined by the Bureau researchers at time 1. Variables were entered in two separate blocks (the 'involvement' variables and the assessment category) and also together. This latter procedure produced the results shown in Table 12.9, explaining 26 per cent of the residual cost variation. Direct involvement in assessment from an Intermediate Treatment worker and from health professionals tended to lower costs of care at time 2, whereas intervention from the psychiatrist was associated with higher costs at follow-up. There was no correlation between psychiatric involvement at assessment and emotional problems reported at the time of event. The remaining variable in the equation indicates whether the young person was referred to the specialist Assessment Service. Having standardised for the outcomes, needs and characteristics of the young people in the sample, young people assessed through this service

Table 12.9   Analysis of residual cost at follow-up[1]

Variable Description	% satisfying this condition[2]	Coefficient value	p value
Constant term		−49.46	.2267
Intermediate Treatment worker[3]	19	−133.35	.0631
Psychiatrist[3]	11	178.84	.0380
Health professional[3]	15	−181.14	.0176
Case referred to Assessment Service	51	160.42	.0047

Notes:
1. Dependent variable: residual cost.
   $R^2 = 0.317$, adjusted $R^2 = 0.260$, F = 5.578 (significance .0009).
2. Sample size: 53 young people.
3. Professional involved in assessment process.

received more costly packages of care at time 2 than those who were assessed within the social workers' routine activities.

Conclusion

This research has been able to offer some clear answers to the questions posed at the outset. Some answers are less clear. Although only briefly described here, the service use and costs data for the two time periods show that the social services department provides and finances the greatest part of both assessment services and the care packages received at follow-up. However, the part played by other agencies should not be ignored as they often provide services which cater for the needs of a sub-group of the population studied, perhaps a residential service to meet particular religious requirements. For more details on service receipt and the associated costs at both time periods see Beecham and others (1993a; 1993b).

From a historical perspective, child care services have always been provided by a range of agencies and organisations. It is this *mixed economy of care* which current policy initiatives aim to develop further. In many fields of operation, social services departments are moving towards acting as purchasers or enablers of care, with less emphasis on direct provision. Understanding the implications of the growing schism between financing care and providing care will become more important. In child care services the funding may, and arguably should, continue to be the province of the social services department as they carry out their legal obligations. But the findings from this study suggest that child care incorporates services, therefore resources, from several social services department sections, as well as other agencies, cutting across budget boundaries. This has implications for the way social workers must operate in the future. During the research period they expressed concerns about the difficulties in contacting professionals in other agencies. Without a comprehensive cost study which focuses on individual young people, out-of-department financing responsibilities or hidden subsidies within these organisations may remain uncovered.

The examination of cost variations revealed interesting but mixed results. The relationship between costs at follow-up and outcomes, for example, is tenuous and there are perhaps three reasons for this. First, as suggested earlier, the measurement of final outcomes in child care is not as well developed as, for example, in medical research. It could be that the outcome measures used here are not sensitive enough to pick up subtle changes in the young person's welfare. Second, we must remember that the sample size is small for the kind of analyses undertaken here and, although every care has been taken to ensure the results are robust, this factor should not be ignored. Third, it is possible that the intervening time between the study periods (only 12 months) is not long enough for the ameliorative effect of services to have worked through to changes in the young people's welfare.

There was, however, a close link between resources expended at both time periods and the needs displayed by the young people in this study, suggesting that services are responding to the different characteristics of the young people. It is also interesting to note that some specific interventions during the assessment process have such a strong influence on costs a year later. Although the specialist Assessment Service raised costs at the follow-up period, the results suggest, encouragingly, that a higher expenditure during the assessment period is associated with both the needs of young people and improvements in their welfare in the following 12 months.

Summary points

- This aspect of the study on the costs of child care assessment was undertaken by the Personal Social Services Research Unit (PSSRU), University of Kent, in association with Bureau researchers.

- All elements of service packages were costed at two stages. First, *during the assessment period*, by focusing on three months following the event which precipitated assessment. Secondly, *one year later* the costs of services received were calculated for the four-week period preceding data collection.

- Unit costs were calculated to approximate the *long-run marginal opportunity cost* of providing each service at 1990-91 prices.

- Total costs for the assessment period varied by a factor of 18. Costs *per week* ranged from £79 per week for a young person routinely assessed by a social worker in her family home; to a much more complicated case involving prolonged stays at Regional Resource Centres, costing £1,809 per week.

- Accommodation accounted for some 66 per cent of total assessment costs. Social work costs were the next highest (13 per cent), followed by education (9 per cent).

- Social workers spent between 17 and 875 minutes each week on our sample cases, with an average (mean) of 182 minutes. This was similar for different assessment types. Team leaders allocated for supervision an average of 12 minutes per week on each case. Costs of social work support were calculated as between £14 and £17 per 'team hour'.

- In addition to the direct fieldworker input, social services provided a range of other services to more than four-fifths of our sample during the assessment period. This dropped to just over half the sample at follow-up.

- Detailed multivariate analysis revealed strong association between the costs of assessment and the needs and circumstances of young people, suggesting that packages were individually tailored.
- For cases still 'open' at follow-up, costs ranged from £105 to £1,437 per week. Once again, accommodation-related costs accounted for the bulk of this (79 per cent). Average weekly costs at follow-up were slightly lower than at assessment (£593 compared with £634) but this difference was not statistically significant.
- It was also encouraging to discover that higher assessment costs were associated with meeting needs of young people and an improvement in emotional state at follow-up. However, the links between assessment or follow-up costs and outcomes were more tenuous.

13. Social work and assessment with adolescents

Structure of chapter

This final chapter is presented in three parts. In Part One we return first to the aims of the study and ask how far these have been achieved. In particular we review our findings on the comparison between different types of assessment. In Part Two we draw together the key themes that emerge from the research and in Part Three we point to issues for the future, picking up the discussion initiated in Chapter 2 on the meaning of assessment and its purpose in contemporary social work practice.

Part One: The aims and findings of the study

In this study we set out to undertake a systematic comparison of the process, procedures, practice and outcomes of different forms of assessment within one local authority. More specifically we set out to find answers to the following questions:

- what are the main components of the different forms of assessment for adolescents;
- which children or young people are allocated to which form of assessment and why;
- who participates in the assessment and what are the participants' perspectives on the assessment process;
- what is the outcome of these assessments in terms of their impact on young people's circumstances one year later;
- what are the relative costs of the various assessment packages – is there a relationship between costs and outcomes in terms of the child's subsequent care career?

Seventy-five adolescent young people who had undergone an assessment, and whose case was active for a period of at least three months, were included in the sample. A further criteria for inclusion was that the assessment had taken place following one of three events – the young person had been considered for care, was admitted to care, or had experienced a breakdown in placement.

The definition of assessment used in the study was *a significant preparation for decision making*. Assessments were then classified on two dimensions; those assessments which were undertaken by social workers as part of their normal case responsibilities and those cases which were referred for assessment to a specialist assessment service. These types are named *Routine* and *Referred*. The second dimension on which cases were classified was venue. Both Routine and Referred assessments could take place in any one of three venues – residential, foster care or while the young person was living at home or elsewhere in the community. This then gives the basis on which the comparative analysis was conducted. A brief overview of this comparison is presented in the next section.

Information was gathered at two points in time; approximately three months after the 'event' which precipitated the assessment and again one year later. At both points in time data were collected on the circumstances of the young person, the services that they were receiving and the costs of these services. Other data collected at round 1 related to the assessment and decision making process, while at round 2 data collection was directed towards measures of outcome.

The definitions employed, and the criteria used to select the sample, are indicative of the nature of social work on which this study focuses. In brief, this is case work with adolescents where the most common causes of concern are relationship and behavioural problems experienced by the young people. Child protection or offending were rarely the most significant immediate presenting problem. The characteristics of these cases is reflected in the purpose for which assessments were undertaken, and in the assessment process.

In conducting this research it has been possible to address all the research questions. However, as we have indicated earlier in the text, the findings relating to the systematic comparison of assessment type need to be interpreted carefully, due to the uneven distribution of cases by type and location. While it was possible to structure the sample to include a roughly equal number of cases of each type of assessment, the flow of work to the department meant that it was not possible to construct a sample equally distributed within the 'three by three' matrix of type of case and assessment venue. The distribution of cases from different categories (considered for care, admitted to care, and placement breakdown) by type of assessment is detailed in Chapter 7. This shows that the Referred assessment process was more likely to be used for young people who were admitted to care (23 out of a total of 39 cases) whereas the Routine assessments were least likely to be used in this instance, but were used where a young person was considered for care or had a placement breakdown (18 and 15 cases respectively out of 36). The sample therefore is more representative of the actual work undertaken by the department than simply reflecting a theoretical construct. As such, the study has much to say, more generally, about the nature of social work interventions with troubled adolescents at a point of crisis.

Although the study was conducted in only one local authority, it should not be viewed simply as an evaluation of that Authority. Rather it seems clear from this and other research literature that these findings are relevant to all local authorities. Similarly, although the study was conceived, and the first round of data gathered, prior to the implementation of the Children Act in 1991, the findings remain pertinent to the practice of social work within the statutory framework of the Children Act 1989.

Types of assessment compared

Chapters 7 to 11 report detailed comparisons between the Routine and Referred forms of assessment. Here we present, in summary form, broad-based conclusions on the differences and similarities between these two assessment systems.

The first general conclusion is that overall the *outputs from the two assessment types are very similar*. For instance, no major differences were found in terms of the proportion of assessments which were successfully completed, the extent to which the objectives of the assessments were felt to be met, the comprehensiveness of the identification of needs which was undertaken, nor in the quality of the plans which were recorded after assessment. However differences were noted in three areas – the process of undertaking assessment, the venues used and, related to this, the costs of the assessment packages.

The Referred assessments were undertaken in a way that was more explicit and more systematic, based on a written procedural guide. There was a recognised timetable, more systematic record keeping and they were more likely to consider interdisciplinary involvement.

There were marked differences in the venues for each of the assessment types. Almost two-thirds of the Routine assessments were carried out while the young person was still living at home, which was true for less than a quarter of the Referred assessments. In contrast, for over half the Referred assessments the venue was residential care, mostly within the Authority, although a small number were referred for assessment to a regional resource. These contrasting patterns were mostly related to differences in the 'events' which precipitated an assessment, although the limited availability of assessment foster places was also a factor.

The third marked difference was in the relative costs of the assessment packages for each of the assessment types, with Referred assessments costing, on average, £250 more per week than Routine assessments. The total mean costs per week of assessment packages varied from £235 for Routine assessments which were home- or community-based, to £962 for Referred assessments where the venue was residential care. However the major factor in determining these costs was the accommodation component. As the majority of Referred assessments were residential the average cost of these assessments was correspondingly greater than that of Routine assessments, which mainly took place while the young person was living at home.

The similarities that were found in the outputs from the assessments, despite differences in the processes, does require further explanation. With reference to the 'elements of good practice' presented in Chapter 2, the more systematic procedures of the Referred assessments would seem better able to meet these criteria, yet this was not reflected in the actual assessment performance. Our research points to several reasons for this.

A divergence between intention and practice: Application of the assessment service procedures was not always reflected in practice. For instance, the AAS always invited young people and their families to attend planning meetings, in comparison to the more arbitrary way in which this was approached in Routine assessments. However when we examine *actual* attendance at meetings we find very little difference between the two assessment types. These results reflect the tenor of the findings of Marsh and Fisher in *Developing Partnerships in Social Services*, where they suggest that the DATA (Doing All That Already) syndrome – where workers fail to take on board the full implications of new approaches or practices, under a misapprehension that they are currently working in that way – can mask gaps between good intentions and outcomes (Marsh and Fisher, 1992).

Social workers are the main actors in each case: Irrespective of whether cases were Referred or not, the district social worker held case responsibility and was therefore the key individual in the progress of the case and the outcome following the assessment process.

Under both assessment types, there was an equal neglect of certain components: Our analysis of the assessment processes indicates that there were significant gaps in the content of the assessment and that this was equally true whether the assessment was undertaken within the AAS or routinely by the social worker. We identified four areas where this was most apparent:

● taking and recording of family history;
● dealing with health issues;
● assessing the needs of young people from minority ethnic groups;
● lack of focus on long-term needs.

Aspects of the assessment process were outside the control of those involved in either assessment process: Although there was an assumption that the AAS was better placed to bring all those involved in a case together, in practice there was little difference between the Referred and Routine assessments in terms of their ability to obtain effective input from other agencies. Similarly the research indicated that, in practice overall, the Referred assessments were no better than the Routine ones in engaging with or gaining the cooperation of young people and their families.

Given that Referred assessments meant that additional professional input was available for each case, one could expect the outcomes from these assessments to be more successful. This was not the case; as the research has shown, except for those assessments carried out by the DAU, there was no difference in the extent to which objectives for the assessment were met. However, as explained in Chapter 12, from the case information gathered, it can be said that, in general, the Referred assessments involved young people who were experiencing a greater degree of crisis and hence the assessments set more challenging objectives, and dealt with a more complex range of issues.

We must also stress that, even where assessments did not meet their primary objective, they were still regarded by social workers as being of value – even more importantly, during the assessment period there were measurable improvements in the circumstances of many of the young people. For instance, twice as many were attending school regularly at the three month period as at the beginning of the assessment period. Once again this suggests that it is inappropriate to regard assessment as a separate activity, one which is distinct from intervention, either conceptually or in practice.

Re-examining previous research questions

Even with the major changes in the concept and practice of assessment which we reported in Chapter 2, there are several research questions which constantly re-emerge – the old chestnuts of assessment. We examine these again briefly in the light of the new research findings from this study.

Residential assessments lead to a recommendation for residential care: In general there was no evidence that this was the case; the only exception being that assessments in regional resources did tend to recommend other specialist residential care. However, as shown by the statistical analysis of needs in Chapter 12, the nature of these cases suggests that a specialist placement was warranted.

Specialist assessment gives better access to other professionals: This research suggests the social workers carrying out assessments Routinely can have as much access to other professionals as those assessed by the specialist service.

Special assessment placements tend to get 'silted-up': One of the criticism of the O & As centred around the difficulty in moving young people on to their recommended placement, resulting in a blockage of assessment places. This tendency is still apparent with special assessment placements, and was particularly acute in this Authority with regard to assessment foster places.

Undertaking assessments inhibits intervention: As discussed in the previous section, this was neither the intention nor the practice of either the Referred or Routine assessments in this study.

Specialist assessments tend to be overelaborate: No evidence was provided by the research to support this view. While the specialist assessment service did have a timetabled procedure, they operated flexibly enough to adjust this to suit the needs of the young person.

Limited use is subsequently made of assessment reports: Here the evidence is fairly complex. We know that many of the young people had been the subject of previous assessments; also over half of the assessments had not been completed within the intended time-scale. Nonetheless plans were made in almost all cases (even if these did not cover as many aspects as could be expected) and most social workers reported finding the assessments useful for making plans and subsequently.

While this suggests the information was used, perhaps the more important question is whether, in all instances, an appropriate balance was achieved between gathering sufficient information to meet the young person's current needs while giving fuller consideration to those young people with more deep-seated or complex needs.

These older research questions tend to address the outputs from assessments, rather than the outcomes – which was the focus of this current research. Here we concluded overall that, while there may be marked variation in some aspects of the different categories of assessments, *the type of assessment undertaken in itself is not a significant factor in the outcomes for the young person, as measured one year later*. Rather this study indicates that the factors that are more likely to contribute to positive outcomes for young people depend less on the procedural framework, per se, and more upon the quality of the social work intervention – continuity of social work input; persistence and advocacy by the social worker on behalf of the young person; a capability to engage in direct work with the young person and their family; and, the extent to which social services are dependent upon other agencies.

This analysis suggests that the categorisation of assessment – in this instance, into Routine and Referred – is perhaps a false dichotomy. More important is an explicit framework for undertaking assessments that applies across all child care (see Marsh and Fisher, 1992, on the importance of frameworks for practice). However an assessment framework is not of itself enough – our evaluation makes clear that a prerequisite to a good assessment is a thorough understanding, on the part of the social worker, of the purpose for which they are undertaking an assessment. Such an understanding was not always apparent with either the Referred or Routine assessments undertaken in this Authority. We would suggest that only with a clear understanding of its purpose can the task of assessment be undertaken in a way that is relevant to each individual case.

These findings also indicate the need for a fresh appraisal of the relationship between procedures and social work practice. The nature of the systems for assessment and planning must be such that they allow the time for and promote the skills needed to work closely and directly with young people and their families. We return to this in Part Three, when we consider issues for the future. First, in Part Two, we identify some of the broad themes to emerge from the research.

Part Two: Themes from the research

In several previous chapters we have detailed the factors that inhibit and enhance a good assessment and promote good outcomes for the young people. Here we abstract these findings and present them as several themes that run throughout our conclusions from this study.

Engaging with young people

The purpose of social work interventions with adolescents is to bring about change in the current situation. It seems self-evident that such interventions are unlikely to be successful unless professional staff (including carers) are able to undertake direct work with the young person and to relate to the young person in a way that is meaningful to them. Yet there is much evidence throughout this study of failure to achieve this level of engagement, but also examples of the positive outcomes when this does occur. Undoubtedly, many of the sample group found it difficult to settle in placement or to make constructive use of the help that was offered. And as a group of young people moving towards the age of majority it is right that they should be taking increasing responsibility for themselves. However the nature of the case work undertaken suggests that direct work to help with specific problems was given a low priority and that the skills required to undertake direct work are both undervalued and underemployed. One exception to this, as reported by many sources, was the work of the Day Assessment Unit, including that of the art therapist.

The low priority accorded to direct work and involvement with young people was not only apparent from the case records and interviews with staff but is indicated by other data. For instance, as we saw in Chapter 8, the level of contact between social workers and their clients, even at these points of crisis, was not high. Furthermore much of this contact related to 'resource management', making decisions or arrangements relating to identifying and gaining access to resources.

> 'What we have got good at is juggling demands, client brokering, we call it; and making decisions – we are very good at making decisions … the bit we have got bad at is the in-depth stuff … it can be very easy to get into superficial work, you make decisions, make plans, you problem solve … but I feel that there are not enough people who have experience of working at great depth with the young people and who are therefore able to ascertain with ease what are the young people's needs and to work with them.' (ASS staff member)

As reported in Chapter 11, social workers often acknowledged their inability to meet the emotional needs of the young people. Often the department's main contribution was seen as the provision of material support, including that of a 'bed', an expression which contains little sense of the fact that this also served the young person as 'home'. There were also some concerns about emphasis on immediate problems, which tended to neglect more fundamental needs.

'It seems to me that we place too much emphasis on strategies and case conferences and don't think enough about the case working ... getting to know the young person and the dilemmas they are facing. Often we make decisions around 'control' and 'behaviour' when these are often peripheral to what really troubles the young person.' (District social worker)

However young people themselves did not always find it easy to accept this. An earlier study in the Authority asked young people what they found helpful; their responses were summarised in the following way:

... although they wanted to be listened to and sometimes wanted to be helped they did not usually want therapy. They wanted someone who cared about them, but they didn't want to be someone's professional case. (Dennington and Pitts, 1991)

However the study does include examples where the ability of social workers or others to work with the young person was a significant contributing factor in a positive outcome. Our findings echo those of Farmer and Parker (1991):

... where social workers were successful in affecting the course of events they relied upon ingenuity, influence and persuasion; in short, upon gaining the trust and collaboration of the youngsters.

This lack of ability to work directly with young people is also very evident from other professionals; for example, in the repeated acknowledgement that referrals to family therapy, or child and adolescent psychiatric services, rarely led to a sustained programme of work with young people or their families. Indeed only one out of six psychiatric assessments were completed, often with no alternative resource or work taking its place when this planned specialist help failed. The inability of these professionals to engage with young people – to work in a way that was understandable, meaningful and acceptable to the young people and their families – was the most cited reason for this.

Engaging with parents

Our research would suggest that not only are adolescents, as a group, accorded low priority within social services, but within these cases work with parents is also given little attention. This too is reflected within the social work literature where writings on partnership with parents has tended to concentrate on younger children and child protection work. Again our findings concur with those of Farmer and Parker's study of disaffected adolescents 'home on trial'.

> ... there is little evidence that the experience and skills that are being developed in working with adolescents are being extended to work with them together with their families. (Farmer and Parker, 1991)

We mentioned above the limited contact the staff have with young people; there was even less contact between social workers and the parents. In interviews, workers suggested several reasons for this. Firstly, they found the work difficult. This stemmed, in part, from an uncertainty about their position, as many felt they had very little leverage with many of the parents, who were often not too unhappy about being separated from their children. There was also a feeling that it was largely up to the families and the young people themselves to work out their own relationships. However, this may well not be the view of many parents, and some undoubtedly felt there was little attempt by social workers to appreciate their point of view.

> 'No, I don't think they (social workers) gave me as much help as they could; I don't think they should believe the child straight away. I think they should have listened to us (parents) more.' (Parent)

> 'Instead of coming round to my house to do an assessment of all of us they should have said – have said to (daughter) – you are in your mother's care, if your mother is responsible for you, then you should try to abide by her rules. Instead everyone is busy trying to blame it all on me ... how can they help me if they are not interested in hearing what I have to say ... no-one is interested in hearing what it is like to live with (daughter).' (Parent)

This reflects the earlier work at Sheffield, which highlighted the very different perceptions of social workers and parents about the immediate problems which faced the families. Unless this is clarified early on when the intervention is being negotiated then it is unlikely that the social worker will be able to engage successfully with the parents (Fisher and others, 1986). Our findings suggest that if the principle of partnership with parents, which is a key element of the Children Act, is to have any meaning for parents of adolescents then social services departments need to acknowledge this, accord it a much higher priority and equip social workers with the skills needed to undertake this work.

Ethnicity, culture, religion and language

The local authority in which the research was conducted served a population with great ethnic diversity, yet a large number of staff interviewed felt that the Authority gave race and culture a very low priority, as evidenced by the lack of any clear policies around these issues. Indeed it was not until influenced by the Children Act that the Authority was prepared to consider adopting a policy on monitoring the ethnic origin of those receiving its services. This is not to say that practitioners and their managers did not take account of race and culture in working with and making decisions for young people. However many felt they were doing this without the explicit help or support of the Authority and welcomed the Children Act as a way of enabling social workers and carers to place a much higher degree of importance on these matters.

There was no explicit policy within the Authority on ethnicity and child care placements, although there were policy statements which pointed to the importance of race and culture. 'Children need to be aware of those positive aspects of identity that are based upon a cultural, religious or racial background or upon established family relationships. In providing services a high priority will be given to the need to respect these aspects of identity, so long as this is consistent with the overall welfare of the child.'

Neither was there an explicit policy of matching children and young people with social workers of the same ethnic background; indeed given the diversity of the child care group this would not be possible. The Authority did not have any comprehensive statistics on the ethnic origin of its social work staff; of the social workers allocated to the young people in our sample, 14 per cent of these were black or from minority ethnic groups – two were African-Caribbean, one African and three Asian. This compares to 63 per cent of the group of young people who were black or from minority ethnic groups.

The ethnic diversity of the sample group demonstrates the importance of considering all four elements of ethnicity contained in the Children Act, 'a child's religious persuasion, racial origin, and cultural and linguistic background' (Section 22(5)(c)). It also suggests that the broad categorisation of 'black' and 'white' is over simplistic not only in relation to children of mixed parentage, but because it tends to disguise the heterogeneity within those terms

(Smith and Berridge, 1994). Certainly in carrying out an assessment and in making care plans, generalised assumptions about race and culture based on stereotypical ideas must be replaced by specific knowledge relating to the individual child (Ahmed, 1989).

The extent to which this happened in the cases included in this study was variable. As noted in early chapters there was no uniform overt consideration of race and culture, and plans to ensure young people maintained contact with their own ethnic community were recorded in only a minority of cases. Nonetheless, for some staff and managers, addressing the needs of young people included needs relating to the young person's ethnicity as a matter of course. Within the sample, therefore, there are examples of excellent practice, together with cases where failure to take account of ethnicity was a serious omission. It is also an area where social workers expressed a lack of confidence, particularly in working with young people from Muslim families.

Lack of written decisions or comprehensive plans

The assessments which were undertaken did not always result in clearly written decisions which were comprehensive in their coverage of key aspects of the lives of the young people. The summary of decision making presented in Table 11.3 shows that this was only marginally less true of those assessments that were undertaken Routinely compared to those Referred to a specialist service. This is of some concern given that the Referred assessments, in general, were undertaken in a much more systematic way, and very much anticipating the requirements of the Children Act.

The gaps in decision making were most obvious in three areas – education, promoting ethnic identity and in health. Indeed so infrequently was a health plan recorded that decision implementation in this area was not included in that particular outcome measure.

The lack of plans around ethnicity and racial identity, in many ways, is consistent with the findings summarised in the two previous sections. It suggests, first, that the lead must come from the top in establishing the right climate throughout the Authority, so that policies and practices around race and culture are given a higher priority. Second, an awareness of the importance of race and culture needs to be translated into a capability by individual practitioners to engage in direct work with young people to enhance a positive ethnic identity, a prerequisite to building self-esteem (Small, 1991; Maxim, 1993).

The third area in which there were significant gaps in plans was education, training or employment. Although Table 11.1 shows that the lack of decisions concerning education (just over one in four) is not the topic area with fewest decisions, it is a subject which is crucial to all the young people in this group. The description of the sample in Chapter 6 highlighted the prevalence of serious educational problems prior to assessment. Data from the follow-up period demonstrated the continuing lack of educational input. The damaging consequences for young people from a lack of educational opportunity is now more evident than ever, although ironically at a time when the willingness of individual schools and the capacity of the LEAs to act effectively has been eroded by the Education Reform Act 1988 and the 1993 Education Act (Utting, 1991; The Who Cares? Trust, 1993; Sinclair, Grimshaw and Garnett, 1994).

Looking to the future, one would hope that the requirements of the Children Act that Care Plans should specifically include an educational plan, would reduce the likelihood of these gaps in decision making continuing to be a feature of future practice. However it has to be said that at follow-up, which was post-Children Act implementation, there was no evidence from case files that Care Plans, let alone educational plans, had been drawn up in respect of this group of young people. Perhaps this was too soon after the implementation of the Act to expect major changes. However the early results from another research project by the National Children's Bureau suggests this picture may persist in some authorities for some time (Sinclair and Grimshaw, 1995).

Foster care

Much has been written in recent years about the quality of residential services for adolescents and undoubtedly some of those concerns apply to this Authority (Utting, 1991; Bullock, 1992; Berridge, 1994). However in distilling the themes that have arisen from this research it is the issues relating to foster care that seem more pertinent.

Although the research Authority has proportionally fewer foster placements than other authorities (see Chapter 4), foster care is still a major resource for the placement of adolescents. However, ensuring that the supply of foster homes matches the demand is not always an easy task. The formula devised by Bebbington and Miles predicts that of all local authorities, the research Authority will experience the greatest discrepancy between potential foster carers and the demands of the child care system (Bebbington and Miles, 1990). The research study highlights four concerns that arise from the limited availability of foster carers. These are problems that are likely to be experienced by other authorities and which need to be overcome if the fostering service is to fulfil its expectations. However before these four problem areas are identified it is important to remind ourselves that, throughout this report, we have included several case studies which illustrate the very positive outcomes that can result when placement in a suitable foster home is secured and supported.

The first issue of concern is the location of foster homes. *None* of the foster placements used by the young people throughout the research was actually within the local authority boundary – which, in contrast, was true for the majority of residential placements. For many of these young people placement in foster care meant unwelcome disruption to the pattern of their lives – long journeys to visit family and friends and to attend school. This does beg the question of whether, in these circumstances, residential care rather than foster care is more appropriately regarded as 'care in the community'?

However for many young people even a foster home out of borough did not seem to be a possibility. Reminiscent of *Children Who Wait*, this study, nearly 20 years later, shows that the most likely cause for placement plans not to be fulfilled is an inability to find suitable long-term foster homes (Rowe and Lambert, 1973). For many young people in the study this meant unacceptable delays in implementing their care plans or in preparing contingencies. Clearly stated within the Children Act is the principle that delay in decision making is detrimental to the child; this principle can equally be applied to delay in implementing decisions, and this research indicates that a prime cause of such delay is the limited supply of suitable long-term foster homes.

A further significant consequence of the difficulty in finding long-term foster placements was the 'silting up' of the assessment foster care service. Ideally young people were placed in assessment foster homes for an initial period of six weeks, with the presumption that a further six weeks was likely to prepare for transition to the placement recommended by the assessment. In practice many young people remained in these assessment placements for several months, some for periods of over a year. This had major implications for the efficacy of this specialist service, both in reducing the number of assessment foster places available and in creating great insecurity for those waiting for a new placement. This in turn raises questions about the role of highly rewarded specialist assessment foster carers within a foster service that needs to be responsive to demand – and to offer maximum stability to the young people it cares for.

The fourth issue of concern is the lack of choice when the supply of placements is limited, a major finding also from the evaluation of Warwickshire's policy to close all its children's homes (Cliffe with Berridge, 1992). This is of particular concern when the young people requiring accommodation are from minority ethnic groups. The enormous ethnic diversity of the care population of this Authority highlights the complexity of implementing a policy of 'ethnic matching', especially in taking due account of the four elements of race, culture, religion and language. Where exact 'matching' is not possible, carers must, as a minimum, demonstrate an awareness of the importance of promoting, within young people, a positive racial and cultural identity.

> 'It's like the classic thing, if you're white you often don't talk about your identity – it's taken for granted. Whereas this is a very live issue in this family ... about who you are and where you've come from, so the young people feel value in that ... I'm an immigrant and I've got my own culture, they feel that they can relate and identify themselves with me on these issues.' (Foster carer, from a family with one black and one white carer)

With the intention of actively promoting the welfare of children and young people, most local authorities have adopted policies which advocate, where possible, ethnic matching in placements and a preference for foster homes for long-term care. If these policies are not backed by adequate resources, leading to implemented and implementable planning decisions, then the results may in fact lead to a diminution of the young person's welfare (Caesar, Parchment and Berridge, 1994).

Liaison with different agencies

Interagency cooperation is a statutory requirement when dealing with child protection cases or children with special needs and in other cases would be regarded good practice (Department of Health, 1991g; Department for Education, 1994). For the adolescents in our sample, social services staff tended to seek help from other agencies when their own resources had been exhausted or were thought to be inappropriate, or when they believed that they did not have the necessary skill or expertise to help the young person themselves. Our analysis of both the assessment process and the subsequent making and implementation of decisions points to the problems that interdisciplinary working can have for Social Services Departments, a finding which accords with other studies (Audit Commission and HM Inspectorate, 1992; Audit Commission, 1994a; Kurtz, Thornes and Wolkind, 1994). As a result, many young people with the most complex needs are not receiving the specialist help they require. It is clear that if the needs of this group of young people are to be met, that staff in social services will have to work with other agencies, especially education and the psychiatric and psychological services. Working in partnership with other professionals is one of the key principles on which the success of the Children Act is predicated. However, this research suggests that there is still a long way to go before such relationships produce a genuinely interdisciplinary service that is able to appear relatively seamless to its users. In particular, our findings suggest that working in partnership will require:

- that relationships between different services are formalised rather than dependent on *ad hoc* arrangements. In addition, to avoid the current level of frustration and wasted resources, staff must be familiar with these arrangements so they can get ready access to resources;
- a greater appreciation of the realities under which different professionals operate. For instance, social workers often have over-optimistic expectations of the impact that other professionals will have on the problems of families and young people. Equally, other professional agencies fail to appreciate that the unfamiliarity of the more clinical style and the slower pace at which their services are delivered causes problems for social services clients;
- that there is a clear understanding of the expected roles of each worker, whatever their professional expertise or agency base, and that this is negotiated separately for each individual case;
- greater understanding of the pace at which each profession works – ideally these should be matched – to reduce the probability of one aspect of a Care Plan being held up by the slower pace of delivery of other services;
- a challenge to the unequal power between professions, which is still problematic, especially where the distribution of power does not equal that of responsibility for the management of the case;
- enhancement of the function of case management, ensuring coordination of the input from different services, in particular monitoring the uptake of services and where necessary ensuring alternative sources of help are offered.

Although social services departments have statutory responsibility for helping and supporting these young people, to do so they are often required to call upon the help of other specialists, which is clearly recognised in Section 27 of the Children Act. Yet the experience of the sample group indicates that on many occasions that help is not forthcoming quickly enough or that the practitioners in other agencies have particular difficulties in engaging the attention of these young people long enough for them to benefit from the help offered.

Young people and decision making

This Authority, even in pre-Children Act days, had a clear policy of involving young people in decision making, although the procedures for doing so were unclear in relation to some of the multifarious planning meetings. Given the commitment to this philosophy it was disappointing that there was such a low level (less than 50 per cent) of actual attendance at planning meetings by young people.

Most young people we interviewed were clear that they could attend meetings but not all choose to do so; some had difficulty in understanding the purpose of meetings or did not find them meaningful or useful. Perhaps we need to question whether a reliance on such procedures helps us meet the aim of involving young people in decisions; whether 'meetings' can ever be truly 'child-centred' and whether there is sufficient focus on preparation and work outside the meeting structure.

Following through what happened to each of these 75 young people, it soon became apparent that in many cases the young people themselves, or their families, were responsible for initiating many of the changes that occurred, either in accordance with agreed plans or in contradiction to it. Often this happened without reference to the social worker or with the social worker, sometimes supported by the planning system, confirming a de facto decision taken by the young person.

In other instances, especially in relation to contact with family and with others from the same ethnic background, many social workers believed that these young people were old enough – that is of sufficient age and understanding – to decide these matters for themselves. In this sense, some felt that intervention (though not necessarily support) in these areas should not be the business of the social services. More pragmatically, they believed that the motivation to work towards the goal they wanted to achieve had to come from the young people themselves; decisions made by others were unlikely to succeed (see Marsh and Fisher, 1992). When working with older adolescents, especially on a voluntary basis, this poses a dilemma. What is the right balance between the positive of enabling young people to be more involved in making decisions for themselves and the negative of passive non-intervention? When does giving young people the power to choose (and to carry responsibility for that choice) without reference to their social worker or care plan, become neglect?

While the Children Act makes clear the principles on which such issues should be resolved, and as such was welcomed by all those participating in this study, translating that into decisions on a day to day basis still needs to be thought through carefully. Involving young people appropriately is a definite skill (Hodgson, 1995). This entails getting the balance right between taking full account of the young person's views without abdicating the department's responsibility for decision making.

The costs of assessment

The implications of our findings on the costs of child care assessment were discussed in detail in the last chapter. Earlier in this chapter we summarised the major differences in costs between the two assessment types. Here we add some more general observations.

Initially, we are convinced that the desire to collaborate in this study between social work researchers and social care economists has been justified. Child care researchers from different disciplines work together too infrequently on individual studies and our efforts here have provided useful complementary information. Sharing, in the main, a common methodology has also been an interesting and valuable development.

In addition, we feel that the specific aims for this aspect of the research have been fully met. We demonstrated that assessment is often a complex activity, reflected in the high costs of some cases and approaches. However, some assessments are much more straightforward and less intensive. It was important to discover that social services bears the brunt of assessment costs and, perhaps surprisingly, that so much of the costs of assessment can be attributed to accommodation expenses given the general move in child care away from the more costly residential care options.

Overall, the conclusions from this costs analysis strike us as encouraging. Social work is a complex, unenviable task and practitioners, it seems, are frequently and unreasonably blamed for society's ills. Nonetheless it is clear, as one would expect, that professional standards could be improved (see for example, Department of Health and Social Security, 1985). But there are two findings in particular that demonstrate important elements of rationality in social work assessments with adolescents. First, higher expenditure on assessment packages is linked to greater needs in young people and, secondly, while the link between assessment costs and outcomes was more tenuous, there was some evidence to suggest that higher costs are associated with an improvement in a young person's welfare in the following 12-month period. At the outset of the research, these two results could by no means have been assumed. Any of us who, on occasions, may doubt the efficacy of social work with adolescents should find this reassuring.

Part Three: Issues for the future

In this final chapter our first task has been to report on the research objectives that we set out to achieve. Secondly we summarised several themes that arose from those research findings. We turn now, in the last part of the chapter, to some of the broader questions which arise from this research study concerning both the future of social work with adolescents and the continuing relevance of assessment.

What priority should be given to social work with adolescents?

Our research evidence points to the generally low priority that was given in the study Authority to social work with adolescents, a conclusion reported in other studies (Farmer and Parker, 1991). One instance of this was the way in which cases were allocated within area teams; only experienced workers on higher scales are allowed to deal with child protection cases. As a result the only team members left to work with adolescents – where the presenting problems though complex are rarely a protection issue – were new and inexperienced staff. Similarly, striving to meet the very appropriate requirement that all child protection cases should be allocated often meant that many teenagers, even those on care orders, were without allocated social workers for considerable periods of time. The need for social services departments to reconsider the current balance in their work between child protection and services to other young people is now a pressing matter. This was certainly the view of the Audit Commission, and seems to be reflected in recent Department of Health thinking (Audit Commission, 1994a; Rose, 1994).

The current low priority of this age group not only contrasts with that of child protection cases, it is also very different to the situation a decade ago when much of the new thinking in social work organisation and practice was focused upon this particular group. Has this occurred because of a change in the perceived needs of young people or is it more to do with organisational imperatives? The considerable, yet unfortunately often unacknowledged, success which social services have experienced in dealing with juvenile offenders may well have contributed to some of the decrease in attention to adolescents (Morris and Giller, 1987). However, as indicated by the case studies presented here, the needs of adolescents are still very real, with many facing very complex and intractable problems (Bullock, 1992).

> 'When the AAS started at first they offered a new way of working with adolescents which was important – about being prepared to take risks, not always going for security, but thinking of other imaginative ways of working – I think that now we (as a department) have lost some of the sense of how to work with adolescents ... we have lost sight of some of the things we were trying to achieve for them.' (Service Manager)

A substantial proportion of the cases in this sample fall into the category that is now referred to as 'children in need' – that is cases where social services are offering support services or short periods of accommodation in the hope of preventing longer-term family break-up. Although the provision of such services is a requirement of the Children Act, the fact that most social services staff still referred, incorrectly, to these as non-statutory cases reflects the priority that is accorded to them. The second report to Parliament on the operation of the Children Act, together with several recent studies, suggests that the very limited provision of services to 'children in need', under Section 17 of the Children Act, is a cause for some concern (Department of Health, 1994). While the emphasis in these discussions has tended to fall on younger children, this research suggests that these problems are equally significant for adolescents.

The limitations of social work with adolescents

In working with adolescents, especially older adolescents, social workers always need to balance the extent to which they can offer prescriptive choices to young people with that of enabling them to decide for themselves, even if this does not always turn out to be in their best interests. At a purely pragmatic level, if the young person is unhappy with a decision or with their current situation, they will simply remove themselves or effect their own choices.

> 'It is not down to me to tell him what to do, but to counsel him into

making a realistic choice and to sustain him in achieving that.' (Social worker)

Very often the power of social workers to control or influence the behaviour of teenagers is very limited, as the report into the death of Elaine Foley concluded. Elaine, a young woman in care, was murdered by a stranger on one of her many visits to central London. The report concluded:

'... over the previous year she had received many warnings and counselling from her social worker and others about the risks her life style exposed her to ... there is no reason to believe that alternative courses of action would have afforded her better protection .... Decisions made whilst Elaine was in care were made with due debate and made corporately with appropriate consultation.' (Goodall, 1992)

The findings of this current research also point to the limited success that many social workers have in meeting the emotional needs of this group of young people. Recognition of this, and the long history of involvement for some, did lead a few social workers to question whether, for some young people, a fuller assessment at an earlier point would have been beneficial. In fact in many cases this had been offered, but had not been effective. As we noted an important factor was the limited success of psychological and psychiatric assessments. Hence many staff saw that the successful contribution of social services was more likely to lie in meeting the very real material needs of the group. This is not intended simply as a criticism of the workers or the department, but more as a recognition of the realities of the situation. However this does mean that some young people are reaching adulthood and losing the support of social services while they still have severe unresolved emotional needs or relationship difficulties.

Making and implementing comprehensive Care Plans

This research reports a significant degree of failure in making comprehensive plans for young people and in implementing them fully. These findings relate to the period immediately prior to the implementation of the Children Act and the introduction of the new statutory requirement to draw up a Care Plan for every child and young person looked after by the local authority. Are there any grounds for thinking that the new regulations will significantly alter the extent to which plans are made and implemented? Good practice in child care planning would seem to require three components: a clear understanding of the purpose and principles of social work planning; a planning system which facilitates the exercising of those principles and which does not give undue weight to process over content; and the necessary resources to do the job well. It is also important that Care Plans should be comprehensive 'care packages' that address the full range of a young person's needs and not just those of placement. When this research was undertaken staff, particularly those in the Assessment Service, were very aware of the imminent requirements of the Act, so there is little reason for thinking that any of these components would be significantly altered solely by the implementation of the Children Act in 1991.

It seems unlikely that any further regulation on planning is necessary; indeed over-prescriptive regulation carries the danger of promoting a 'bureaucratic' approach to planning rather than one motivated by a thorough understanding of the sound principles of social work planning (Sinclair and Grimshaw, 1995). The often changing circumstances of adolescents require a very flexible planning system, one which can take account of the realities of a dynamic life pattern, still ensuring that decisions are made and implemented, so that young people are not left for any length of time in a dangerous planning vacuum.

With the introduction of the Children Act staff have had to take on new terminology, new procedures and new paperwork. Much of the early training was directed towards gaining a familiarity with these aspects. Perhaps the time has come for training that will reassert the importance of the key principles of social work planning in influencing positive outcomes for young people. It is clear that planning procedures are a necessary but not a sufficient component; they can guide the intervention, but cannot replace the need for a consistent exercising of social work skills. Of equal importance is the distribution of departmental resources in a balanced way, such that the effort directed towards the making of Plans does not outweigh that given to implementation and to working closely and directly with young people to actually effect change and thereby address needs.

Should assessment be a specialised activity?

It seems that restructuring is now the natural state of affairs within social services departments. In the past few years this has resulted in an increasing number of specialisms within child care. This is most widespread in relation to child protection, but more recently several departments have introduced the model of purchaser/provider split to child care services. Under such a model one worker assesses the needs of a client and then 'purchases' these from a separate section of the department or other agency whose function is to supply services.

What are the implications of such a functional split for child care assessment? Ultimately this is a matter of balancing the potential advantages against the disadvantages. First the possible advantages. A separation of the function of assessment from the delivery of services has the potential for staff to undertake intensive or in-depth assessments; to enable them to develop their skills in assessment; to increase the focus on case management and decision implementation; and to encourage a needs-led rather than resource-led pattern of decision making. Additionally it can give young people and their families more than one point of contact within social services.

On the negative side the first question to be faced is whether it is possible to distinguish between the two activities of assessment and intervention to address a young person's immediate problems. As we saw in earlier chapters the staff in the AAS are firmly of the view that assessment and intervention are intertwined. This would imply modifications in the understanding of the role of care manager as articulated in relation to adult services (Department of Health, 1991g). It has been suggested that for success in children's services, the role of care manager as a care provider of an interactive, dynamic and therapeutic assessment process needs to be accepted and established (Walby, 1994).

Other drawbacks from a functional split are the greatly increased possibility of fragmentation in decision making, with confusion over who is responsible for taking and implementing decisions (Ballard, 1994). Any such confusion will cause difficulties for staff but more importantly may present real problems to young people and their families. In addition, a needs-led approach to decisions that is totally divorced from resource planning and allocation must take account of the very negative consequences for young people if the recommended placements are not available within a reasonable period.

However, one of the main contrasts between the models of assessment that have developed for Community Care and those in use with adolescents is in the different assumptions about the dynamic nature of the lives of those being assessed. Though reassessments can be undertaken, Community Care assessments often seem to assume that the needs of the client are relatively static or cumulative, even predictable, and therefore that assessment can be undertaken as something of a discrete task which will then lead to a Care Plan. This is far from the case with adolescents, where assessments are usually initiated by a crisis and are frequently punctuated by major changes in circumstances – running away, offending, making and breaking significant relationships. Hence, assessment with this particular client group is also about immediate intervention. It is particularly because of these characteristics of work with adolescents that it seems problematic to simply transfer across the purchaser/provider model of Community Care. The value of separating the purchasing and providing function does appear to be closely related to the passivity of the user, which is not an attribute readily associated with adolescents.

Do we need a new word for 'assessment'?

The discussions presented throughout this report have pointed to the lack of any single concept or common understanding of what is meant by assessment. Rather we find the term being used in a variety of ways to describe very different processes, with an implicit acknowledgement of the range of functions inherent in assessment. Does a term which has so many meanings lack any value and need to be replaced? Our conclusion is no. There is sufficient understanding of the essence of assessment for it to remain a useful term – even if the consensus of understanding is no more than suggested by the definition used in this research – namely, a preparation for decision making. However attached to that core definition it is necessary to have a very clear understanding of the particular purpose of any individual assessment and to match the style of the assessment to suit that purpose. More importantly the term assessment conveys an awareness of a particular set of competences – competences that have a common core but which can be tailored to meet the needs of different assessment purposes.

The purpose of assessment

In Chapter 2 we noted several different forms of child care assessment that are currently in use in many social services departments: assessment of a 'child in need'; assessment of risk; assessment of special educational needs; comprehensive assessments, using the 'Orange Book' approach; assessment of the standards of parenting for 'looked after' children using the Assessment and Action Records. Further, we suggested that perhaps the term assessment is meaningless if it is detached from an indication of its purpose. Depending on why they are being undertaken, assessments are likely to take on a different form. No single pattern for assessment will be applicable to every circumstance.

Most of the emphasis on assessment in the 1970s focused on

adolescents, while in the past decade greatest attention has been on child protection. However, with the passage of the Children Act, social services departments have had to consider fresh approaches or systems for the assessment of 'children in need', many borrowing from the new concepts applied to Community Care. While there are numerous variations in the way in which these systems are described in departmental procedures, they have many similar features. Usually the sequence is first to assess whether a referral relates to a 'child in need', and the priority that should be assigned to the case and then to consider the appropriate service option. Hence many departments have developed three-tiered assessment systems; screening: initial assessment; comprehensive assessment (see Social Information Systems, 1993).

Beyond establishing the immediate criteria for each of these stages and the corresponding paperwork, there is limited evidence from social services departments of more developed or integrated assessment systems. Most often there is a procedural separation of the assessment of 'children in need', from child protection assessment, or the ongoing assessment of 'looked after' children. Similarly the documentation tends to concentrate on procedures with less emphasis on the concept or principles of assessment. While it is perhaps invidious to single out individual examples, for illustrative purpose we have included some documentation from two Authorities.

First, we include a statement of the principles of assessment which the London Borough of Hackney has included within its multi-agency Children's Service Plan (London Borough of Hackney, 1994). Given that assessments will be undertaken for different purposes and probably under different procedures, it is important that this variety of activity is based upon a common set of principles. In defining 18 principles of assessment the Hackney document makes clear that these should apply to all assessments, regardless of the agency, the worker or the purpose of undertaking the assessment. We have included these principles of assessment in Appendix B.

Our second illustration is the model of assessment developed by Staffordshire Social Services Department with the help of the Bridge Consultancy, which we feel represents a relatively complete design.

> The purpose of the model is to provide a clear and consistent, conceptual and practical framework for assessment work with children and their families. It starts from legal, theoretical and philosophical state-

ments and moves on to identify details of practice and process. (Staffordshire Social Services Department, 1993)

This statement of the general purpose of assessment and the process of assessment is not very different from many others. However the complete pack includes a more detailed consideration of these components, set within clear principles, integrated with the Care Planning and Review systems and presented with suggested tools for practice and information for service users. The outline of that model is reproduced in Appendix C.

A flexible process for assessment

While much recent thinking on assessment has centred around assessments of 'children in need', it illustrates our contention that no one rigid model of assessment will be appropriate in every case, whether that is a new referral for support services, or a complex child protection case, or a young person already known to the department but for whom new decisions need to be made. So what model of assessment is appropriate for which purpose? It seems unlikely that a simple classification by type of case or even presenting problem will be sufficient. Rather than looking for a series of different models, or sets of procedures, perhaps it is more helpful to see child care assessment as falling along a series of dimensions, and selecting the appropriate point on each continuum according to the individual circumstances of the case. In this way it is possible to establish a set of general principles that will apply to all assessments but to allow the actual process to vary according to individual cases.

We would suggest that there are eight dimensions along which cases vary and which need to be considered in deciding what form of assessment is appropriate; these are presented diagrammatically (Figure 13.1).

Which form of assessment is appropriate will depend upon the characteristics of the case, the purpose of the assessment and how these are located on the dimensions of assessment. For instance, where the needs of the child are clearly articulated a limited assessment may be adequate. If the issues are more complex or are likely to involve several agencies then the level of investigation necessary to gather the appropriate information will need to be different. We can find a useful illustration of that within the Staffordshire model, where a distinction is drawn between simple, brief, once and for all events and assessments which may be *cumulative* or *cyclical*.

A *cumulative* assessment may be the best approach where infor-

Figure 13.1   Variable dimensions of the assessment task

knowledge already available
little information ◄─────────────► much information

depth of knowledge required
limited ◄─────────────► comprehensive

range of issues
limited ◄─────────────► complex

time-scale
short/immediate ◄─────────────► long/less urgent

applicability
all referrals ◄─────────────► specific referrals

specificity of task
continuous ◄─────────────► discrete task

specialist task
with intervention ◄─────────────► separate from treatment

professional involvement
multidisciplinary ◄─────────────► SSD only

mation from all sources is gradually brought together and built up – here one thinks of the process of assessing for special educational needs. A *cyclical* pattern, depicted in Figure 13.2, may be appropriate if action is necessary before all the information can be gathered. This pattern is particularly relevant to child protection referrals.

Indeed one might take this model a stage further and give greater emphasis to the notion of intervention or change by depicting the assessment process as *helical*, in that each interpretation of new information actually generates progress, in the way that a screw moves forward with each turn (see Figure 13.3). The image of the screw turning within its surrounding environment also reminds us that assessments do not take place in a vacuum, but are interactive processes. However as is clear from the picture

Figure 13.2   Cyclical assessments

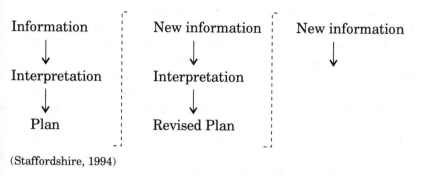

(Staffordshire, 1994)

presented by this study, not all assessments will move forward in this fashion; there will be many deflections and blockages along the way.

However the point about these particular descriptions of assessment forms is that they are not isolated alternatives; rather they represent a range of options to be deployed as fits any particular situation. Viewing assessment thus, as a flexible process, also helps to lessen the perception of assessment as an isolated activity attached to a particular procedure. Rather it promotes the importance of assessment as a social work task governed by a set of competences which the worker is required to deploy appropriately according to the circumstance of any case.

Figure 13.3   Helical assessments

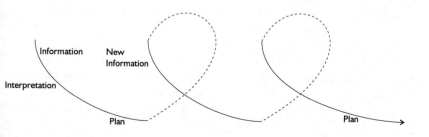

An integrated assessment, planning and review system?

We would also suggest that such an approach to identifying the right form of assessment might help to deal with the problems thrown up by the increasing specialisation and, therefore, fragmentation of assessment and decision making within the child care system. Not only have restructuring and reorganisations of service response led to the development of multiple child care assessment systems in most departments, in many instances these have been replicated in multiple decision making or planning arrangements. Often different processes, personnel and paperwork will be used for decision making for child protection cases from those used for children 'looked after' or 'children in need'. As this study shows, coordination of assessment within a continuing process of planning and review is particularly important in work with adolescents living turbulent lives.

The dynamic nature of many adolescent cases means that assessment processes must be responsive. This in turn requires a planning system that is flexible enough to deal with changing circumstances, but systematic enough to ensure that the management of cases retains a clear structure and purpose. This study clearly demonstrates the importance of the relationship between assessment and planning and review systems if knowledge about young people is to be used effectively to make plans with them and to work with them to fulfil these. But the planning and review systems that have been developed under the Children Act are most often used solely for children who are 'looked after'. This means that the separate assessment process for children and young people who are 'in need' but not looked after, are not linked into any systematic planning or review system.

It seems then that departments need to think about developing assessment systems that are capable of being adapted for individual cases, rather than operating a series of different models of assessment depending on how a case is classified. Without this flexible, unitary approach to assessment there is a danger that the current fragmentation of assessment and its reflection in complex planning arrangements will continue.

The Guidance within the Children Act on the making of Care Plans is compatible with, even conducive to, the development of coordinated, almost seamless, planning and review systems, which see planning and reviewing as processes rather than events. Within that Guidance, assessment is identified as one of the four components of planning, further promoting the value of a unified system for assessment, planning and review. Of course this is not to suggest that the format of assessments will not vary, simply that variation should be possible within a single procedural system that meets necessary statutory requirements. But most important of all, everyone engaged in such a system should have a clear understanding of its purpose and the fundamental principles which underpin good child care practice. These then act as the criteria by which the procedural framework is adapted to match the circumstance of the particular case.

Conclusion

This study paints a picture of the day to day work in undertaking social work with adolescents; it describes the context of that task, its complexities, its limitations, some of its successes and failings. More specifically it focuses on the role of assessment as part of the social work process, comparing a more procedural form of referred or specialist assessment with those undertaken routinely by district-based social workers.

The study contains many research messages: about the low priority given to work with adolescents; the importance of addressing the racial, cultural, religious and linguistic needs of young people and the need to enhance social workers' ability to do this; the consequences of failing to provide sufficient long-term foster homes; the need to develop practice to involve actively young people in making and implementing decisions, without expecting them to carry all responsibility; the continuing difficulties in securing appropriate educational provision; major problems for young people in receiving effective help from psychological or psychiatric services. But running throughout the study are two interlinked themes: a lack of clarity in both the concept and practice of assessment; and the appropriate balance between the procedural, managerial aspects of providing a social work service and that of working directly with young people.

Too often assessment is understood solely in terms of the specific procedures that guide it or the paperwork that records it. This can overshadow the need to enhance the skills required to gather and appraise information, and to do so by working in partnership with young people and their families. Certainly assessment must be a part of the child care planning process; that process needs to be an integrated and flexible one. Only then can it provide the necessary framework for demonstrating clearly the purpose of a particular assessment and support social workers in deploying their social work skills in undertaking an assessment appropriate to the particular circumstances of each case.

The relatively positive outcomes for this group of adolescents are encouraging. Also important is the conclusion that these outcomes are more likely to be associated with the quality of social work input than solely the style of the assessment. This suggests that the very proper attention paid to procedures and working in a planned and participatory way will only be effective when it also encourages and supports working directly with young people and their families to address their concerns.

Appendix A

Working Together Under the Children Act

Definitions of assessment

Initial assessment: An agreed multidisciplinary composite report on the child's current health and welfare in the context of his/her family which will enable participants at a case conference to plan the child's immediate future.

Medical assessment: A specific examination by a doctor for a definite purpose, e.g. a court request or as part of a child's health surveillance programme. The medical assessment may be more wide-ranging than a physical examination of the child and may in addition include comment on development and behaviour. The medical assessment may include recommendations for the ongoing care of the child within a medical context.

Developmental assessment: An objective assessment of a child, often to some agreed protocol, carried out by a doctor, health visitor or child psychologist, for the purpose of determining the child's developmental level. Such assessments carried out in a serial way would provide information on a child's developmental progress. Developmental assessments are normally part of the DHA child health surveillance programme, but may be carried out at other times.

Special educational needs assessment: A compilation of reports from various professionals to assist the local education authority to place the child in an educational setting compatible with his/her abilities. This assessment is carried out under the Education Act 1981.

Health assessment: An examination undertaken by the health visitor or school nurse to ascertain the child's health status. The health assessment will include information on height and weight, immunisation status, and vision and hearing.

Comprehensive assessment: A structured time-limited exercise to collect and evaluate information about the child and his/her family on which to base long-term decisions (see *Protecting Children: A Guide for Social Workers Undertaking a Comprehensive Assessment*, Department of Health, 1988).

Family assessment: A report prepared over a period of time to assess the functioning of a particular family in relation to the needs of a child. The assessment is usually undertaken by a social worker but may be undertaken by a psychologist or family centre worker.

(Department of Health, 1991g)

Appendix B

The First Hackney Children's Plan
The key principles of assessment

1. All assessments of need must have a clear and stated purpose within the context of safeguarding and/or promoting the child's welfare.

2. All assessments will be undertaken in partnership with parents and other carers. Parents or carers will be encouraged to participate actively in the assessment process. This will include attendance at assessment and review meetings which should take place at a time and location convenient to them.

3. The views and wishes of children and young people will in every case be sought and taken seriously.

4. Assessments must not be informed by stereotypical or value-laden judgements.

5. All assessments should acknowledge and seek to enhance the strengths within families, recognising that lifestyles may vary according to race, culture, religion, class, sexuality and family composition.

6. Assessments must incorporate alternative forms of communication where a child or family's particular needs indicate this is necessary, for example, by use of interpreters, signers, or by the use of advocates.

7. All assessments must be undertaken within a timescale which avoids unnecessary delay and does not prejudice the needs of the child. In practice this will mean that no assessment of need should take longer than a month. In some cases, for example, child protection, assessments of young homelessness, there will be much stricter timescales. The 1993 Education Act also demands that the statementing process for Children with Special Educational Needs must not take longer than six months. This, like all other detailed

assessment procedures can be obtained from those agencies directly concerned.

8. All assessments should be conducted in a way which takes account of the special needs of a child or family.

9. All assessments of need must be based on the needs of children and children's families and not determined by resource or financial implications.

10. Assessments must be co-ordinated both within and between agencies to avoid duplication and to develop consistency and clarity of communication and service delivery.

11. Assessments should not be 'static' but should be constantly reviewed to take account of changing needs and circumstances.

12. All assessments should be undertaken within existing inter-agency policies and procedures.

13. All new Council, departmental or agency policies and procedures must be informed by this set of key assessment principles.

14. All assessments must be properly recorded and form the basis of written agreements between the particular agency and the child and/or her/his parents or carers.

15. Parents and/or children and young people have the right to challenge assessments made on their behalf.

16. All assessments must be treated in confidence and information only shared on a 'need to know' basis.

17. Any child or young person, parent or carer may request an assessment of their needs.

18. Any child, or parent, has the right to refuse an assessment (or the right to participate, if there is a statutory reason for the assessment to proceed without the child/or parents agreement).

(London Borough of Hackney, 1994)

Appendix C

A Model of Assessment (Staffordshire Social Services Department, 1994)

The purposes of assessment are:

- 'to support good professional practice;
- to establish whether the child is "in need";
- to fulfil legal duties and expectations of the Local Authority and others in relation to such need;
- to ensure equity of access and the appropriate use of resources as above and, more importantly;
- to ensure that the needs of the individual child are appropriately identified in order that he/she may receive the best possible individualised response'.

The process of assessment:
Assessment is a process which focuses on individual need, current difficulties, individual and family strengths and the range of help that may be available. Essentially it is concerned with how the key people around a child come to conclusions about needs and how to meet them. The process is represented graphically as shown in Figure C.1 on page 312.

Figure C.1   The process of assessment

Collection of relevant information

Collation, ordering and recording of information

Explanation or interpretation of information

Identification of (a) category of need and (b) individual personal needs

Identification of possible relevant responses from within and outside the family
⇓

(Staffordshire Social Services Department, 1993)

References

Adcock, M (1980) *Terminating Parental Contact*. British Association for Adoption and Fostering

Adcock, M and White, R eds (1985) *Good Enough Parenting. A Framework for Assessment*. British Agencies for Adoption and Fostering

Ahmad, B 'Child care and ethnic minorities' *in* Kahan, B ed. (1989) *Child Care Research, Policy and Practice*. Hodder & Stoughton

Ahmad, B (1990) *Black Perspectives in Social Work*. Venture Press in association with the Race Equality Unit and the National Institute for Social Work

Ahmed, S (1980) 'Selling fostering to the black community', *Community Care*, 305, 21-22

Ahmed, S 'Cultural racism in work with Asian women and girls' *in* Cheetham, J and Small, J eds (1986) *Social Work with Black Children and their Families*. Batsford in association with British Agencies for Adoption and Fostering

Ahmed, S 'Children in care: the racial dimension in social work assessment' *in* Morgan, S and Righton, P eds (1989) *Child Care: Concerns and Conflicts*. Hodder & Stoughton

Aldgate, J 'Identification of Factors Influencing Child's Length of Stay in Care' *in* Triseliotis, J ed. (1980) *New Developments in Foster Care and Adoption*. London and Boston: Routledge and Kegan Paul

Allen, C and Beecham, J 'Costing services: ideals and reality' *in* Netten, A and Beecham, J eds (1993) *Costing Community Care: Theory and Practice*. Ashgate

Association of Directors of Social Services/Commission for Racial Equality (1978) *Multiracial Britain: the Social Services Response*. ADSS/CRE

Association of Metropolitan Authorities (1994) *Mental Health Services: Issues for Local Government*. AMA

Audit Commission (1994a) *Seen But Not Heard: Coordinating Child Health and Social Services for Children in Need.* HMSO

Audit Commission (1994b) *Taking Stock: Progress with Community Care.* HMSO

Audit Commission and HM Inspectorate (1992) *Getting In On the Act – Provision for Pupils with Special Educational Needs: The National Picture.* HMSO

Ballard, R (1994) 'Double trouble', *Community Care,* 1032, 26-27

Bamford, F and Wolkind, N (1988) *The Physical and Mental Health of Children in Care.* Economic and Social Research Council

Barn, R (1993) *Black Children in the Public Care System.* Batsford in association with British Agencies for Adoption and Fostering

Batta, I and Mawby, R (1981) 'Children in local authority care – monitoring of racial differences in Bradford', *Policy and Politics,* 9, 2, 137-50

Bebbington, A and Miles, J (1989) 'The background of children who enter local authority care', *British Journal of Social Work,* 19, 5, 349-68

Bebbington, A and Miles, J (1990) 'The supply of foster families for children in care', *British Journal of Social Work,* 20, 4, 283-307

Beecham, J, Dansie, A and Knapp, M (1993a) *Child Care Assessment in Social Services: A Study of the Costs,* Interim Report to the Department of Health, Discussion Paper 903/3, Personal Social Services Research Unit, University of Kent at Canterbury

Beecham, J, Dansie, A, Knapp, M and Carter, S (1993b) *Child Care Assessment in Social Services: A Study of the Costs,* Second Report to the Department of Health, Discussion Paper 944/3, Personal Social Services Research Unit, University of Kent at Canterbury

Berridge, D (1985) *Children's Homes.* Blackwell

Berridge, D and Cleaver, H (1987) *Foster Home Breakdown.* Blackwell

Berridge, D (1994) 'Foster and residential care reassessed: a research perspective', *Children & Society,* 8, 2, 132-50

Bilson, A and Thorpe, D (1987) *Child Care Careers and their Management: A Systems Perspective.* Fife Regional Council Social Work Department

Blyth, E and Milner, J (1993) 'Exclusion from school: A first step in exclusion from society', *Children & Society,* 7, 3, 225-68

Brent Borough Council (1985) *A Child in Trust: the Report of the Panel of Inquiry into the Circumstances Surrounding the Death of Jasmine Beckford.* The Council

British Agencies for Adoption and Fostering (1994) *Preparing Schedule 2 Reports under Adoption Rules 1984*. BAAF Practice Note 31. BAAF

British Association of Social Workers (1983) *Effective and Ethical Recording*. BASW

British Refugee Council (1990) *Unaccompanied Refugee Children: A Monitoring Report*. BRC

Brummer, N 'White social workers/black children: issues of identity' *in* Aldgate, J and Simmonds, J eds (1988) *Direct Work With Children*. Batsford

Buist, M and Mapstone, E (1985) *Choosing for Children – a Study of Interprofessional Decision-making*. Department of Social Administration, University of Dundee

Bullock, R (1992) 'Research review – residential care', *Children & Society*, 6, 4, 382-84

Bullock, R, Little, M and Millham, S (1993) *Going Home: The Return of Children Separated from their Families*. Dartington Social Research Unit, Dartmouth

Bunyan, A and Sinclair, R (1987) 'Gatekeepers to care', *Practice*, 1, 2, 116-28

Butler-Sloss, E (1988) *Report of the Inquiry into Child Abuse in Cleveland 1987*. HMSO

Caesar, G, Parchment, M and Berridge, D (1994) *Black Perspectives on Services for children in need*. National Children's Bureau

Central Statistical Office (1991) *Family Expenditure Survey*. HMSO

Challis, D and Ferlie, E (1987) 'Changing patterns of fieldwork organisation: The team leaders' view', *British Journal of Social Work*, 17, 2, 147-68

Charles, M, Rashid, S and Thoburn, J (1992) 'The placement of black children with permanent new families', *Adoption and Fostering*, 16, 2, 13-19

The Chartered Institute for Public Finance and Accountancy (1991) *Survey of Social Services Departments Expenditure*. CIPFA

The Children's Society (1994) *The Children's Planning Initiative*.

Cliffe, D with Berridge, D (1991) *Closing Children's Homes: An End to Residential Childcare?* National Children's Bureau

Clifford, D (1994) 'Towards an anti-oppressive social work assessment method', *Practice*, 6, 3, 226-38

Commission for Racial Equality (1989) *Race Equality in Social*

Services Departments: A Survey of Equal Opportunities Policies. CRE

Commission for Racial Equality (1990) *Social Services and Race: Guidelines for Social Services/Work Departments.*

Dennington, J and Pitts, J *eds* (1991) *Developing Services for Young People in Crisis.* Longman

Department For Education (1994) *Code of Practice on the Identification and Assessment of Special Educational Needs.* DFE

Department For Education and Department of Health (1994) *Pupils with Problems: Circulars.* DFE

Department of Health *Annual Statistical Returns on Children in Care of Local Authorities.* HMSO

Department of Health (1988) *Protecting Children: A Guide for Social Workers Undertaking a Comprehensive Assessment* (Orange Book). HMSO

Department of Health (1989) *Caring for People: Community Care in the Next Decade and Beyond.* HMSO

Department of Health (1991a) *Patterns and Outcomes in Child Placement: Messages from current research and their implications.* HMSO

Department of Health (1991b) and (1995) *Looking After Children: Assessment and Action Records.* Second edition 1995. HMSO

Department of Health (1991c) *Child Abuse: A Study of Inquiry Reports 1980-1989.* HMSO

Department of Health (1991d) *The Children Act (1989) Guidance & Regulations, Vol. 2, Family Support.* HMSO

Department of Health (1991e) *The Children Act (1989) Guidance & Regulations, Vol. 3, Family Placements.* HMSO

Department of Health (1991f) *The Children Act (1989) Guidance & Regulations, Vol. 4, Residential Care.* HMSO

Department of Health (1991g) *Working Together Under the Children Act 1989: A guide to arrangements for inter-agency cooperation for the protection of children from abuse.* HMSO

Department of Health (1991h) *Care Management and Assessment.* HMSO

Department of Health (1993a) *The Children Act Report 1992.* HMSO

Department of Health (1993b) *Profiles of Local Authority Social Services.* HMSO

Department of Health (1993c) *National Review of Mental Health Services for Children and Young People.* HMSO

Department of Health (1994) *The Children Act Report 1993.* HMSO

Department of Health and Social Security (1981) *Observation and Assessment. Report of a Working Party* (Tutt Report). HMSO

Department of Health and Social Security (1982a) *Observation and Assessment. Some Styles of Method and Practice* (Report of a seminar at Scarborough in March 1982). DHSS

Department of Health and Social Security (1982b) *Observation and Assessment. Some Styles of Method and Practice* (Report of a seminar at Bristol in July 1982). DHSS

Department of Health and Social Security (1982c) *Child Abuse: A Study of Inquiry Reports 1973-1981.* DHSS

Department of Health and Social Security (1983) *Non-Residential Assessment of Children Referred to Social Services Departments.* DHSS

Department of Health and Social Security (1985) *Social Work Decisions in Child Care. Recent Research Findings and their Implications* (Pink Book). HMSO

Department of Health and Social Security (1986) *Inspection of the supervision of social workers in the assessment and monitoring of cases of child abuse where children, subject to a court order, have been returned home.* DHSS

Doel, M and Marsh, P (1992) *Task Centred Social Work.* Ashgate

The Dolphin Project (1993) *Answering Back – Report by Young People Being Looked After under the Children Act 1989.* CEDR, Department of Social Work Studies, University of Southampton

Eaton, L (1994) 'No hiding place', *Community Care*, 1013, 20

Farmer, E and Parker, R (1991) *Trials and Tribulations: Returning Children from Local Authority Care to their Families.* HMSO

Fenyo, A and Knapp, M (1988) *New Directions in the Assessment of Child Care: Counting the Costs*, Discussion Paper 568, Personal Social Services Research Unit, University of Kent at Canterbury

Fisher, M, Marsh, P, Phillips, D and Sainsbury, E (1986) *In and Out of Care: the Experiences of Children, Parents and Social Workers.* Batsford in association with the British Agencies for Adoption and Fostering

Fletcher-Campbell, F and Hall, C (1990) *Changing Schools? Changing People? A Study of the Education of Children in Care.* NFER

Fox, L (1982) 'Two value positions in recent child care law and practice', *British Journal of Social Work,* 12, 3

Fox-Harding, L (1991) 'The Children Act 1989 in context: four perspectives in child care law and policy', *Journal of Social Welfare and Family Law*, 3, 179-93

Fratter, J, Rowe, J, Sapsford, D and Thoburn, J (1991) *Permanent Family Placement: A Decade of Experience*. British Agencies for Adoption and Fostering

Freeman, M (1984) *The Rights and Wrongs of Children*. Frances Pinter

Frost, N and Stein, M (1989) *The Politics of Child Welfare: inequality, power and change*. Harvest Wheatsheaf

Fuller, R (1985) *Issues in the Assessment of Children in Care*. National Children's Bureau

Gardner, R (1987) *Who Says? Choice and control in care*. National Children's Bureau

Gardner, R 'Consumer views' in Kahan, B ed. (1989) *Child Care Research, Policy and Practice*. Hodder & Stoughton

Gardner, R (1992) *Supporting Families: Preventive Social Work in Practice*. National Children's Bureau

Garnett, L (1992) *Leaving Care and After*. National Children's Bureau

George, V (1970) *Foster Care: Theory and Practice*. Routledge and Kegan Paul

Gibbs, G (1990) 'True to type?', *Community Care*, 801, 18-19

Goodall, P (1992) *Elaine Foley: Independent Review into the Management of Work by Brent Social Services Department*. Brent Council and National Children's Bureau

Grimshaw, R and Sumner, M (1991) *What's Happening to Child Care Assessment? An Exploratory Study of New Approaches*. National Children's Bureau

Grimshaw, R with Berridge, D (1994) *Educating Disruptive Children: Placement and Progress in Residential Special Schools for Pupils with Emotional and Behavioural Difficulties*. National Children's Bureau

Hallett, C and Birchall, E (1992) *Coordination and Child Protection: A Review of the Literature*. HMSO

Hardiker, P and Curnock, K (1984) 'Social work assessment procession work with ethnic minorities', *British Journal of Social Work*, 14, 1, 23-48

Hardiker, P, Exton, K and Barker, M (1991) *Policies and Practices in Preventive Child Care*. Avebury

Heath, A, Colton, M and Aldgate, J (1989) 'The education of children in and out of care', *British Journal of Social Work*, 19, 447-60

Hodgson, D (1991) *Planning in Social Work and Children's Participation*, Internal Report, National Children's Bureau

Hodgson, D (1995) *Young People's Participation in Social Work*

Planning: A Research Pack. National Children's Bureau (forth-coming)

Hoghughi, M (1980) *Assessing Problem Children: Issues and Practices*. Burnett Books

Hoghughi, M (1992) *Assessing Child and Adolescent Disorders: A Practice Manual*. Sage

Holman, R (1980) *Inequality in Child Care*. Child Poverty Action Group

Home Office (1968) *Children in Trouble*. HMSO

House of Commons Home Affairs Committee (1993) *Juvenile Offenders: Memoranda of Evidence*. HMSO

House of Commons Social Services Committee (1984) *Second Report from the Social Services Committee. Children in Care* (Short Report). HMSO

Hussell, C (1983) 'Contracts', *Adoption and Fostering*, 7, 3, 22-24

The Islamic Foundation (1993) *Caring About Faith. A Survey of Muslim Children and Young Persons in Care*. The Islamic Foundation

Jackson, S (1987) *The Education of Children in Care*. University of Bristol, School of Applied Social Studies

Kahan, B (1989) *Child Care Research, Policy and Practice*. Hodder & Stoughton

Kavanagh, S (1988a) 'Foster carers have allowed themselves to be used to subsidise child care', *Foster Care*, 53, 16-17

Kavanagh, S (1988b) 'The true cost of caring', *Foster Care*, 56, 8-10

Kind, P (1992) *Caring for Children – Counting the costs*. Discussion Paper 97, Centre for Health Economics, University of York

Kirby, P (1994) *A Word From the Street. Young People Who Leave Care and Become Homeless*. Centrepoint and Community Care

Knapp, M, Brysan, D and Lewis, J (1984) *The Comprehensive Costing of Child Care: The Suffolk Cohort Study*, Discussion Paper 335, Personal Social Services Research Unit, University of Kent at Canterbury

Knapp, M (1984) *The Economics of Social Care*. Macmillan

Knapp, M and Fenyo, A (1985) *Residential Child Care in the Voluntary Sector: Demand and Supply Explanations of Fee and Utilisation Differences*, Discussion Paper 378, Personal Social Services Research Unit, University of Kent at Canterbury

Knapp, M and Smith, J (1985) 'The costs of residential child care: explaining variation in the public sector', *Policy and Politics*, 13, 127-54

Knapp, M 'The relative cost-effectiveness of public, voluntary and private providers of residential child care' *in* Culyer, A.J and

Jönsson, B eds (1986a) *Public and Private Health Services.* Blackwell

Knapp, M (1986b) 'The field social work implications of residential child care', *British Journal of Social Work,* 16, 25-48

Knapp, M (1987) *Child Care Outcomes: the Basic Principles Underlying Practical Measurement,* Discussion Paper 557, Personal Social Services Research Unit, University of Kent at Canterbury

Knapp, M and Baines, B (1987) 'Hidden costs multipliers for residential child care', *Local Government Studies,* July/August, 53-73

Knapp, M and Fenyo, A 'Economic perspectives on foster care' *in* Carter, P, Jeffs, R and Smith, M eds (1989) *Social Work and Social Welfare Book.* Open University Press

Knapp, M 'Background theory' *in* Netten, A and Beecham, J eds (1993a) *Costing Community Care: Theory and Practice.* Ashgate

Knapp, M 'Principles of applied costs research' *in* Netten, A and Beecham, J eds (1993b) *Costing Community Care: Theory and Practice.* Ashgate

Kurtz, Z, Thornes, S and Wolkind, S (1994) *Services for the Mental Health of Children and Young People in England: A National Review.* South Thames Regional Health Authority, Department of Public Health

London Borough of Hackney (1994) *The First Hackney Children's Plan* 1994/95. London Borough of Hackney

MacDonald, S (1991) *All Equal under the Act? – A Practical Guide to the Children Act 1989 for Social Workers.* National Institute for Social Work

Macdonnel, P and Aldgate, J (1984) *Reviews of Children in Care.* University of Oxford, Department of Social and Administrative Studies

Malek, M (1993) *Passing the Buck: Institutional Responses to Controlling Children with Difficult Behaviour.* The Children's Society

Maluccio, A N ed. (1981) *Promoting Competence in Clients – a New/old Approach to Social Work Practice.* Free Press

Marchant, C (1993) 'Muslim first', *Community Care,* 982, 9

Marsh, P and Fisher, M (1992) *Good Intentions: Developing Partnership in Social Services,* Joseph Rowntree Foundation in association with Community Care

Maximé, J (1993) 'The importance of racial identity for the psychological well-being of black children', *Association for Child*

Psychology and Psychiatry Review (ACPP) and Newsletter, 15, 4, 173-79

Millham, S, Bullock, R, Hosie, K and Haak, M (1986) *Lost in Care: The Problems of Maintaining Links Between Children in Care and their Families.* Gower Press

Millham, S, Bullock, R, Hosie, K and Little, M (1989) *Access Disputes in Child-Care.* Gower Press

Mind Working Party (1975) *Assessment of Children and their Families.* Mind/King's Fund Centre

Morris, A and Giller, H (1987) *Understanding Juvenile Justice.* Croom Helm

National Foster Carers' Association (1991) 'The cost of caring', *Foster Care,* 7, 6-7

Netten, A and Smart, S (1992) *Unit Costs of Community Care 1992-93,* Personal Social Services Research Unit, University of Kent at Canterbury.

Office of Population Censuses & Surveys (1992) *1991 Census. Great Britain.* OPCS

Oxford Review of Education (1994) *Special Issue: The Education of Children in Need,* 20, 3

Packman, J (1981) *The Child's Generation: Child Care Policy in Britain.* Basil Blackwell and Martin Robertson

Packman, J and Jordan, B (1991) 'The Children Act: looking forward, looking back', *British Journal of Social Work,* 21, 4

Packman, J with Randall, J and Jacques, N (1986) *Who Needs Care? Social Work Decisions About Children.* Second Edition. Blackwell

Parker, R (1966) *Decision in Child Care: A Study of Prediction in Fostering.* National Institute for Social Work/Allen & Unwin

Parker, R (1987) *A Forward Look at Research and the Child in Care.* School of Applied Social Studies, University of Bristol

Parker, R 'Residential care for children', *in* Sinclair, I ed. (1988) *Residential Care: The Research Reviewed,* Wagner Committee Report, 2. HMSO

Parker, R and others eds (1991) *Looking After Children: Assessing Outcomes in Child Care.* Report of an independent working party established by the Department of Health. HMSO

Parton, N (1991) *Governing the Family: Child Care, Child Protection and the State.* Macmillan Education

Platt, D (1994) 'Split decisions', *Community Care,* 1016, 30-32

Polnay, L (1994) *Children in Community Homes: Health, Mental Health and Health Promotion Needs*

Reinach, E, Lovelock, R and Roberts, G (1976) *First year at Fair-*

field Lodge: A Children's O & A Centre in Hampshire. SSRIU: Portsmouth Polytechnic

Reinach, E, Lovelock, R and Roberts, G (1979) *"Consequences", the progress of sixty-five children after a period of residential observation and assessment.* SSRIU: Portsmouth Polytechnic

Research Authority (1992) *Perfomance and Indicators.*

Rhodes, P (1992) *Racial matching in fostering: the challenge to social work practice.* Avebury

Robbins, D (1990) *Child care policy: putting it in writing: a review of English Local Authorities child care statements.* Social Services Inspectorate: HMSO

Rose, W (1994) *The Relationship Between Protection and Family Support and the Intentions of the Children Act.* Paper at Sieff Conference

Rowe, J and Lambert, L (1973) *Children Who Wait: A Study of Children Needing Substitute Families.* Association of British Adoption Agencies

Rowe, J and others (1984) *Long-term fostering and the Children' Act: a study of foster parents who went on to adopt.* British Agencies for Adoption and Fostering

Rowe, J, Hundleby, M and Garnett, L (1989) *Child Care Now: A Study of Placement Patterns.* British Association for Adoption and Fostering

Shaw, M and Hipgrave, T (1983) *Specialist Fostering.* Batsford/British Associaton for Adoption and Fostering

Sinclair, R (1984) *Decision-making in Statutory Reviews on Children in Care.* Gower Press

Sinclair, R (1987) 'Behind the numbers: an examination of child care statistics', *Policy and Politics,* 15, 2, 111-17

Sinclair, R, Grimshaw, R and Garnett, L (1994) 'The education of children in need: the impact of the Education Reform Act 1988, The Education Act 1993 and the Children Act 1989', *Oxford Review of Education,* 20, 3, 281-92

Sinclair, R and Grimshaw, R (1995) *Plans and Reviews for looked after children: Shaping a Framework for Practice.* National Children's Bureau (forthcoming)

Small, J (1991) 'Ethnic and racial identity in adoption in the UK', *Adoption and Fostering,* 15, 4, 61-69

Smith, P and Berridge, D (1994) *Ethnicity and Childcare Placements.* National Children's Bureau

Social Information Systems (1989) *The Children Act 1989: Priorities for Management Information.* SIS

Social Information Systems (1993) *Children in Need: Definition, Management and Monitoring.* SIS

Social Services Inspectorate (SSI) (1989) *A Sense of Direction: Planning in Social Work with Children.* Department of Health

Social Services Inspectorate (1993a) *Corporate Parents: Inspection of Residential Community Care Services in 11 Local Authorities* Department of Health

Social Services Inspectorate (1993b) *Enpowerment, Assessment, Management and the Skilled Worker.* National Institute for Social Work

Staffordshire Social Services Department (1994) *Assessment Process Document.* Children and Families Division

Stein, M and Carey, K (1986) *Leaving Care.* Blackwell

Thoburn, J, Lewis, A and Shemmings, D (1993) *Family Participation in Child Protection: a Report to the Department of Health.* University of East Anglia

Tizard, B and Phoenix, A (1993) *Black, White or Mixed Race? Race and Racism in the Lives of Young People of Mixed Parentage.* Routledge

Triseliotis, J, Borland, M, Hill, M and Lambert, L (1994) *Care Service for Teenagers – Research Report to the Department of Health.* Universities of Edinburgh and Glasgow

Tunstill, J (1989) 'Written contracts' *in Using Written Agreements with Children and Families.* Family Rights Group

Tunstill, J 'Local authority policies on children in need' *in* Gibbens, J ed. (1993) *The Children Act 1989 and Family Support.* HMSO

Utting, W (1991) *Children in the Public Care: A Review of Residential Child Care.* Department of Health and Social Services Inspectorate

Vernon, J and Fruin, D (1986) *A Study of Social Work Decision Making.* National Children's Bureau

Walby, C (1994) 'More than a system of honest brokerage', *Care Plan*, 1, 1, 22-23

Walker, M and Xanthos, P (1982) *The Functioning of O & A Centres in Yorkshire and Humberside.* Centre for Criminological Studies and Socio-legal Studies, University of Sheffield

Warner, N (1992) *Choosing with Care, The report of the Committee of Inquiry into the Selection, Development and Management of Staff in Children's Homes.* HMSO

Whittaker, D (1987) *The Experiences of Residential Care: from the Perspectives of Children, Parents and Caregivers.* University of York

Who Cares? Trust and the National Consumer Council (1993) *Not just a name, the views of young people in care*. The Trust/NCC

Wilding, P (1982) *Professional Power and Social Welfare*. Routledge and Kegan Paul.

Index

Entries are arranged in letter–by–letter order (hyphens and spaces between words are ignored). Principal page references are printed in bold type.